MURDER UNDER TRUST

or

THE TOPICAL MACBETH

and other Jacobean Matters

THE GOWRIE CONSPIRACY as illustrated by JAN LUYKEN, 1649-1712

MURDER UNDER TRUST

or

THE TOPICAL MACBETH
and other Jacobean Matters

ARTHUR MELVILLE CLARK

Awake, awake!
Ring the alarum-bell. Murder and treason!
Macbeth, II, iii, 78-79

1981

SCOTTISH ACADEMIC PRESS
EDINBURGH

Published by
Scottish Academic Press Ltd
33 Montgomery Street, Edinburgh EH7 5JX

First published 1981
ISBN 0 7073 0312 5

Printed in Great Britain by
Clark Constable Limited, Edinburgh

Contents

In Piam Memoriam

J. C. et M. M. C.

A.D. MCMLXXXI.

Preface

I have worked intermittently, during forty years or more, on the fascinating tragedy of *Macbeth* and on various related matters. But the final organisation and writing of the Chapters which follow has been done in the last five or six years.

Mr. Douglas Grant must share in the credit or the blame, at least to the extent of having encouraged me to develop themes I had outlined to him and of keeping an octogenarian at his job till it was finished. Now he deserves from me sincere thanks for all the skill he has devoted to the publication of this book.

The more I pondered on *Macbeth*, the more I realised that Shakespeare had "treated his Scottish story in a Scottish setting as something of a special case requiring special treatment" (page 6). The tragedy is unique among Shakespeare's plays for many reasons, out of which I would choose three in particular for mention in this Preface.

The first is the peculiar care, extending down to minute details, with which Shakespeare has built up his picture of Scotland north of the Highland Line, its inhabitants and their ethnic characteristics, its landscape, climate, and conditions of life, in a way entirely different from the setting and substance of any of his other plays and deliberately calculated for an audience to whom the country and its circumstances were virtually unknown.

Secondly, there are in this tragedy on an eleventh-century story so many derivatives from late sixteenth-century Scotland as to make "*Macbeth* the play with the greatest topical content in the Shakespearian canon" (page 7). Among the most remarkable echoes of a Scotland contemporary with the play's composition are these: the very surprising and hitherto-unrecognized[1] weaving-in of specialities from recent Scots Law and procedure in relation to treason and murder under trust or *homicidium sub praetextu amicitiae*; the familiarity with conditions of life in the Highlands illustrated by the terrible clan feud which directly occasioned the legislation in question; and the similarities between *Macbeth* and the Gowrie Conspiracy, the sequels of which provided the most signal instance of that legislation in operation.

1. Except in my own article, *Shakespeare and Scots Law. A Statute of 1587*, in *The Scotsman*, 31st December 1953.

The third uniqueness of *Macbeth* is that it was obviously written to compliment and appeal to one particular person, James VI. It has in fact the quality of a commissioned work, by reason of its repeated allusions to the descent of the House of Stewart from Banquo, its emphasis on legitimacy and lineal succession, its acceptance of James's own ideas of monarchy, its approval of his policy of peace, and its manifest catering for his intense interest in demonology and witchcraft; all of these topics being interwoven into a plot of treason and murder under trust which, as I have said, reflected the Gowrie affair.

In addition to examining *Macbeth* along the lines indicated, I discuss "other Jacobean matters", as my title says. There is a considerable variety of them; including perplexing facts about the shadowy Shakespeare and his relation to Scotland, and other facts about the highly idiosyncratic James VI, his patronage of players and the war it provoked with his clergy, and his achievement of his long-cherished hopes in the Union of the Crowns.

Owing to the onset of an incapacitating illness during the last stages of preparing this book for the press, I have been unable to provide it with an index but in conclusion, I acknowledge with a deep appreciation the kindly and expert offices of Dr Robert Schlapp and Mr J. Geoffrey Sharps in taking such trouble to free the printed text of this book from errors; leaving me, however, responsible for what is said in it and so

> cabin'd, cribb'd, confined, bound in
> To saucy doubts and fears (III, iv, 24-25)

as to its reception.

Arthur Melville Clark

Edinburgh, 1981.

Abbreviations

Aberdeen B.	*Register of Burgesses of the Burgh of Aberdeen, 1399-1631.* Edited by A. M. Munro and James Moir. In *The Miscellany of the New Spalding Club,* I, 1890.
Aberdeen C. R.	*Extracts from the Council Register of the Burgh of Aberdeen.* Edited by John Stuart for the Spalding Club. 2 vols. 1844-48.
Arbuckle.	*The "Gowrie Conspiracy".* By Sir W. F. Arbuckle in *The Scottish Historical Review,* XXXVI, 1957.
Buchanan.	*The Jephtha and Baptist.* By George Buchanan. Translated by Alexander Gibb. 1870.
B.U.K.	*The Booke of the Universall Kirk of Scotland.* Edited by Alexander Peterkin. 1839.
Calderwood.	*The History of the Kirk of Scotland.* By David Calderwood. Edited by Thomas Thomson for the Wodrow Society. 8 vols. 1842-49.
Chambers, ed.	*Macbeth.* Edited by Sir E. K. Chambers for The Warwick Shakespeare. 1893.
Chambers, *Sh.*	*William Shakespeare: A Study of Facts and Problems.* By Sir E. K. Chambers. 2 vols. 1930.
Chambers, *Stage.*	*The Elizabethan Stage.* By Sir E. K. Chambers. 4 vols. 1923.
C.S.P.	*Calendar of the State Papers, relating to Scotland.* Edited by M. J. Thorpe. 2 vols. 1858.
Dibdin.	*The Annals of the Edinburgh Stage.* By J. C. Dibdin. 1888.
D.W.	*Macbeth.* Edited by John Dover Wilson for The New Shakespeare. 1951.
En. Brit.	*The Encyclopaedia Britannica.* Fourteenth Edition. 24 vols. 1929.
Fasti.	*Fasti Ecclesiae Scoticanae. The Succession of Ministers in the Church of Scotland from the Reformation.* By Hew Scott and others. 9 vols. 1915-61.
Halliday.	*A Shakespeare Companion, 1550-1950.* By F. E. Halliday. 1952.
Henderson.	*The Royal Stewarts.* By T. F. Henderson. 1914.
Holinshed.	*The Scottish Chronicle; or, A Complete History and Description of Scotland.* 2 vols. 1805.
Hume, *Commentaries.*	*Commentaries on the Law of Scotland, Respecting the Description and Punishment of Crimes.* By David Hume. 2 vols. 1797.
Hume Brown.	*History of Scotland.* By P. Hume Brown. 3 vols. 1911.
Knight.	*William Shakspere; a Biography.* By Charles Knight. 1843.
Lee.	*A Life of William Shakespeare.* By Sir Sidney Lee. 1915.
Mackenzie, *Institutions.*	*The Institutions of the Law of Scotland.* By Sir George Mackenzie. 1723.

Mackenzie, *Laws*.   *The Laws and Customes of Scotland, in Matters Criminal*. By Sir George
                Mackenzie. 1678.
Mackenzie, *Observations*.   *Observations on the Acts of Parliament*. By Sir George
                Mackenzie. 1686.
Macmillan.   *George Buchanan: A Biography*. By D. Macmillan. 1906.
Mill.   *Mediaeval Plays in Scotland*. By Anna Jean Mill. 1927.
Murray.   *English Dramatic Companies, 1558–1642*. By J. T. Murray. 2 vols. 1910.
Pitcairn.   *Criminal Trials in Scotland*. Edited by Robert Pitcairn for the Maitland
                and Bannatyne Clubs. 3 vols. 1833.
R.P.C.   *The Register of the Privy Council of Scotland, 1545–1625*. Edited by
                John Hill Burton and David Masson. 14 vols. 1877–98.
S.D.   Stage direction(s).
Spottiswoode.   *The History of the Church of Scotland*. By John Spottiswoode. Edited by
                Michael Russell and Mark Napier for the Spottiswoode Society and
                the Bannatyne Club. 3 vols. 1847–51.
S.R.   *A Transcript of the Registers of the Company of Stationers of London,
                1554–1640*. Edited by Edward Arber. 5 vols. 1875–94.
Stewart, *Cron.* *The Buik of the Croniclis of Scotland*. By William Stewart. Edited by
                W. B. D. D. Turnbull for the Rolls Series. 3 vols. 1858.
Stopes.   *Shakespeare's Industry*. By Charlotte Carmichael Stopes. 1916.

I

Shakespeare and Topicality

Stay, you imperfect speakers, tell me more.
Macbeth, I, iii, 70.

The existence of an active censorship of plays and playing on the Elizabethan-Jacobean stage proves, not that current topics were never handled or living persons represented, but that, on the contrary, they were sometimes introduced and that the authorities kept a watchful eye on the theatres. The dramatists and the acting companies who bought their plays were not hostile to the government or to influential persons in general. They were, in fact, sympathetically biased towards the royal establishment and its entourage; and, as an institution largely dependent on the support of persons about the Court, they knew too well on which side their bread was buttered to quarrel deliberately with their patrons and protectors. But they also knew the drawing-power of topical allusions, and from time to time they took the risk of introducing them. What they did not know was when and on what the authorities would come down. That is to say, the playwrights or the players sometimes blundered into an offence and had to pay the penalty, through misreading situations or miscalculating the authorities' shifting policy in relation to them.

However, not every topical allusion could possibly be interpreted as adversely critical of government policy or of influential persons. Many were affirmative and complimentary; and many had a highly acceptable patriotic ring. Others bore no vital relation to affairs of State or of Church at all, but simply reflected the interest of a public that had no newspapers in current ongoings, vogues and fashions, rumours and gossip.

Such were the circumstances of the theatres for which Shakespeare wrote his plays; and it might be presumed that he would be no more averse to the topical than were his fellow-dramatists. But, rather surprisingly, it has been held that he concerned himself little with such an ingredient. "I do not myself believe," says Sir Edmund Chambers, "that, apart from some passages of obvious satire in comic scenes, there is much of the topical in Shakespeare, whose mind normally moved upon quite another plane of relation to life. What little there is, probably remains for the most part irrecoverable."[1]

No worker in the field of the sixteenth- and seventeenth-century drama should rashly query the opinions, let alone the facts, in the works of Chambers, than whom nobody in this century or before has had such an unrivalled command of the subject. In venturing myself to do any querying of his views on the amount of topicality in Shakespeare, I can at least plead that I have been slow and cautious in doing it, especially in relation to *Macbeth* which has been for me a fascinating study for nearly fifty years.

Frankly, then, I believe that there is a good deal of the topical in Shakespeare. But I would at once add that it is always, so to speak, only a secondary or transient consideration. So I would agree with Chambers in holding that Shakespeare's "mind normally moved upon quite another plane of relation to life" from, let us say, Spenser's or that of John Barclay, the author of the almost-forgotten *Argenis*, a *roman à clef* which had an extraordinary European vogue and ran through some forty editions between its publication in 1621 and the end of the century. Their main concern was to construct an allegorical symbolism in story-form which would present, in new terms and by ingenious parallels, men and things, partisanships and tensions, negotiations and conflicts, ideologies and doctrines.

But Shakespeare's primary and over-riding purpose was the dramatic and convincing presentation of his characters and their reactions to each other and to their circumstances. Admittedly, the plots in which his characters move often do not conform to everyday experience. *Macbeth*, for example, and *A Midsummer Night's Dream* are full of impossibilities to the workaday world; and *The Winter's Tale* and *As You Like It* include improbabilities bordering on the incredible. Such departures from the matter-of-fact belong quite appropriately to the kind of poetic or heightened drama Shakespeare was writing. All the same, though his plots may be far from realistic and may plunge his men and women in decisions and events in which no man or woman ever was or could be involved, he regularly made his characters speak and behave, soliloquize and decide in a psychologically plausible and consistent way. Shakespeare, as much as Coleridge, "aimed at . . . the interesting of the affections by the dramatic truth of such emotions, as would naturally accompany such situations, supposing them real."[2] Indeed the unusualness of some of his situations set Shakespeare some of his most interesting problems in characterization and expression. It would be untrue to say that Shakespeare is invariably plausible; for he sometimes stretches the acceptable to avoid labouring a transition or to polish his play off, and gets away with even such legerdemain better than any other dramatic illusionist. But the fact remains that the peculiar greatness of Shakespeare is the all-but-constant psychological truth—the consistency of a character to his or her nature through whatever stresses they may be taken or on whatever lines they may develop in consequence of the stresses; the unpredictable rightness of everything said in relation to everything felt and done; the play of mind which accompanies the action and is manifested in the reactions of every character to his or her particular situations.

All of this amounts to saying that Shakespeare was interested above all in human nature in order to illustrate it and present it; not to draw any lessons from it like Bacon in his *Essays*; not to typify it like Earle and the other character-writers; not to analyse out and isolate ruling "humours" like Ben Jonson; but, without taking sides in moral approval or disapproval, to give every character a square deal, be it to Lear or Goneril, Othello or Iago, Malvolio or Sir Toby, Shylock or Portia.

The only way in which human nature can be so objectively mirrored is by not allowing a secondary purpose, didactic or satirical or allegorical or propagandist, to usurp the first place in the dramatist's regard. And undoubtedly Shakespeare, for almost all of the time, left his unparalleled genius for presenting real persons in the round to work completely unimpeded by secondary considerations.

I have put in "for almost all of the time," because there are times when Shakespeare's divine impartiality is withheld, in some degree at least, from certain characters, and they are presented as somewhat less than whole individuals. The occasions I mean are all of a comic kind; and, as I have said in another context, they reveal Shakespeare's attitude 'to the whole gamut of persons below the level of gentry. I have to confess that Shakespeare was a bit of a snob. The line between gentle and simple was the great gulf in his sociology; and his "even-handed justice"[3] stops short with his gentlefolk. However varied his gentles may be in human dignity, from the sublime of Lear to the ridiculous of Polonius, his simples are invariably undignified, comic or absurd, illiterate and ignorant even when smart, likable as individuals, but contemptible in the mass. Kindly as Shakespeare is to Bully Bottom and Dogberry, it is a condescending kindness at most. He never presented any of their class seriously. They lift and lay for their superiors; but they belong to a different order of being. When they pass across Shakespeare's tragic stage, like the Gravediggers in *Hamlet* or the Porter in *Macbeth*, they never rise to the tragic level. Still less did it ever occur to Shakespeare to present them in their own tragedies. Tragedy in Shakespeare is a royal and aristocratic preserve';[4] as are also in their ways history and romantic comedy.

As to Shakespeare's topicality, which Chambers would minimize almost to nothing, I find it fairly frequent and sometimes of great significance, though always harmonizing with and subdued to the purely dramatic requirement. I venture to give a few instances in plays other than *Macbeth* which seem to me to be incontestably topical.

The English chronicle-histories are all examples of a kind of diffused topicality, since they were a response to the patriotic tide of the age which flowed from the rivalry with Spain and especially from the triumph over the Armada. To take one of the chronicle-histories in particular, *Henry V*: it contains a highly specific topicality in the lines in which Shakespeare likens the actual reception of the victorious Henry on his return from Agincourt to the reception which he, very wrongly as things turned out, anticipated for the Earl of Essex on his return from Ireland:

> As, by a lower but loving likelihood,
> Were now the general of our gracious empress,
> As in good time he may, from Ireland coming,
> Bringing rebellion broached on his sword,
> How many would the peaceful city quit,
> To welcome him![5]

The lines must have been written between Essex's departure to take up his duties as Lieutenant and Governor-General on 27th March 1599 and his ignominious return on 28th September, probably indeed before the end of June by which time doubts about the success of his mission were stirring in London. In addition to the specific topicality, the whole play has an appositeness to a critical national situation in 1598-99. The tension was of an exhilarating kind. The last fears of Spain had been dissipated by the news of the death of the bogey Philip II in November 1598. And, as Dover Wilson says in his edition of *Henry V*, "there was being fitted out . . . the largest and most elaborate military expedition launched from these shores during Elizabeth's reign, with the object of effecting the final conquest of Ireland".[6] The whole country was busy with preparations and recruiting and poised for a national triumph across the seas, not in France like Henry V's, but in the troubled and troublesome country of Ireland. So the mood of England while Shakespeare was writing was precisely what he represented as obtaining in the England of Henry V.

In *Love's Labour's Lost* Shakespeare has quite a variety of topical allusions;[7] but one illustration will suffice. At the time of the play's composition in the early fifteen-nineties, the English people were more than a little interested in the civil wars in France which ran for years, especially from the assassination of Henry III in 1589 to Henry of Navarre's reception by Paris as its King in 1594. Their sympathies lay with Henry of Navarre. Shakespeare set his light-hearted comedy in a Navarre as far removed from wars and politics as is the equally idyllic Illyria in *Twelfth Night*, and made its king and several of his nobles the principal male characters. Two are called by the names of two of Henry of Navarre's stoutest supporters: Biron, otherwise Charles de Gontant, Duc de Biron; and Longaville, otherwise Henri d'Orléans, Duc de Longueville. The third nobleman in the court of Navarre is called by Shakespeare Dumain, which is an anglicizing of de Mayenne and stands for Charles de Lorraine, Duc de Mayenne. He was, in fact, the Lieutenant-General of the Holy League, the party opposed to Henry of Navarre's claim to the French throne. But it was only too easy for Shakespeare in England to be mistaken about the personalities and who adhered to what in the confusion of the warring factions in France.

The Merchant of Venice was Shakespeare's remarkable reaction to the antisemitism which sprang from the trial in February and the execution in June 1594 of Roderigo Lopez. This accomplished linguist was a Portuguese Jew, who had become physician to Queen Elizabeth in 1586. In 1590 Lopez acted as interpreter to Antonio Perez, who had fled from Philip II's persecution and had been brought to England by the Earl of Essex in order to help to rekindle the hostility to Spain. Spanish agents in London tried to bribe Lopez to poison the Queen and also Antonio Perez. The evidence that Lopez yielded to the temptation is inconclusive; but there is no doubt of the effect of the allegations on public opinion. So far, however, from Shakespeare's going with the antisemitic tide and presenting his Jew as a monster of iniquity like Barabbas[8] in Marlowe's *Jew of Malta*, he made his Shylock the most impressive personage in the play and "despite his mercenary instinct . . . a penetrating and tolerant interpretation of racial characteristics which are degraded by an antipathetic environment".[9] This did not prevent Shakespeare's giving his Merchant the same Christian name as Antonio Perez bore. And from an outburst by Gratiano, it

looks as if Shakespeare worked in a pun of sorts on the name Lopez as though it
derived from *lupus*:

> Thou almost makest me waver in my faith
> To hold opinion with Pythagoras,
> That souls of animals infuse themselves
> Into the trunks of men: thy currish spirit
> Govern'd a wolf, who, hang'd for human slaughter,
> Even from the gallows did his fell soul fleet,
> And, whilst thou lay'st in thy unhallow'd dam,
> Infused itself in thee; for thy desires
> Are wolvish, bloody, starved and ravenous.[10]

The final illustration I offer of topicality in Shakespeare comes from
Hamlet and relates to the Poetomachia or War of the Theatres, which raged from
1599 to 1602. The champions in the War were John Marston and Thomas
Dekker on the one hand and Ben Jonson on the other, though several more of
the playwrights were involved in a greater or less degree. Most of the plays,
which appealed less to the general public than to the habitués of the theatres,
were performed by companies of boy-actors: the Children of Paul's (*i.e.* the
choristers of St. Paul's Cathedral) and the Children of the Chapel Royal.
Shakespeare in *Hamlet* transports, as it were, the Poetomachia to Denmark.
According to Rosencrantz, who is Hamlet's informant about theatrical matters
in the capital, the troupe of adult actors on their way to Elsinore had taken to
the road because of an "inhibition" coming "by the means of the late innovation".[11] An "inhibition" was an official prohibition of playing in and about
London. "Innovation" in other Shakespearian contexts means a political up-
heaval of some sort; and if the word has the same meaning in *Hamlet*, it could
be an allusion to the abortive rising of the Earl of Essex on 8th February 1601.
But this is most unlikely. Shakespeare's own colleagues, the Lord Chamberlain's
men, were certainly not inhibited in consequence of the rising, and in fact performed before Elizabeth on 24th February, the day before Essex's execution. I
think that the "inhibition" and the "innovation" were somehow both connected
with the theatrical rivalry which Rosencrantz goes on to describe. The adult
company, he says, does not enjoy its former metropolitan esteem; nor does it
draw audiences so large, though its "endeavour keeps in the wonted pace";
because "there is, sir, an aery of children, little eyases, that cry out on the top of
question, and are most tyrannically clapped for't: these are now the fashion,
and so berattle the common stages—so they call them—that many wearing
rapiers are afraid of goose-quills and dare scarce come thither . . .'Faith, there
has been much to do on both sides; and the nation holds it no sin to tarre them
to controversy: there was, for a while, no money bid for argument, unless the
poet and the player went to cuffs in the question".[12]

> *Guildenstern.* O, there has been much throwing about of brains.
> *Hamlet.* Do the boys carry it away?
> *Rosencrantz.* Ay, that they do, my lord; Hercules and his load
>   too.[13]

That is to say, the boys had scored over the Globe Theatre itself, which had a

B

figure of Hercules carrying the globe as its sign and which was the regular base of Shakespeare's own company.

Chambers was led to a minimal estimate of the topical in Shakespeare by taking the word in a sense too narrow, as covering only such allusions to their contemporary world as Shakespeare knew his audience would pick up, in the way of penetrable disguises of living persons or references to controversial questions of the day. But the topical need not concern persons or the controversial; and it need not be meant to be taken by the audience as an echo or reflection of their contemporary interests. I believe that in *Macbeth*, which is the focus of this book, there is, besides the topicality that was there for all to appreciate, much that would not be recognized by English audiences and was not meant to be, though some of it would be caught by Scottish ones. In my submission, Shakespeare used, simply as contributory material for "the ingredients of [his] cauldron" (IV, i, 34), appropriate data and suggestions from the Scotland of James VI to fill in his picture of the Scotland of Duncan and Macbeth and to give local colour and atmosphere, without expecting anyone to nod a knowing head when he spotted a parallel. In so doing Shakespeare treated his Scottish story in a Scottish setting as something of a special case requiring special treatment. He did nothing comparable for Hamlet's Denmark, or for Othello's Venice and Cyprus. But topical as *Macbeth* may be, Shakespeare never swerved in it from his primarily dramatic end and never worked at a greater creative intensity.

Notes

1. Chambers, *Sh.*, I, 67.
2. *Biographia Literaria*. Edited by J. Shawcross. 2 vols. 1907. II, 5.
3. *Macbeth*, I, vii, 10.
4. *Sir Walter Scott. An Edinburgh Keepsake*. Edited by Allan Frazer. 1971. 120.
5. V, Prologue, 29-34.
6. ix.
7. *Cf.* Lee, 103-4, which condenses the substance of two earlier articles.
8. "Barabas" is the spelling in the first extant edition, the 1633 quarto.
9. Lee, 133.
10. IV, i, 130-38.
11. II, ii, 346-47.
12. II, ii, 353-60, 369-73.
13. II, ii, 375-79.

2

'Macbeth' for Scottish and English Quidnuncs

> Of dire combustion and confused events
> New hatch'd to the woeful time.
> *Macbeth*, II, iii, 63-64.

I should like to develop in this Chapter some aspects of the topical in *Macbeth* to which I referred in the last paragraph of the previous Chapter,[1] leaving still other topical considerations for discussion later. The topicalities discussed in this Chapter are mainly such as knowledgeable spectators in England or in Scotland would catch and recognize. Those to be discussed in later Chapters[2] would probably ring a louder bell in Scotland than in England. The two categories together may be said to make *Macbeth* the play with the greatest topical content in the Shakespearian canon.

As a preliminary to my argument, I must refer at some length to two vexed questions:—the state of the text of *Macbeth*; and the date of the play's composition.

Macbeth was one of eighteen plays by Shakespeare not printed until their inclusion in the 1623 Folio. The text for it may have been that of the prompt-copy. But it was a very defective copy, and the off-print from it is far from being true to Shakespeare's holograph. The extant *Macbeth* is the shortest of all the plays in the Folio except two of the comedies, *The Comedy of Errors* and *The Tempest*, and is only about two-thirds of the length of *Antony and Cleopatra* or *Hamlet*.

The shortness is, in the main if not entirely, due to some kind of abbreviation early in the play. The abridging, if that term may be used as meaning something less than voluntary shortening, has had the result, more fortuitous in my opinion than calculated, of hurrying us to an unusually early climax in II, iii; that is to say, in a scene before the end of the second act. This rapid crescendo has undoubtedly an impressive effect. But it has come about only by the loss of what Hamlet calls "some necessary question of the play".[3]

For example, in I, ii there are two reports to Duncan, one by "*a bleeding Captaine*"[4] and the other by Ross. Even together they give but a sketchy account of the victories of Macbeth and Banquo over Macdonwald on the one hand and Sweno of Norway leagued with the thane of Cawdor on the other, expatiating mainly on the valour of Macbeth. It was absurd to assign the first of these

reports to a man almost fainting on his feet from loss of blood.[5] He comes
to Duncan, who appears to be in the Forres neighbourhood,[6] from a battlefield which could not have been more than a few miles away; whereas Ross
announces that he has come "From Fife "(I, ii, 48), which is obviously a considerable distance away, so far indeed that many dispatches had been sent
ahead of Macbeth and Banquo:

> As thick as hail
> Came post with post; and every one did bear
> Thy praises in his kingdom's great defence,
> And pour'd them down before him.
> (I, iii, 97-100).

Or again, how was Ross, who was only the bearer of tidings from the
battlefield, able to report to Duncan the thane of Cawdor's treason (I, ii, 52-53);
but Macbeth, who was one of the two victorious generals, thought that, so far
from his being himself the thane of Cawdor as the witches had greeted him,

> the thane of Cawdor lives,
> A prosperous gentleman (I, iii, 72-73)?

The most striking piece of evidence for the shortening of the original play
occurs in the intense scene in which Lady Macbeth screws her irresolute husband's "courage to the sticking-place" (I, vii, 60) by retrospective taunts and
the contrast of what he was *then* with what he is *now*:

> Lady Macbeth.   Was the hope drunk
> Wherein you dress'd yourself? hath it slept since?
> And wakes it now, to look so green and pale
> At what it did so freely? From this time
> Such I account thy love. Art thou afeard
> To be the same in thine own act and valour
> As thou art in desire? Wouldst thou have that
> Which thou esteem'st the ornament of life,
> And live a coward in thine own esteem,
> Letting 'I dare not' wait upon 'I would',
> Like the poor cat i' the adage.
> Macbeth.   Prithee, peace:
> I dare do all that may become a man;
> Who dares do more is none.
> Lady Macbeth.   What beast was't, then,
> That made you break this enterprise to me?
> When you durst do it, then you were a man;
> And, to be more than what you were, you would
> Be so much more the man. Nor time nor place
> Did then adhere, and yet you would make both:
> They have made themselves, and that their fitness now
> Does unmake you. I have given suck, and know
> How tender 'tis to love the babe that milks me:
> I would, while it was smiling in my face,
> Have pluck'd my nipple from his boneless gums,

And dash'd the brains out, had I so sworn as you
Have done to this.

(I, vii, 35-59).

The whole passage is taut between *then* and *now*, past tenses and present tenses. Lady Macbeth seems almost to cast in Macbeth's teeth the very words of his resolution when he "broke the enterprise" to her, ere "time and place" had "adhered" for its consummation. But there is no such corresponding passage in the extant play. I cannot believe that Lady Macbeth's retrospection is an instance of a character referring back to something merely assumed to have been said or done off-stage. As to the appropriate place in the play for the dialogue in which Macbeth "broke his enterprise" to his wife, it must have been before the present opening scene of the witches lying in wait for a man whose entertainment of a murderous ambition had already made him their potential victim.

The three examples I have cited are only the more obvious signs of tampering with or patching and compression of the defective first act of *Macbeth*.

It has been suggested that the play was deliberately shortened to fit into the timing of a special occasion, say a performance at Court. But why, in that case, were all the more obvious abridgements made in the beginning of the play and none later, at least none that the scrutineers have detected? Indeed, so far from there having been any later shortening, the original text, as we shall see,[7] has actually been augmented. It is, of course, not unlikely that *Macbeth* was performed, perhaps several times, at Court.[8] But the text in the hands of the printer of the Folio was, I am sure, from the mutilated prompt-copy for the ordinary public performances in the Globe Theatre, not from a copy of the play as shortened for a special occasion.

I suggest, as an explanation of the state of some of the early scenes, that the first page or perhaps considerably more of the prompt-copy had been lost through wear and tear by the time the text for the Folio was being prepared; and that the editors, being left with a jagged edge, set a play-cobbler to gather the strands together as well as he could from the tatters or from one or two actors' parts or from a mixture of memory and invention. The result, however Shakespearian (with qualifications) it may be, is anything but satisfactory, particularly in I, ii, but also in I, iii and I, iv, with gaping holes, abrupt transitions, and glaring discrepancies, as well as broken lines, irregular metre, and obscurities or oddities of expression.

The internal evidence for the rehandling of the text of the play does not end with these early scenes. But for the rest of the play, it is different in kind. There is little doubt that any play in the hands of a theatrical company was liable to undergo a greater or less degree of revision, sometimes but by no means always at the hands of the original author. And *Macbeth*, in which there are quite a number of suspected passages, is no exception.

The most unequivocal evidence of rehandling consists of passages of additional witch-business: the whole of III, v and IV, i, 39-43 and 125-32. In them appears a totally unnecessary Hecate, who rebukes the witches and orders them about, but who is otherwise without any integration into the action. The metre in these additions is mainly iambic, whereas in the genuine witch-passages it is mainly trochaic; and what is said runs incongruously "to favour and to prettiness".[9] Besides, the stage directions in the additional passages require the witches to dance and to sing two songs, "Come away, come away, &c." (III, v) and "Black Spirits, &c." (IV, i). "One can hardly imagine", says Chambers, "the awful beings, who meet Macbeth and Banquo on the blasted heath, singing little songs and dancing 'Like elves and fairies' "[10] (IV, i, 42). The songs in question occur in full in Thomas Middleton's *The Witch*, in which they are sung by Hecate and in which the witch-passages echo *Macbeth*. The date of Middleton's play, which was not printed till 1778, is uncertain; but it may have been written in 1609 or 1610.[11] I would date the Middletonian tampering with *Macbeth* after Shakespeare's death in 1616, not before it.

For other passages suspected of being not by Shakespeare, I refer the curious reader to the edition of the play by Sir Edmund Chambers.[12] I agree with his conservative findings and do not think that further contamination than he picks out can be proved.

But the retention of the passages in question as genuinely Shakespearian still leaves us with the possibility and indeed the likelihood that Shakespeare himself rehandled *Macbeth* to some slight extent after its original composition.

I think, for example, that he added a phrase or two to the Porter's maundering at the beginning of II, iii.[13] It is obvious that the entry of the Porter was necessary for the dramaturgy from the very beginning of the play's existence; and he would have to be given something to say. But I believe that into his inconsequential babble Shakespeare later slipped these words: " 'Faith, here's an equivocator, that could swear in both the scales against either scale; who committed treason enough for God's sake, yet could not equivocate to heaven: O, come in, equivocator" (II, iii, 9–13). That passage is an unquestionable allusion to Father Henry Garnett, the English Provincial of the Society of Jesus, who, after many examinations before the Privy Council, was condemned for complicity in the Gunpowder Plot on 28th March 1606[14] and hanged on 3rd May. At his trial he confessed to or, more correctly, justified the use of equivocation.[15] The allusion to Garnett implies that he was already dead when it was made. But it is not enough to date the original composition of the play as late as 1606.

As it happens, equivocation or false-swearing, traitors, and hanging are again linked in the dialogue of Lady Macduff and her son:

Son. Was my father a traitor, mother?

Lady Macduff. Ay, that he was.

Son. What is a traitor?

Lady Macduff. Why, one that swears and lies.

Son. And be all traitors that do so?

Lady Macduff. Every one that does so is a traitor, and must be hanged.

Son. And must they all be hanged that swear and lie?

Lady Macduff. Every one.

Son. Who must hang them?

Lady Macduff. Why, the honest men.

Son. Then the liars and swearers are fools, for there are liars and
swearers enow to beat the honest men and hang up them.
Lady Macduff. Now, God help thee, poor monkey!
    But how wilt thou do for a father?
Son. If he were dead, you'ld weep for him: if you would not, it
were a good sign that I should quickly have a new father.
                                                            (IV, ii, 44-63).

But this prose passage occurs in a scene which is otherwise in verse; and "hanging" has no relevance to Macduff, who was "a traitor" and "one that swears
and lies" only metaphorically. My conclusion, then, is that both this passage
and the sentence in the Porter's speech are topical insertions in an already-
existing text.[16]

What are almost certainly other Shakespearian insertions are: the brief and
adroit allusion to the Union of the Crowns (IV, i, 119-21)[17]; and the description
of Edward the Confessor's healing touch (IV, iii, 140-59).[18]

To turn now to the second vexed question, the date of the main composition of *Macbeth*: the most commonly-held opinion is for early in 1606.
This dating of the play has largely been done by English editors and researchers,
with a limited interest in or knowledge of things Scottish. It has sprung from
an unexamined assumption that the idea of writing *Macbeth* could have rever-
berated in Shakespeare's mind only from an English sensation, the Gunpowder
Plot of 1605. My contention, which I develop in Chapter 7,[19] is that the suggestion for his treatment of the Macbeth story came to Shakespeare from
quite a different attempt on James's life, an attempt made in Scotland, the
Gowrie Conspiracy of 1600. The parallels between the Conspiracy and *Macbeth*
are many and striking; whereas the parallels between the Plot and *Macbeth* are
non-existent, beyond the simple fact that the Plot, like the Conspiracy, was an
abortive attempt to kill a king.

When, then, did Shakespeare decide to reflect the Gowrie Conspiracy in a
play based on an eleventh-century episode in Scottish history? I venture to
suggest that it was done earlier rather than later; at least that the substantive
composition of the play was completed soon after accounts of the Conspiracy
were published in late 1600,[20] whatever modifications may have been made by
revision, cutting, augmentation, and wear and tear in the years up to the Folio
of 1623.

Apparently Scotland had not much interested the Elizabethan dramatists
during the sixteenth century, to judge from the scanty data that are known to
us. In fact only three plays set in Scotland are recorded before 1600. The first,
of which we know only the name, was "a Tragedie of the Kinge of Scottes",
presented at Court in the Christmas season of 1567-8.[21] It could well have been
a drama on the midnight murder on 9th February 1567 of Mary, Queen of
Scots's husband, Lord Darnley, who had been conceded the courtesy title of
King.

The second play in the sixteenth century with a Scottish or, more correctly,
an allegedly Scottish plot is Robert Greene's *The Scottish Historie of Iames the
fourth, slaine at Flodden. Entermixed with a pleasant Comedie, presented by Oboram,*

King of Fayeries, to quote the 1598 title-page.[22] It was probably written in 1590 or 1591. The title is quite misleading; for the play proper is not a chronicle-history of James IV at all, but a dramatization of a novella by Giraldi Cinthio;[23] and there are no deaths, at Flodden or elsewhere. Nor is the play proper presented by Oboram, but by the Scottish misanthrope Bohan to Oboram, in these words which reveal both Greene's anti-Scots bias and his ignorance of Scottish history: "I will shew thee whay I hate the world by demonstration. In the yeare 1520 was in Scotland a king overruled with parasites, misled by lust, and many circumstances too long to trattle on now, much like our court of Scotland this day. That story haue I set down; gang with me in the gallery and Ile shew thee the same in action by guid fellowes of our countrey-men; and then, when thou seest that, iudge if any wise man would not leaue the world if he could."[24]

The third play on an allegedly Scottish theme was "Robart the second kinge of Scottes tragedie" or "the Scottes tragedie", of which but little is known, for it was apparently never published. The only references to it are under the dates 2nd, 15th, 16th, 27th, and 28th September 1599 in Henslowe's Diary.[93] The five payments he made are all called "earnests", which would normally imply that work on the play was incomplete and still in progress. But the total paid was £6. 10s. which was about Henslowe's going rate for a complete play. The play in question was a collaboration of Thomas Dekker, Ben Jonson, Henry Chettle, and a fourth whose name is not given but who was probably John Marston. The title, "Robart the second kinge of Scottes tragedie" suggests that its "history" was of the same fictitious kind as is supplied by Greene's *James IV*; for the reign of the historical Robert II was uneventful by Scottish standards and did not end in a tragedy. Robert in fact died in his bed at the age of seventy-four in 1390. It is possible and indeed likely that the play was never finished or, if finished, was never staged because of the outbreak in 1599 of the Poetomachia in which Jonson was ranged on the one side and Dekker and Marston on the other.[94]

Elizabethan dramatists, then, practically ignored Scotland before 1600. But in that year the first-class sensation of the Gowrie Conspiracy focused English, and European interest as well, on Scotland and her King, the man who everybody, including the demurring and procrastinating Elizabeth, knew would soon succeed her.

I submit that *Macbeth* was one of the results of that interest and the original date of its composition was 1601. This dating more or less agrees with Dover Wilson's: "In a word, my guess is a very daring one, viz. that the earlier *Macbeth* was the next play undertaken after *Hamlet*, i.e. that it was written in the second half of 1601 or early in 1602."[25] His reasons for reaching that conclusion are, however, very different from mine. They are almost entirely stylistic; and they do not include any reference to the all-important Gowrie Conspiracy. Moreover, Dover Wilson appears to think that more revision by Shakespeare was carried out on the original *Macbeth* than I do.

In addition to the parallelism between *Macbeth* and the Gowrie Conspiracy, and as further support of my dating, I draw an inference from the existence of a play that has never been mentioned in connection with *Macbeth*. It is the lost *Malcolm, King of Scots*, written by Charles Massey in April 1602 for the Lord Admiral's company of which he was at that time a member.[26] It seems to me that there could have been only one reason for any minor playwright in 1602 choosing the unlikely reign of Malcolm Canmore,[27] namely an attempt to cash in on the success of *Macbeth* with a sequel to it.[28]

Another play, which I discuss more fully in Chapter 9,[29] is the anonymous and lost *Tragedy of Gowry*. It is known to have been acted to large crowds at least twice by the King's men by 18th December 1604. It apparently dramatized the actual episode of 1600, introducing the participants in it under their own names, and therefore going a step further than *Macbeth* in mirroring the Gowrie Conspiracy well before the Gunpowder Plot.

Very naturally and almost inevitably Shakespeare, in search of a suitable Scottish theme, went in the first instance and for his main story to his usual historical source-book, Raphael Holinshed's *The Chronicles of England, Scotland, and Ireland*, which had been his stand-by for all his English histories from *King John* to *Richard III*. The first edition appeared in 1577; but Shakespeare seems to have used the second, published in 1587. *The Chronicles* are really a compilation from histories written by many others with more or less of modification by Holinshed acting as the general editor. *The Scottish Chronicle*, which Shakespeare used in *Macbeth*, is in the main a translation into Elizabethan English by William Harrison from John Bellenden's *Croniklis of Scotland with the cosmography and dyscription thairof*, 1535. Bellenden's *Croniklis* are themselves a translation into the Scots vernacular from Hector Boece's Latin *Scotorum Historiae*, 1526, which in its turn drew on various still earlier sources.[30] In translating Bellenden, Harrison often adds material taken from the fuller narrative by Boece as well as from other early chronicles.

In *Macbeth* Shakespeare did not aim at producing a Scottish chronicle-history play; that is to say, at a fairly loose dramatic structure based on the events of a reign such as he had derived from the reigns of English kings; but at a unified tragedy in which he would feel himself quite free to depart from his source or otherwise modify it or add to it in accordance with a purely dramatic purpose. So into what he took from the chronicles of Duncan (died A.D. 1040) and Macbeth himself (died A.D. 1057) he wove matter from the chronicles of two earlier kings, Duff (died A.D. 967) and Kenneth (died A.D. 1005), and also from *The English Chronicle* of Edward the Confessor (died A.D. 1066).

As for what Shakespeare added, it is incomparably more important, dramatic, and impressive than what he derived from his source. What he got was humdrum statement: what he gives is supreme drama. The characterization and the inter-character relationships, especially the wonderfully conceived personalities of Macbeth and his wife, were evolved by Shakespeare out of almost nothing. It was he who invented such gripping situations as: the psychological tension in Inverness Castle with the hallucinatory dagger, the voices in the night, the ineffable Amen, and the knocking on the gate; the startling appearance of Banquo's ghost at the feast; the double-talking apparitions and the show of kings in the witches' cavern; and Lady Macbeth's sleep-walking. And, of course, Shakespeare's and his alone is the poetic vesture from beginning to end.

It is worth remarking that in choosing his plot he wisely avoided any period in which the age-long Scottish-English discord figured too prominently. Indeed in the play the feud is in abeyance, and England, so far from evincing hostility and taking advantage of Scotland's difficulties,[95] is anxious to afford such help as will restore to the Scottish throne the rightful King Malcolm after the overthrow of the usurping Macbeth.

While, then, Holinshed or Harrison provided Shakespeare with the general lines of his plot, however much he shaped and added to it, there is good reason to believe, as Charlotte Carmichael Stopes first maintained,[31] that he drew on another telling of the same story. This other source could have been consulted only in manuscript; for it was not printed till 1858[32] from what appears to be a unique original.[33] It is *The Buik of the Croniclis of Scotland*, a quaint versification of Hector Boece's *Scotorum Historiae*. The author, William Stewart (?1481-?1550), was one of the minor Scots Makars, to whom are ascribed various poems in the Bannatyne and Maitland collections. He is said to have made his *Buik* for the young James V at the command of James's mother, Margaret Tudor, and to have finished it in 1535. It is likely that the manuscript *Buik* remained in royal hands and that it can be identified with "the Scottis Chronicle, wrettin with hand" which was in James VI's library at Holyroodhouse.[34]

Throughout his *Buik* Stewart made notable additions to Boece, possibly from tradition but more probably from invention. They have a tendency to glorify the House of Stewart, whose protégé he was and whose surname he shared. Stewart is much more expansive than Boece or Holinshed on the thoughts and feelings, characters and motives of his persons; and he introduces whole conversations which do not figure in his original and are, so to speak, more like the raw material of drama.

Among the amplifications are many points and details which considerably supplement both the story of Macbeth and his wife on the one hand and on the other the stories from the earlier reigns of Duff and Kenneth which, as has already been noticed,[35] Shakespeare fused into a single plot. The material from Stewart is worked into the play, mostly but not entirely, in I, v-vii and II, i-iii; that is to say, in the rising excitement of the lead-up to the murder of Duncan and the shock of its discovery.[36]

It is of great interest as contributing to the characterization of Macbeth and not less to that of Lady Macbeth. The wife of Macbeth is but a shadowy figure in Holinshed, as in Boece. All that Holinshed says about her is: "speciallie his wife lay sore upon him to attempt the thing, as she that was verie ambitious, burning in unquenchable desire to beare the name of a queen".[37] Incidentally, Shakespeare ignores this trait of character and makes his Lady Macbeth selflessly devoted to her husband's advancement. In Stewart the wife of Macbeth is a much more potent and developed personality with a command of words, the kind of woman that Shakespeare made his Lady Macbeth.

In the play the reluctant and half-hearted Macbeth almost pleads with his wife not to urge him on to the murder of Duncan, on the ground of his good standing in the esteem both of the king and of others:

We will proceed no further in this business:
He hath honour'd me of late; and I have bought
Golden opinions from all sorts of people,
Which would be worn now in their newest gloss,
Not cast aside so soon.

(I, vii, 31-36).

This recalls the general picture of Macbeth in Stewart:

This Makcobey, quhilk wes bayth wyss and wycht [= strong],
Strang in ane stour [= battle], and trew as ony steill,
Defendar als with [= likewise] of the commoun weill,
So just ane juge, so equale and so trew
As be [= by] his deidis richt weill befoir ay schew,
Syne [= afterwards] throw his wyfe consentit to sic thing,
For till [= to] destroy his cousing and his King,
So foull ane blek [= black mark] for to put in his gloir,
Quhilk haldin [= held] wes of sic honour befoir.[38]

As Dover Wilson says, "Boece and Holinshed have nothing corresponding to this, and yet how well it sums up the pity of Macbeth's fall as Shakespeare represents it!"[39]

It is Stewart, not Holinshed or Boece, who tells us of the wife of Macbeth "chastising her husband with the valour of her tongue" (I, v, 28) and taunting him with unmanliness and cowardice:

"Thow neidis nocht", scho said, "uther [= otherwise] presume
Bot it maun be as God hes gevin dume [= decreed],
In to the self [= indeed] quhilk is so just and trew",
Be [= by] sindrie ressones that scho till [= to] him schew [= explained].
"Traist weill," scho said, "that sentence is so leill [= reliable]
Withouten place fra it for to apeill [= without ground for appeal
     against it],
That it ma nocht retreittet be agane [= be rescinded],
Quhilk in the self [= indeed] so equal [= just] is and plane."
Quhen this was said, than scho begouth [= began] to flyt [= scold]
With hym that tyme, and said he had the wytt [= was to blame]
So cowartlie that durst nocht tak on hand,
For to fulfill as God had gevin command.
Thairfoir, scho said, "revenge yow of yon King,
Sen [= since] gratious God decreittit hes sic thing.
Quhy suld thow dreid or stand of him sic aw,
So blunt [= dull], so blait [= stupid], berand [= bearing] himself
     so law [= humbly],
That war nocht [= were it not] thow and thi aucthoritie,
With all his liegis he wold lichtlied [= slighted] be?
And now to the sin [= since] he is so unkynd,
Thairfoir," scho said, "I hold the by [= in] thi mind
To dreid the man the quhilk for the is deid [= who but for thee
     would be dead],

And throw thi power oft of his purpois speid [= have success].
Now tarie nocht thairfoir; speid hand [= make haste], haif done
　　[= be done with it],
And to thi purpois se thow speid the sone [= soon];
And haif no dreid, for thow hes all the rycht
Grantit to the be [= by] gratious God of mycht".[40]

I have already quoted the parallel to this passage in the play, in discussing the
state of the text.[41]

　　　It should be noticed that Stewart, like Boece and Holinshed but more
emphatically than they, makes Macbeth feel himself wronged and defrauded
by Duncan's nominating Malcolm as Prince of Cumberland and so heir-
apparent; and also that Stewart goes on, in the lines quoted, to make the wife
of Macbeth tell him that he would be only fulfilling God's will in killing
Duncan. Shakespeare, on the other hand, in order to make Macbeth's treason
the more hideous, leaves him with no justification whatever and with no more
than a sense of vexation at Malcolm's elevation:

　　　　The Prince of Cumberland! that is a step
　　　　On which I must fall down, or else o'erleap,
　　　　For in my way it lies. Stars, hide your fires;
　　　　Let not light see my black and deep desires:
　　　　The eye wink at the hand; yet let that be,
　　　　Which the eye fears, when it is done, to see.
　　　　　　　　　　　　(I, iv, 48-53).

　　　So much for Shakespeare's debt to Stewart in respect of the relationship
of Macbeth and his wife. But Shakespeare, drawing on both Holinshed and
Stewart, conflated the story of their crime with that of an earlier one in which
King Duff was killed by servants at the command of their master Donwald
who was himself driven on by his wife. In Stewart Donwald's wife is just such
a one as he made Macbeth's wife, as urgent and dominating, in words that
have no place in Boece or Holinshed:

　　　This wickit wyffe, that bitter wes and bald,
　　　Consauit [= conceived] hes with greit crudelitie
　　　Ane wickit wyle for to revengit be.
　　　And to hir husband in the tyme scho said,
　　　"Blyn of your baill [= cease from your sad looks], se ye be blyth
　　　　and glaid,
　　　And slaik [= give over] also of all your syte [= sighing] and sorrow:
　　　All salbe [= shall be] weill, I find yow God to borrow [= I
　　　　promise you by God],
　　　To [= according to] my counsall, and heir I tak on me
　　　Of all injure thow sall revengit be.
　　　Considder now thow hes at thi command
　　　Of all this castell ilk syre [= every man] and seruand,
　　　Rycht bisselie for to obey the till [= obey thee],
　　　To satisfy all thi desyre and will,
　　　At thi plesour intill [= in] all gudlie haist.

Hes thow nocht Duffus for to be thi gaist [= guest],
Without belief [= suspicion] of tressoun in thi cuir [= care, hold],
Quhilk hes the wrocht sic malice and injure?
Hes thow nocht seruandis also at thi will,
All thi command at plesour to fulfill?
How can thow find", scho said, "ane better tyme,
To be revengit of this cruell cryme?
Hes thow nocht now this Duffus in thi cuir,
Hes [= who has] done us baith so greit harme and injure?
Dreid nocht", scho said, "suppois he be ane King,
Tak litill tent [= notice] or terrour of sic thing,
Sen [= since] mony ane with litill red [= considering] full sone
    [= without delay]
Siclike [= in the same way] befoir to sic tirannis [= tyrants] had done.
Thairfoir," scho said, "as all the cace now standis
And he umschew [= escape] at this tyme fra thi handis
In all thi lyfe, thocht [= though] thow wald neuir so fane [= so
    much desire]
Thow sall nocht get so gude ane tyme again".[42]

Passages in I, v and I, vii of *Macbeth* are much in the same strain:

             To beguile the time,
Look like the time; bear welcome in your eye,
Your hand, your tongue: look like the innocent flower,
But be the serpent under't.   (I, v, 64-67).

         Only look up clear;
To alter favour ever is to fear.   (I, v, 72-73).

            We fail!
But screw your courage to the sticking-place,
And we'll not fail. When Duncan is asleep . . .
         his two chamberlains
Will I with wine and wassail so convince
That memory, the warder of the brain,
Shall be a fume, and the receipt of reason
A limbeck only: when in swinish sleep
Their drenched natures lie as in a death,
What cannot you and I perform upon
The unguarded Duncan? what not put upon
His spongy officers, who shall bear the guilt
Of our great quell?   (I, vii, 59-61, 63-72).

After the murder of Duffus in Stewart's *Buik*, Donwald, like Shakespeare's Lady Macbeth, pretended to swoon. On recovering he ran distractedly up and down, shouting and screaming, just as Lady Macbeth plans for herself and her husband:

    Macbeth. . . . Will it not be received . . .
      That they [*i.e.* the grooms] have done't?

Lady Macbeth. Who dares receive it other,
   As we shall make our griefs and clamour roar
   Upon his death?   (I, vii, 74, 77-79).

These and other correspondences between Stewart and Shakespeare are too many and too close to be dismissed as coincidental. For a discussion of how, where, and when Shakespeare had access to Stewart's *Buik* I must refer to the last Chapter.[43]

Shakespeare had several understandable reasons, some of them decidedly topical, for fixing on the Macbeth story out of all the lurid annals of Scotland. In the first place, it is eminently suitable for dramatic presentation. George Buchanan had already realized this incidentally when narrating the events in his *Rerum Scoticarum Historia*, 1582. The translation of the passage, which Shakespeare was a good enough Latinist to have read in the original, is as follows: "Some of our writers do here record many fables, which are like Milesian tales, and fitter for the stage than a history, and therefore I omit them".[44] And Milton likewise realized the story's potentialities, for he included Macbeth in a list of ninety-nine subjects from Biblical and British history suitable for dramatic treatment,[45] drawn up between 1640 and 1642 at a time when he had not yet abandoned the drama in favour of the epic for his *magnum opus*.

A more particular reason for Shakespeare's choice of plot is that the historical events dramatized were closely associated with James VI and I's family history. Holinshed in fact has a long digression, in his account of Macbeth's reign, on the alleged origin of the House of Stewart from Banquo and Fleance and on all the generations down to James himself.[46] The earlier part of the genealogy was invented to dignify the royal line, perhaps at the instance of one of the first of the royal Stewarts, Robert II or Robert III. But Boece seems to have been the first to have incorporated it in a written history.

The Stewarts in the person of Robert II had come to the throne by the marriage of Robert's father, Walter Stewart who was the Lord High Steward of Scotland like five or more of his direct ancestors, and Princess Marjory, daughter of Robert I (The Bruce). The chroniclers, or perhaps the High Seannachies (predecessors of the Lords Lyon) whose duty it was on occasions to recite the royal genealogy, extended the Stewart line back, not to the undistinguished Flaald or Fledaldus (Seneschal of Dol in Brittany) who was the real progenitor, but by some dubious generations to Fleance and so to Banquo. Banquo was reputed to be, on both the male and the female sides, of the royal stock of Scotland like Duncan and Macbeth, a true descendant of Kenneth MacAlpine and Fergus MacErc and innumerable generations before that. But he was in fact an unhistorical fiction.

Shakespeare accepted his historicity without question, and on from the witches' hail—

First Witch. Lesser than Macbeth, and greater.
Second Witch. Not so happy, yet much happier.
Third Witch. Thou shalt get kings, though thou be none.
         (I, iii, 65-67)—

reminds us by a phrase, again and again, of Banquo as the ancestor of kings-to-be.

And he makes much of Macbeth's bitterness and heartache at his own child-lessness:

> He chid the sisters
> When first they put the name of king upon me,
> And bade them speak to him: then prophet-like
> They hail'd him father to a line of kings;
> Upon my head they placed a fruitless crown,
> And put a barren sceptre in my gripe,
> Thence to be wrench'd with an unlineal hand,
> No son of mine succeeding. If't be so,
> For Banquo's issue have I filed my mind;
> For them the gracious Duncan have I murder'd;
> Put rancours in the vessel of my peace
> Only for them; and mine eternal jewel
> Given to the common enemy of man,
> To make them kings, the seed of Banquo kings!
> Rather than so, come fate into the list,
> And champion me to the utterance!
>
> (III, i, 57-72).

When, in the witches' cavern, Macbeth sees "*A show of Eight* Kings, *the last with a glass in his hand; Banquo's Ghost following*" (IV, i, S.D., after 111),[47] he is aghast:

> Thou art too like the spirit of Banquo; down!
> Thy crown does sear mine eye-balls. And thy hair,
> Thou other gold-bound brow, is like the first.
> A third is like the former. Filthy hags!
> Why do you show me this? A fourth! Start, eyes!
> What, will the line stretch out to the crack of doom?
> Another yet! A seventh! I'll see no more:
> And yet the eighth appears, who bears a glass
> Which shows me many more; and some I see
> That two-fold balls and treble sceptres carry:
> Horrible sight! Now, I see, 'tis true;
> For the blood-bolter'd Banquo smiles upon me,
> And points at them for his.   (IV, i, 112-24).

The eight kings, with a family resemblance to each other and to Banquo, are the eight Stewart monarchs from Robert II to Mary whose husband Lord Darnley, also a Stewart, enjoyed the Crown matrimonial and the title of King Henry. It is unlikely that Shakespeare omitted the generation of Mary and Darnley from his count and intended the last of the kings to be James VI and I himself. I think that we are meant to recognize James as the first of the sovereigns seen only in the mirror carried by the last of the eight. The "two-fold balls and treble sceptres" have been variously interpreted; but it cannot be doubted that in some way they allude to the Union of the Crowns under James. That Union can be said to have been a constitutional fact from the death of Elizabeth on 24th March 1603, and before the triple style of King of Great Britain, France, and Ireland was announced by a proclamation of 20th October 1604.

The plot which Shakespeare chose for his Scottish tragedy also allowed him to emphasize legitimacy and lineal succession. As Queen Elizabeth grew older without naming her successor, there was a mounting anxiety as to who it would be. The better-informed statists knew that James was unquestionably the true heir, though in fact Elizabeth herself refused to admit his claim until she was *in articulo mortis*; and there may well have been doubts as to the ready acceptance of a sovereign from a foreign land, good as his title might be. That James did succeed peacefully was the occasion for general rejoicing. Shakespeare expressed his own satisfaction and relief in *Sonnet* 107.[48]

In *Macbeth*, which I believe to be earlier in the main, he ignores or makes as little as he can of the fact that the Scottish monarchy in the eleventh century was still of a semi-elective nature within the options of tanistry; that is to say, the system by which the Crown passed, not to an heir-apparent, but to the male member of the royal House most fitted by age and capacity to rule. As I have already said,[49] in Holinshed, as also in Boece and Stewart, Macbeth felt himself defrauded by Duncan's nominating Malcolm as Prince of Cumberland "as it were thereby to appoint him his successor in the kingdome, immediatelie after his decease. *Makbeth* sore troubled herewith, for that he saw by this means his hope sore hindered (where, by the old laws of the realme, the ordinance was, that if he that should succeed were not of able age to take the charge upon himself, he that was next of blood unto him should be admitted) he began to take councell how he might usurp the kingdome by force, having a just quarrell so to do (as he tooke the matter) for that *Duncane* did what in him lay to defraud him of all manner of title and claime, which he might in time to come, pretend unto the crowne".[50] Shakespeare's Macbeth, on the other hand, though vexed by the proclamation of Malcolm as Prince of Cumberland, never in soliloquy or otherwise thinks of himself as cheated or of Duncan as having acted arbitrarily and contrary to constitutional usage.

Immediately after the discovery of Duncan's murder occurs this passage:
Ross. Is't known who did this more than bloody deed?
Macduff. Those that Macbeth hath slain [*i.e.* the grooms].
Ross.   Alas, the day!
   What good could they pretend?
Macduff.   They were suborn'd:
   Malcolm and Donalbain, the king's two sons,
   Are stol'n away and fled; which puts upon them
   Suspicion of the deed.
Ross.   'Gainst nature still!
   Thriftless ambition, that wilt ravin up.
   Thine own life's means! Then 'tis most like
   The sovereignty will fall upon Macbeth.
Macduff. He is already named, and gone to Scone
   To be invested.   (II, iv, 22-32).
This is more or less in line with Holinshed: "Then having a companie about him of such as he had made privie to his enterprise, he caused himself to be proclamed king, and foorthwith went unto *Scone*, where (by common

consent) he received the investure of the kingdome according to the accustomed maner . . . *Malcolme Canmore* and *Donald Bane* the sons of king *Duncane*, for fear of their lives (which they might well know that *Makbeth* would seeke to bring to end for his more sure confirmation in the estate) fled".[51]

But there are some differences which are not without significance. Shakespeare's Macbeth has no accomplices except his wife, and no nucleus of supporters in the expectation of an election. His Malcolm and Donalbain forfeit, in the opinion of the notables, their own prior and higher claims to the Crown by their flight and the suspicion it excited of their complicity. And his Macbeth has no need to proclaim himself king first and trust to the "common consent" following on thereafter. Macbeth in the play is of royal descent, Duncan's "peerless kinsman" (I, iv, 58); and so far as the text of the play goes and so far as Shakespeare's audience with its settled notion of monarchy as strictly hereditary would understand, Macbeth inherited as the man next in succession, not as a man elected.

The disablement of Malcolm and Donaldbain from the succession on account of their alleged instigation of their father's murder is further emphasized in a speech by Macbeth to Banquo, in which for the first time he assumes as of right the royal plural:

> We hear, our bloody cousins are bestow'd
> In England and in Ireland, not confessing
> Their cruel parricide, filling their hearers
> With strange invention: but of that to-morrow,
> When therewithal we shall have cause of state
> Craving us jointly.   (III, i, 30-35).

He infers that the forfeited princes are working treasonable malice against himself as lawful king, and that their activities abroad is proper "cause of state" for the Council to consider.

In the interests, then, of a wider topical purpose, Shakespeare makes the eleventh-century monarchy of Scotland depend on a right in blood, a right, however, which could be forfeited by treason, parricide, and flight.

From II, iv to III, iv the other characters accept Macbeth as a king with an undoubted title. It is only with III, vi that the revolt against him begins. He is openly declared a "tyrant" (III, vi, 22 and 25; IV, iii, 12, 36, 45, 104, 178, and 185) and a "usurper" (V, viii, 55). Malcolm's "down-fall'n birthdom" (IV, iii, 4) is asserted. And in the last scene of all Macduff, with Macbeth's head symbolically held aloft, hails Malcolm as King:

> Hail, king! for so thou art: behold, where stands
> The usurper's cursed head: the time is free:
> I see thee compass'd with thy kingdom's pearl,
> That speak my salutation in their minds;
> Whose voices I desire aloud with mine:
> Hail, King of Scotland!

All.   Hail, King of Scotland!
>   (V, viii, 54-59).

C

This is no election by one claiming by right of conquest. It is the acknowledge-ment and proclamation of a king by right of blood and descent.

And such James VI and I was. But Shakespeare and all his audience knew that treason had raised its head in very recent days against James; and Shake-speare wanted a plot with treason and its consequences as the pivot of a play. As already said,[52] it is a false assumption that the treason which bulked large in Shakespeare's mind when he was writing *Macbeth* was the Gunpowder Plot of 1605: it was, on the contrary, the Gowrie Conspiracy of 1600, as I try to demonstrate in Chapter 7.[53]

Shakespeare shared the almost religious detestation with which men in general, and King James himself in particular, regarded regicide. The murder of an anointed king was a crime and sin of a peculiarly appalling character:

> *Macduff.* O horror, horror, horror! Tongue nor heart
> Cannot conceive nor name thee! . . .
> Confusion now hath made his masterpiece!
> Most sacrilegious murder hath broke ope
> The Lord's anointed temple, and stole thence
> The life o' the building! . . .
> Approach the chamber, and destroy your sight
> With a new Gorgon: do not bid me speak;
> See, and then speak yourselves.
>   (II, iii, 69-74, 76-78).

James's extraordinary and protracted measures for the signal punishment of persons adjudged guilty in the Gowrie Conspiracy,[54] as later in the Gunpowder Plot, if they manifest in the main the King's own feelings in the matter, also reflect a universal abhorrence.

Besides his horror at regicide, Shakespeare proclaims in play after play his profound reverence for the mystique of kingship. He could not but be well aware of James's no less exalted notions of the royal office. James had in fact expounded them in several places, but most fully in *The true Lawe of Free Monarchies; or the reciprocle and mutuall dutie betwixt a free king and his naturall subjects*, 1598. He makes much of royal anointing. In his opinion "once a king has been anointed, be he 'an idolatrous persecuter' like Nebuchadnezzar or 'a bloody tyrant' and 'monster to the world' like Nero, his subjects' duty, as laid down in Holy Writ, is perfect obedience and even prayers for his prosperity".[55]

Shakespeare can be said to illustrate such a concept in relation to Macbeth, even though he was "*the* tyrant of Scottish history"[56] according to the chroniclers.[57] Hence Banquo, who has better cause than anyone else to suspect, nevertheless accepts the unalterable fact that Macbeth has indeed become his king, even though he may have played "most foully for't" (III i, 3), and behaves with the utmost respect to the anointed and crowned usurper. He was not, as some have misinterpreted him, an ambiguous time-server, but simply such a one as both King James and Shakespeare believed a subject should be.

At the same time, and in contrast to Macbeth, Shakespeare wanted to paint a picture of a good and beloved king, which King James at least might take to be a true likeness of himself and which, in the climate of opinion then obtaining, would be generally accepted as seemly. Shakespeare's Duncan is such an amiable sovereign; he is "the gracious Duncan" (III, i, 66; III, vi, 3), who

> Hath borne his faculties so meek, hath been
> So clear in his great office, that his virtues
> Will plead like angels, trumpet-tongued, against
> The deep damnation of his taking-off.
>   (I, vii, 17-20).

But Duncan and James are not meant to be specially equated. However, there is another good king off-stage, the saintly Edward the Confessor, "gracious England" (IV, iii, 189).

The passage in the play on his miraculously healing touch (IV, iii, 140-59) is based on one in Holinshed's *English Chronicle* dealing with the Confessor's reign, which is not in *The Scottish Chronicle*. But Shakespeare seized on it for reasons quite other than relevance to the story of Macbeth; for indeed it has no relevance and the twenty lines given to it are an excrescence from a dramatic point of view. The spectators were meant to shuttle their minds between the Confessor and James, his lawful, though not lineal, successor; notably in respect of his curative touch for "the King's Evil" or scrofula, which James began to exercise not later than 6th November 1604; but also no doubt in respect of the "heavenly gift of prophecy" (IV, iii, 157), with which the British Solomon was credited by the bishops at the Hampton Court Conference of January 1604;[58] and generally in respect of piety and prayerfulness and

> sundry blessings . . . about his throne,
> That speak him full of grace.
>   (IV, iii, 158-59).

Moreover, Shakespeare's contemporaries were also meant to associate "the king-becoming graces", which Malcolm lists as proper to a king:

> As justice, verity, temperance, stableness,
> Bounty, perseverance, mercy, lowliness,
> Devotion, patience, courage, fortitude,
>   (IV, iii, 91-94).

with James, extravagant as the attribution of some of them in particular might be. The list in Holinshed which suggested the passage is shorter: "there is nothing that more becometh a prince than constancy, verity, truth, and justice, with the other laudable fellowship of those fair and noble vertues which are comprehended onlie in soothfastness".[59] There is something more like the list in the play in James's own list of royal attributes in *Basilikon Doron*: "Iustice . . ., Clemencie, Magnanimitie, Liberalitie, Constancie, Humilitie, and all other Princelie vertues".[60]

But Shakespeare knew, as all did, that James's favourite motto was one of the Beatitudes, *Beati pacifici*, and that his foreign policy in particular was directed by a genuine desire for peace. In alluding to this, Shakespeare deliberately departs from a sequence in Holinshed.

He follows Holinshed in making Malcolm in the scene in England accuse himself of certain vices to Macduff, in order to put the latter's loyalty and reliability to the test and to make certain that he himself was not being led into a trap. Then, when Malcolm is convinced of Macduff's complete integrity, he "unspeaks his own detraction" (IV, iii, 123). The first two self-accusations of Holinshed's Malcolm are "immoderate lust and voluptuous sensualitie" and "unquenchable avarice". The third (this last with particular emphasis) is "dissimulation, telling of leasings, and all other kinds of deceit, so that I naturally rejoice in nothing so much, as to betray and deceive such as put any trust or confidence in my words".[61] Shakespeare's Malcolm confesses to the first two vices, bottomless "voluptuousness" (IV, iii, 61) and "stanchless avarice" (IV, iii, 78); but for the third he substitutes a hatred of peace and a love of discord:

> Nay, had I power, I should
> Pour the sweet milk of concord into hell,
> Uproar the universal peace, confound
> All unity on earth.
> (IV, iii, 97-100).

But when Shakespeare's Malcolm does "unspeak his own detraction", it is the three vices in Holinshed which he repudiates without any reference to the hatred of peace:

> I am yet
> Unknown to woman, never was forsworn,
> Scarcely have coveted what was mine own,
> At no time broke my faith, would not betray
> The devil to his fellow and delight
> No less in truth than life: my first false speaking
> Was this upon myself.   (IV, iii, 125-31).

The discrepancy between the self-accusation and the retraction is a sure sign of a somewhat carelessly-made change in an already-existing text. But it is clear that Shakespeare was complimenting by implication a royal peacemaker in changing the Holinshed sequence. The tragedy of *Macbeth* ends, too, on a note of relief and peaceful promise such as the orderly accession of James had brought.

But *Macbeth* was more pervasively complimentary to James, in that it offered a play involving demonology and witchcraft, to a monarch who believed himself to have suffered many things at the hands of diabolists and regarded himself as a witch-doctor of no common order. James was not at all exceptional in his convictions as to the existence of witches and the dire effects of their malign operations. Indeed such beliefs were widespread in the sixteenth and seventeenth centuries. Many witch-trials took place and many wretches were barbarously executed in consequence. Statute followed statute for the more effective suppression of the supposed evil. And a great number of books of every dimension from huge compilations to mere pamphlets were published in which diabolology and witchcraft were taken for granted without question. Only a very few were sceptics, like John Wier or Wierus in his *De Praestigiis Daemonum*, 1563, and other works, and his admirer and debtor Reginald Scot in *The Discovery of Witchcraft*, 1584.

James, who was an avid reader in many fields, had almost certainly delved deep and early in the vast literature of witchcraft. But his zeal against the black arts was greatly quickened in 1590 by reports of a grand assembly of wizards and witches held at North Berwick under the presidency of Satan, in order to raise storms on the sea during James's voyage home from Denmark with his young bride. At the witch-trials which followed, evidence was given to the effect that certain wizards and witches had been approached by the troublesome Francis Hepburn, Earl of Bothwell (nephew of Queen Mary's Bothwell) to get them to practise their arts against the King's life. Many other such trials occurred in different districts throughout the country and during the whole reign, with the King himself sometimes on the bench.

As an avowed opponent of John Wier and Reginald Scot, James published his *Daemonologie, in forme of a dialogue* in 1597.[62] It is in three books, the first on magic and necromancy, the second on sorcery and witchcraft, and the third on the kinds of spirits that trouble and injure men. Unlike many other books at the time on such subjects, which tend to be rambling and long-winded, James's dialogue is concise and well-written; and it provides the best contemporary exposition of the whole belief in witchcraft.

That Shakespeare read *Daemonologie* with attention cannot be doubted. As Mrs. Stopes says, such a book "written by the king whom Shakespeare was planning to honour might not be ignored".[63]

But Shakespeare gleaned suggestions from the abundance of other literature in the same field, including Reginald Scot's book which is crammed with curious lore and accounts of recent witch-trials, cases of demoniacal possession, and the like.

One pamphlet of particular interest in the circumstances is *Newes from Scotland, Declaring the damnable life of Doctor Fian, a notable Sorcerer, burned at Edenborough*, of which three editions appeared in 1591 either in Scotland or in England. Doctor Fian, whose real name was John Cunningham, was said to be the chief figure of the already-mentioned large coven numbering two hundred or more of men and women who, many arriving by sea in sieves,[64] forgathered at North Berwick to swear obedience to the devil and to raise storms to disperse the King's fleet on his return from Denmark in April 1590.[65] The evidence against the many accused is as particular and detailed as it is incredible. It is perhaps worth remarking that the Scottish trials for witchcraft are distinguished from the English ones by being less trite and more imaginative in the details of the evidence led and by the greater prominence in them of the alleged power of witches over the elements and of charges against them of raising storms and causing shipwrecks. And such are Shakespeare's witches.

The question of Shakespeare's own belief or disbelief in witchcraft must remain unsolved. But it would be rash to assume that the great Shakespeare must have been as incredulous of the actuality of witchcraft as we are in these wise days. And it could be plausibly argued that no one could present the supernatural with such imaginative power as he does, unless he went a part of the way at least towards belief in it.

However, it has to be recognized that in *Macbeth* the witchcraft is *sui generis* and very different from the commonplace diablerie of *The Witch, c.* 1609-

1610, by Thomas Middleton, *The Witch of Edmonton, c.* 1621, a collaboration
by Thomas Dekker, William Rowley, John Ford, and perhaps others, and *The
Late Lancashire Witches*, 1634, by Thomas Heywood and Richard Brome. They
all put on the stage the sort of alleged activities of witches, petty and grotesque,
such as were described in trials by witnesses who were mostly uneducated and
unreliable and often scared and malicious.

Shakespeare made his witches, in the uncontaminated scenes of the play,
far more awful and impressive, far more mysterious and powerful than the
common run of the pathetic victims of witch-hunts. The few points which
Shakespeare's witches have in common with the witches of vulgar superstition
do not slant to the comic or absurd, and are suggested quite incidentally, mostly
at the beginning of I, iii and in IV, i.[66] His "instruments of darkness" (I, iii,
124) are never called "witches", apart from the stage directions and this one
line:

> 'Aroint thee, witch!' the rump-fed ronyon cries.
> (I, iii, 6).

Otherwise they are referred to more impressively as: the "weird sisters" (I, iii,
32; I, v, 8-9; II, i, 20; III, iv, 133; IV, i, 136), the "sisters" (III, i, 57), or the
"weird women" (III, i, 2). They strike wonder and awe into even such seasoned
warriors as Macbeth and Banquo. They are invariably addressed or spoken of
in the language of fearful astonishment or fearful revulsion:

> What are these
> So wither'd and so wild in their attire,
> That look not like the inhabitants o' the earth,
> And yet are on't? Live you? or are you aught
> That man may question?   (I, iii, 39-43).
> you secret, black, and midnight hags!
> (IV, i, 48).

They can vanish into thin air:

> The earth hath bubbles, as the water has,
> And these are of them. Whither are they vanish'd?
> (I, iii, 79-80).

They have "more . . . than mortal knowledge" (I, v, 3) and power to

> look into the seeds of time,
> And say which grain will grow and which will not.
> (I, iii, 58-59).

They command spirits which appear and speak for them in equivocating
prophecies. And they read the mind of anyone consulting them: "Thou hast
harp'd my fear aright", says Macbeth (IV, i, 74).

Besides, we are meant to associate the witches in some vague way with all
the storms and portents of the night of Duncan's murder and in the days before
and after (II, iii, 59-68; II, iv, 1-20). And though Macbeth does not state facts
about the witches in his tremendous adjuration, he calls up the fears which their
powers have begotten in his mind:

> I conjure you, by that which you profess,
> Howe'er you come to know it, answer me:

Though you untie the winds and let them fight
Against the churches; though the yesty waves
Confound and swallow navigation up;
Though bladed corn be lodged and trees blown down;
Though castles topple on their warders' heads;
Though palaces and pyramids do slope
Their heads to their foundations; though the treasure
Of nature's germens tumble all together,
Even till destruction sicken; answer me
To what I ask you.   (IV, i, 50-61).

In a real sense, the influence of the witches is as potent when they are off
the stage as when they are on it. For all the murders and massacres, betrayals
and blood, tyranny, war, and carnage of the play are triggered off by their
"supernatural soliciting" (I, iii, 130) and follow in an inevitable sequence of
evil.

As Charles Lamb says, "the hags of Shakspeare have neither child of their
own, nor seem to be descended from any parent. They are foul anomalies, of
whom we know not whence they are sprung, nor whether they have beginning
or ending. As they are without human passions, so they seem to be without human relations. . . . they have no *names*; which heightens their
mysteriousness."[67]

Shakespeare keeps them on a plane of their own. It is to be noted that only
Macbeth himself and Banquo ever see them. Yet they were known dimly by
others to exist: Macbeth had "learned by the perfectest report, they have more
in them than mortal knowledge" (I, v, 2-3). They had a haunt where Macbeth
knew he could find them, as he lets fall in his wife's hearing though more to
himself than to her:

I will to-morrow,
And betimes I will, to the weird sisters:
More shall they speak. (III, iv, 132-34).

When he does consult them in their cave,[68] he is alone with them. But apparently he had been attended as far as the cave by Lennox, who waits outside and
is summoned in when the witches have vanished. To Macbeth's questions,
"Saw you the weird sisters? . . . Came they not by you?" (IV, i, 135-36),
Lennox gives a negative answer; but he is not surprised at the mention of them
or curious as to who they were. Moreover, the galloping which Macbeth had
heard in the cave was caused by the horses of two or three who had come with
news of Macduff's flight to England and who had evidently known where to
come to deliver it.

One Simon Forman, an astrologer, quack doctor, and necromancer of
some notoriety, saw a performance of *Macbeth* on Saturday, 20th April 1611,[69]
and wrote an account of it in his *Booke of Plaies and Notes thereof, for common
Pollicie.*[70] From his interest in the occult, one might have expected him to be
particular and circumstantial about a supernatural play. But there are details in
his account which suggest either that the play Forman saw differed in several
points from the version we possess or (and this is much more likely) that

Forman was an inaccurate observer. His description of Macbeth's first encounter with the witches is puzzling. It is as follows:

"there was to be observed first how Macbeth and Banquo two
noblemen of Scotland, riding through a wood, there stood before
them three women, fairies or nymphs, and saluted Macbeth, saying
three times unto him, Hail, Macbeth, king of Codor, for thou
shalt be a king, but shalt beget no kings, &c. Then said Banquo,
What, all to Macbeth and nothing to me? Yes, said the nymphs,
Hail, to thee, Banquo; thou shalt beget kings, yet be no king.
And so they departed, and came to the Court of Scotland."[71]

But no beings could be less like fairies or nymphs than the mysterious three whom Shakespeare's Macbeth and Banquo meet, not in a wood, but "Upon this blasted heath" (I, iii, 77), or less like the "secret, black, and midnight hags" (IV, i, 48) who concoct a hellish broth and, by their "masters' " aid (IV, i, 63), summon up spirits to speak strange "bodements" (IV, i, 96). Very surprisingly, Forman says nothing about Macbeth's deliberate consultation of the witches in IV, i, the apparitions raised, or their equivocating prophecies; and likewise nothing about the unexpected fulfilment of the prophecies in V, iii-viii.

It is just possible that Forman, perhaps recording his summary of the play after a lapse of time, confused his recollection of the play with his recollection of two other items.

One is Holinshed's narrative of the confrontation of Macbeth and Banquo by three unknown women: when they were passing "without other companie, save onlie themselves, . . . through the woods and fields, . . . suddenlie in the middest of a laund [= glade, open space in a wood], there met them three women in strange and wild[72] apparell, resembling creatures of an elder world". After hailing Macbeth as thane of Glamis, thane of Cawdor, and king-to-be, and promising to Banquo that he would be the progenitor of a long line of kings, "Herewith the foresaid women vanished immediatelie out of their sight. This was reputed at the first but some vaine fantasticall illusion by *Makbeth* and *Banquho*. . . . But afterwards the common opinion was, that these women were either the weird sisters, that is, (as ye would say) the goddesses of destinie, or else some nymphs or feiries, indowed with knowledge of prophesie by their necromanticall science, because every thing came to pass as they had spoken."[73]

The second of Forman's recollections may have been of a complimentary show to welcome James, Queen Anne, and Prince Henry in progress at Oxford before the gate of St John's College on 27th August 1605. This brief device, consisting of speeches in Latin and English, was enacted by three young members of the College, attired as nymphs or sibyls and declaring themselves to be beings similar to the three who had once prophesied to Banquo a long line of royal descendants. There are two triads of hails to the King who is variously designated in them, and a third triad hailing the other members of the royal family. The sibyls foretell, in cloudy terms, a long continuation of the royal line, increasing empire, fame extending to the stars, peace, etc. But, while much is made of James's descent from Banquo, there is no allusion to Macbeth.

The author of *Tres Sibyllae* was Matthew Gwinne or Gwynne, one of the

St. John's fellows. He added his verses to the edition in 1607 of his Latin play, *Vertumnus sive Annus Recurrens*, which James saw at Christ Church on 29th August during the same royal visit to Oxford and which nearly or quite sent him to sleep. The verses as printed have the heading: "Ad Regis introitum, a Ioannensi Collegio extra portam Vrbis Borealem sito, tres quasi Sibyllae, sic (ut a silua) salutarunt".[74]

It has generally been assumed that Shakespeare was influenced towards adopting the story of Macbeth by acquiring some knowledge of Gwinne's show. But this assumption is dependent on another (and in my opinion equally false) assumption that *Macbeth* was not written till 1606 and that it was a reverberation, so to speak, of the Gunpowder Plot. I have already given my reasons for substantially assigning *Macbeth* to 1601 and for regarding it as an echo of the Gowrie Conspiracy.[75] It is far more likely that Gwinne got the idea for his device from seeing Shakespeare's play, which he could have done when the King's men visited Oxford between 7th May and 10th June 1604, than that Shakespeare was set on to write his tragedy on Macbeth by a once-only show which does not even mention Macbeth. Holinshed's *Chronicles* was one of the most-thumbed books in Shakespeare's library and had been so for years. He did not need to be reminded of what was in it by Gwinne. He simply turned to it, possibly at a hint from James himself,[76] when he wanted a plot from Scottish history.

Of course Gwinne, too, knew his Holinshed. That is why he made his three sybils dignified personages in splendid attire for the delivery of complimentary speeches.

The point to notice is that Holinshed distinguishes between the stately three, who give an oracular greeting to Macbeth and Banquo, and the diabolists Macbeth consults later. But all that Holinshed has corresponding to the activities of Shakespeare's witches in IV, i is as follows: "Neither could he afterwards abide to look upon the said *Makduffe*, either for that he thought his puissance over great; either else for that he had learned of certaine wizzards, in whose words he put great confidence (for that the prophesie had happened so right, which the three faries or weird sisters had declared unto him) how that he ought to take heed of *Makduffe*, who in time to come should seek to destroie him.

"And surelie hereupon had he put *Makduffe* to death, but that a certaine witch, whom he had in great trust, had told that he should never be slain with man borne of anie woman, nor vanquished until the wood of *Bernane* came to the castell of *Dunsinane*. By this prophesie *Makbeth* put all fear out of his heart, supposing he might do what he would, without anie fear to be punished for the same, for by the one prophesie he believed it was impossible for anie man to vanquish him, and by the other unpossible to slay him."[77]

In dramatizing a Scottish story with an eye to an English audience,[78] Shakespeare was obviously aware of the differences between the two nationalities and felt that the ethnic characteristics of his Scots must be unmistakably manifested. The result is that *Macbeth* is more of a study of national character than Shakespeare ever attempted elsewhere. For all the persons of the tragedy, with insignificant exceptions, are Scots; and they live, move, and have their being in a Scotland which he set himself to convey, as he did not for, say, Hamlet's Denmark or, for that matter, for any of the other foreign countries which supply a nominal *mise-en-scène*.

It is true that Shylock the Jew and Othello the Moor are what their blood and heredity have made them. But they are only individual representatives of their races among other characters with no particular ethnic colouring.[79] Such other Shakespearian figures as the Welsh Glendower, Fluellen, and Sir Hugh Evans, the Scottish Captain Jamy, the Irish Captain Macmorris, the Spanish Prince of Arragon and Don Adriano de Armado, and the Moorish Prince of Morocco are all only of episodic interest and all only individuals out of context.[80] The great majority of the people in Shakespeare's plays, set in England, France, Italy, Illyria, Vienna, Cyprus, Denmark, or the Never-Never-Land of the Forest of Arden, the sea-coast of Bohemia, the Levant of Pericles, and the island of Prospero, are characterized according to their roles, and not according to race or nationality. As for the Roman histories and other plays with classical or pseudo-classical backgrounds, Shakespeare was not greatly concerned with either national differentiae or local custom, beyond what could be conveyed by a masterly hint here and there.

But *Macbeth* is most intimately related to and embedded in a still primitive Scotland; and the plot, the characters, the ethos, and the locale are inextricably interdependent. In the tragedy, apart from the witches who are beings of a unique kind, Shakespeare presents characters nearly all of high or royal rank and all displaying in varying degrees a temperament with an emotional mobility, an intensity of imagination, and a responsiveness to the mystery of things.[81]

It is distinguished from the temperament he had already illustrated in his English chronicle-histories. As Sir Herbert Grierson says, Shakespeare "recognized in these turbulent kings and thanes" whom he found in Holinshed's *Scottish Chronicle* "a type of criminal quite distinct both from the hard, unscrupulous, remorseless, and ambitious Norman nobles ... of the early 'histories', and from the subtle and soulless artist in crime such as he ... portrayed in Iago. Story after story told him of men driven by an irresistible impulse into deeds of treachery and bloodshed but haunted when the deed was done by the spectres of conscience and superstition."[82] But, as I shall try to show later, Shakespeare was perhaps able to take a closer and more up-to-date view of the Scots than he found in Holinshed.[83]

For his Scottish royalty and nobility, Shakespeare indicates, by skilfully chosen details and phrases, a gaunt and impressive way of life, not without the elements of a noble barbarism, which the spectators were meant to contrast with the softer existence of those whom Macbeth scornfully dismisses as "the English epicures" (V, iii, 8).[84] In his dramatization of eleventh-century events, Shakespeare offered a picture of a primitive Scotland, much as he did of a primitive England in *King Lear*. If the picture was not to be taken quite as a sample of King James's Scotland, nevertheless it was to be seen as not so very different either, and as reflecting a country still savage in many ways, in which law and order were only too frequently violated and deeds "bloody, bold, and resolute" (IV, i, 79) were only too commonly committed.

Shakespeare staged both aspects of the Scottish ethos, the national character and the social organization, in no spirit of depreciation or satire; though
such a treatment of Scots and Scotland on the stage, especially after James's
accession to the English throne, was in many instances carried to a length which
astounded both native and foreign observers and did not stop short of caricatur-
ing the Sovereign himself (his "uncouth speech . . ., his intemperance, his gusts
of passion, his inordinate devotion to the chase"[85]), as well as his following of
beggarly Scots on the make. On the contrary, Shakespeare's Scots (with the
single exception of the Porter, who, however, is not ridiculed) are all dignified.
The two central characters may at the end appear to Malcolm and the rest as
"this dead butcher and his fiend-like queen" (V, viii, 69); but that, despite
everything, is not how they appear to us, on whom they leave an impression
of superb and terrible grandeur and in whom they cleave asunder compassion
and moral judgement.

In addition to the Scottish temperament and manner of life, Shakespeare
relates his *Macbeth* to the Scottish landscape and topography, as he does not,
to anything like the same degree, any other play to its locale. The word "Scotland" is mentioned thirteen times, often very significantly; and there are other
pointed phrases which mean "Scotland" without actually naming it. The seven
uses of "England" and the four of "English" also in a way keep reminding the
audience of a background that Shakespeare never wants them to forget. The
other place-names, all from the rugged northern half of the country with the
exception of Cumberland (which was an appanage of the Scottish Crown in the
eleventh century) are many and are used with effect: Scone where Scottish
kings were crowned (II, iv, 31-32) and Colmekill or Iona where they were
buried (II, iv, 32-35); the Western Isles whence came the "kerns and gallowglasses" of "The merciless Macdonwald" (I, ii, 9, 13); Saint Colme's inch or
Inchcolm where Sweno buried his dead (I, ii, 60-62); Forres near which the
witches lay in wait on the "blasted heath" (I, iii, 39, 76-78); Inverness Castle
where Duncan was murdered (I, iv, 42; I, v to II, iv); "Great Birnam wood"
and "high Dunsinane hill" (IV, i, 93); and the districts which gave their territorial titles to the thanes, Fife, Glamis, Cawdor, Ross, Lennox, Menteith,
Angus, and Caithness. In fact *Macbeth* is not merely set in Scotland: it is set in
Highland Scotland and Shakespeare drew most of his characters on the lines of
Highland chiefs and their clansmen, not at all on Lowland models which would
have presented him with much less in the way of a national idiosyncrasy
different from the English.

The evidence for this is diffused throughout the play. But I would mention
two small visual details which Shakespeare has deliberately introduced, though
no one to my knowledge has previously noted them. The first shows that he
visualized his Scots as wearing clothes that were different from those commonly worn in England (presumably the *breacan-feile* or tartan belted plaid and
the blue bonnet with one or more feathers to indicate rank). It occurs appropriately in the one scene in England:

              Enter Ross.

Macduff.   See, who comes here?

Malcolm. My countryman; but yet I know him not.
Macduff. My ever-gentle cousin, welcome hither.
Malcolm. I know him now. Good God, betimes remove
    The means that makes us strangers.
(IV, iii, 159-63).

The second particularity follows immediately in the same scene, when in answer to Macduff's famous question "Stands Scotland where it did?" (IV, iii, 164), Ross replies with a poignant description of the state to which Scotland had been reduced under Macbeth's tyranny:

Alas, poor country!

Almost afraid to know itself. It cannot
Be call'd our mother, but our grave; where nothing,
But who knows nothing, is once seen to smile;
Where sighs and groans and shrieks that rend the air
Are made, not mark'd; where violent sorrow seems
A modern ecstasy: the dead man's knell
Is there scarce ask'd for who; and good men's lives
Expire before the flowers in their caps,
Dying or ere they sicken.
(IV, iii, 164-72).

The reference to flowers in the cap is an allusion to the clan practice of sticking a sprig of the clan badge in the bonnet, like the lesser periwinkle or the rowan of the MacLachlans or the heather of the MacDonalds and the Macintyres. Shakespeare is unlikely to have read of the details of Highland costume. He may have heard of them. Or he may have seen them for himself.

Another sign of Shakespeare's awareness of odd and unexpected details about Scotland has been noted before,[90] but must be again because of its relevance to my case. Shakespeare in V, iii and v gives Macbeth's armour-bearer the name Seyton. Though the name Seiten does occur in Holinshed in a list of names,[91] its occurrence there is without reference to Macbeth. But the name Seton or Seaton, as it is generally spelled now, was aptly chosen by Shakespeare, because the Setons of Touch, which is about three miles south-west of Stirling, were and, unless the office has lapsed, still are hereditary Armour-bearers and Squires of the royal body to the Scottish Kings.[92]

So Scotland is to be thought of as a country different from England; and by explicit words or by hints or implications, the reader and perhaps still more the spectator of *Macbeth* are made to envisage unmistakably a "Caledonia stern and wild",[86] a chilly[87] and thinly populated land of mountains and shaggy woods rather than ploughed fields, of barren moors and battle-fields and grim fortresses rather than towns, villages, and farms.

The elements in this most atmospheric of plays accord both with the wild setting and with the wild deeds occurring in it. The weather is unpredictable,[88] more often than not stormy and boisterous with thunder and lightning, rain and hail as accompaniments and with dark night or ominous half-light predominant over brief glimpses of the day and the sun.

The one passage painting a gentler picture provides a deliberate and highly effective contrast. It is, by a stroke of dramatic irony, Duncan's fateful arrival before Macbeth's Castle at Inverness:

> *Duncan.* This castle hath a pleasant seat; the air
> Nimbly and sweetly recommends itself
> Unto our gentle senses.
> *Banquo.*   This guest of summer,
> The temple-haunting martlet, does approve,
> By his loved mansionry, that the heaven's breath
> Smells wooingly here: no jutty, frieze,
> Buttress, nor coign of vantage, but this bird
> Hath made his pendent bed and procreant cradle:
> Where they most breed and haunt, I have observed,
> The air is delicate.   (I, vi, 1-10).

How did Shakespeare know that Inverness receives a normally mild air-stream and enjoys a clement microclimate in consequence? None of his known sources would have told him.[89]

And is it too fanciful to suggest that Shakespeare mentioned so many creatures from the animal world (mammals, reptiles, birds, fish, and insects) in order to carry to his spectators the idea of a country in which the inhabitants lived all the time closer to nature than did his Londoners? There are nearly ninety creatures named, some of course being mentioned more than once.

There is one other element of some importance in betokening a Scottish milieu for *Macbeth*; that is to say, the vocabulary, phrasing, and style. Both before and after *Macbeth*, Shakespeare used dialectal differences when they were appropriate, which was usually only for occasional episodes. The most common dialectal difference in Shakespeare is not a regional one at all, but a class one to distinguish the speech of the simple, rustic, and uneducated, who always number only a few, from that of the more important characters, who are always more numerous and gentle, courtly, and educated. Regional differences in language, though they occur, are less common. There is, for example, the speech of the Welshman Fluellen in *Henry V* and of the Scots Captain Jamy and the Irish Captain Macmorris in the same play; to say nothing of the King's broken French and the Princess Katharine's broken English. Sir Hugh Evans in *The Merry Wives of Windsor* is another Welshman with a marked provincial oddity of speech. But still another Welshman, Owen Glendower in *I Henry IV*, is differentiated, not by provincialisms of accent and vocabulary, but by the high-flown and grandiloquent.

Shakespeare does not attempt in *Macbeth* to catch the sounds and phrasing of contemporary Scots, though a few usages have been noticed by editors as having a Scots ring. The one word which is unquestionably Scots occurs in:

> The devil damn thee black, thou cream-faced loon! (V, iii, 11).

It is a contemptuous term for *lad*, *fellow*. Spelling it *lown*, Shakespeare uses the word again in *Othello* and in *Pericles*, both written after *Macbeth*. In *Othello* it occurs in a stanza[97] sung by Iago from what "is supposed to have been originally a Scotch ballad",[98] every stanza of which ends with a variant of Iago's last line:

Then take thine auld cloak about thee.

In *Pericles* the word looks like part of a proverbial phrase: "We should have both lord and lown".[99]

There are also a few words and idioms not so certainly Scots, but interesting enough to be noticed. Thus, according to Lewis Campbell,

How far is't call'd to Forres? (I, iii, 39)

"betrays an intimate knowledge of a land where distances are indefinite and the cautious natives are not ready to commit themselves to positive statement".[100] In

there ran a rumour

Of many worthy fellows that were out (IV, iii, 182-83)

occurs a use of *out = under arms in an uprising*, which is Scots common form in relation to Jacobite rebellions, as in "He was out wi'the Hielandmen in Montrose's time".[101] The use of *while = till* in

we will keep ourself

Till supper-time alone: while then, God be with you!

(III, i, 43-44).

predates that of Scottish judges who in 1656 sentenced a blasphemer "to be hanged on a gibbet while he be dead".[102] Two other usages are common colloquialisms in Scotland to this day: *doubt = fear* in:

I doubt some danger does approach you nearly (IV, ii, 67);

and *want = lack, be without* in:

Who cannot want the thought how monstrous

It was for Malcolm and for Donalbain

To kill their gracious father?

(III, vi, 7-9).

Finally *gout = drop*, which is rare in standard English and which Shakespeare uses only in:

I see thee still,

And on thy blade and dudgeon gouts of blood (II, i, 45-46),

could be a derivative from French *goutte*, like other words of French origin adopted into Scots as a result of the Auld Alliance, such as *ashet = large plate, carving plate* (from *assiette*), *gigot = leg of mutton* (from *gigot*), and *douce = sedate, prudent, agreeable* (from *doux, douce*).

All told, these locutions number about half a dozen. It is conceivable enough that Shakespeare caught them from Scots speakers; but they are too few and insignificant to found on, because of their rarity or even uniqueness. Every play by Shakespeare, *Macbeth* included, has scores of words and usages which are found in it and in no other play by him.

In fact, Shakespeare adopted quite different devices from the dialectal to convey the speech of a noble barbarism set in a bleak and harsh environment, means which would not puzzle either an English audience by unknown provincialisms or a Scottish one unfamiliar with the linguistic plenty of the London stage. Accordingly he limited himself for the most part to what would be intelligible both north and south of the Border. He made do with what is perhaps the shortest vocabulary of any of his plays, using many words again and again contrary to his usual practice. There is a starkness and bareness of phrase, especially in the most intense passages. There is a continual giving of great pregnancy of meaning to very ordinary words, such as *be, do, have, make, know,* and many others, thus:

be:

> yet let that be,
> Which the eye fears, when it is done, to see.
> (I, iv, 52-53).
> To be thus is nothing;
> But to be safely thus.   (III, i, 48-49).

do:

> If it were done when 'tis done, then 'twere well
> It were done quickly.   (I, vii, 1-2).
>
> What's done cannot be undone.   (V, i, 75).

have:

> thou'ldst have, great Glamis,
> That which cries 'Thus thou must do, if thou have it'.
> (I, v, 23-24).
> I have thee not, and yet I see thee still.   (II, i, 35).

make:

> Nor time nor place
> Did then adhere, and yet you would make both:
> They have made themselves, and that their fitness now
> Does unmake you.   (I, vii, 51-54).

know:

> To know my deed, 'twere best not know myself.
> (II, ii, 73).

There is, too, in *Macbeth,* as there is not in Shakespeare's other plays, a very frequent resort to reference by pronominal phrases in place of specific nouns, and to words like *thing, nothing, something, business, matter,* which mean little in dictionary terms but much in their contexts in the play:

> Glamis thou art, and Cawdor, and shalt be
> What thou art promised.   (I, v, 16-17).
> what thou wouldst highly,
> That wouldst thou holily. (I, v, 21-22).
>
> I am afraid to think what I have done. (II, ii, 51).
>
> I should report that which I say I saw,
> But know not how to do it. (V, v, 31-32).
>
> why do you start; and seem to fear
> Things that do sound so fair? (I, iii, 51-52).
>
> Things without all remedy
> Should be without regard. (III, ii, 11-12).
>
> where nothing,
> But who knows nothing, is once seen to smile.
> (IV, iii, 166-67).

> but something
> You may deserve of him through me.
>   (IV, iii, 14-15).
>   you shall put
> This night's great business into my dispatch.
>   (I, v, 68-69).
> Your face, my thane, is as a book where men
> May read strange matters.   (I, v, 63-64).

Even these many quotations cannot indicate the pervasiveness and frequency of the usages and still less their relative rarity in Shakespeare's other plays.

A different characteristic of style in *Macbeth* is the use of certain key-words, their synonyms, and their phrasal equivalents. They emphasize by repetition three central themes of the tragedy. The first theme is a human action surrounded by the supernatural. In addition to the more manifest supernaturalism of the witch-scenes and Banquo's ghost, Shakespeare repeatedly reminds his audience of the mystery of his world by starring the play with the word *strange*. It occurs at least fourteen times, to say nothing of *strangely* and *stranger(s)* which are used several times each. Other words and phrases affirming the abnormality of things are plentiful, as for instance: "weird sisters" (I, iii, 32 and four times more) and "weird women" (III, i, 2); "Against the use of nature" (I, iii, 137); "a breach in nature" (II, iii, 119); " 'Tis unnatural" (II, iv, 10); " 'Gainst nature still" (II, iv, 27), "a death to nature" (III, iv, 28); "He wants the natural touch" (IV, ii, 9), etc. Even more numerous are words with prefixes or suffixes to express the opposite of the normal: "unfix" (I, iii, 135 and IV, i, 96); "unsex" (I, v, 42); "sightless" (I, v, 50 and I, vii, 23); "boneless" (I, vii, 57); "unmake" (I, vii, 54); "thriftless" (II, iv, 28); "unfelt" (II, iii, 142); "unbecoming" (III, i, 13); "fruitless" (III, i, 61); "unlineal" (III, i, 63); "unsafe" (III, ii, 32); "unmann'd" (III, iv, 73); "marrowless" (III, iv, 94); "fatherless" (IV, ii, 26); "unsanctified" (IV, ii, 81); "stanchless" (IV, iii, 78); "untitled" (IV, iii, 104); "unspeak" (IV, iii, 123); "distemper'd" (V, ii, 15); "disseat" (V, iii, 21); "undeeded" (V, vii, 20); "untimely" (V, viii, 16); etc.

Another of the central themes of *Macbeth* is a human action concentrating on violent deaths. The key-words are what one would expect. The words *murder(s)*, *murderer(s)*, *murder'd*, *murderous*, *murdering* occur, if all the instances are counted together, some twenty-two times. And there are many synonymous phrases for killers and killing: "execution" (I, ii, 18 and I, iv, 1); "unseam'd him from the nave to the chaps" (I, ii, 22); "my fell purpose" (I, v, 47);

> if the assassination
> Could trammel up the consequence, and catch
> With his surcease success; that but this blow
> Might be the be-all and the end-all here.
>   (I, vii, 2-5);

"The deep damnation of his taking-off" (I, vii, 20); "our great quell" (I, vii, 72); "this most bloody piece of work" (II, iii, 134);

> *Macbeth.* Is he dispatch'd?
> *First Murderer.* My lord, his throat is cut; that I did for him.

Macbeth. Thou are the best o' the cut-throats. (III, iv, 15-17); "birth-strangled babe" (IV, i, 30); "fell cruelty" (IV, ii, 71); "Savagely slaughter'd" (IV, iii, 205); "Fell slaughter" (IV, iii, 227); "my slaughterous thoughts" (V, v, 14); "this dead butcher and his fiend-like queen" (V, viii, 69).

Of course violent death is associated in the mind with the weapons which effect it and the blood which follows it. There is plenty in *Macbeth* about the arms and armour of war, swords and shields. But the typical and symbolic weapon of the play is the dagger, the chosen weapon of the assassin and murderer. The word comes in two lines which concentrate in themselves the very essence of the play:

> Is this a dagger which I see before me? (II, i, 33);

and

> Give me the daggers. (II, ii, 53).

But that repeated word and its synonyms, "my keen knife" (I, v, 53), "blade and dudgeon" (II, i, 46), "murderous shaft" (II, iii, 147), and the like, keep the image of an "air-drawn dagger" (III, iv, 62) afloat in our minds, as it was before the eyes of Macbeth.

Far more numerous, however, are the words and phrases which call up the ideas of *blood* and *wounds*, *gashes*, *hacked flesh*, and *a severed head*. The tragedy in fact drips with blood; and we are made to see the unmistakable colour of it and its indelible stain which could

> The multitudinous seas incarnadine,
> Making the green one red (II, ii, 62-63);

made to smell the stench of it which "all the perfumes of Arabia" (V, i, 57) could not sweeten; and, in the ghastliest lines of all, made to feel its horrible curding as it dries:

> Now does he feel
> His secret murders sticking on his hands (V, ii, 16-17).

The instances of *blood*, *bloody* and *bloodier*, *bleed(s)* and *bleeding*, *gore* and *gory* amount to forty-eight, without counting the many phrases and images which have the same effect.

The third thematic strain, which is as important and pervasive as the strange and the murderous, is of a dualistic kind. It is the interrelation and counterparting of trust and distrust, loyalty and treason, integrity and duplicity. Every character, in one way or another and to one degree or another, is swung between belief and doubt with respect to others and, in some cases, with respect to himself. Things done by the characters blend plain-dealing and double-dealing, honesty and dissimulation, the open and the secret. Things seen by the characters poise between fact and hallucination, reliability and delusion, waking and dreaming. Things said by the characters confuse the direct and the indirect, the literal and the ironical, the simple and the equivocal. And the frame of reference unites or contrasts the past and the present, the present and the future, the tangible and the intangible, the human and the animal kingdoms, the physical and the metaphysical, this world and the next.

As this dualistic strain is polarized between reality and appearance in the relationship of king and subject, man and man, and man and circumstance,

D

more than words and phrases would have to be quoted in illustration, more indeed than whole sentences and passages. Nevertheless, as with the strange and the murderous, Shakespeare has his key-words to convey the trust-mistrust nexus. They fall into two antithetic categories, which may be called the positive and the negative. I shall keep the lists as brief as possible by giving only the single words with only one line-reference for each word and no comments. The positive list is: "loyalty" (I, iv, 22), "loyal" (II, iii, 115); "trust" (I, iv, 14), "trusted" (I, iii, 120); "service" (I, iv, 22), "allegiance" (II, i, 28), "obedience" (V, ii, 26), "owe" (I, iv, 22), "due" (I, iv, 21), "duties" (I, iv, 24); "deservers" (I, iv, 42), "deserve" (IV, iii, 15), "deserved" (I, iv, 18); "honours" (I, vi, 17), "dignities" (I, vi, 19), and "worthy" (I, ii, 10). The negative list is rather longer: "rebel" (I, ii, 10), "rebellious" (I, ii, 56), "rebellion" (IV, i, 97), "revolt" (I, ii, 2), "conspirers" (IV, i, 91); "traitor" (I, ii, 52), "treason" (I, iii, 115), "treasonous" (II, iii, 138), "treachery" (III, iii, 17); "treacherous" (IV, iii, 18), "disloyal" (I, ii, 52); "deceive" (I, ii, 63), "beguile" (I, v, 64), "put upon" (I, vii, 70), "hoodwink" (IV, iii, 72), "betray" (I, iii, 125), "equivocate" (II, iii, 12), "palter" (V, viii, 20); "false" (I, vii, 82), "false speaking" (IV, iii, 130), "forsworn" (IV, iii, 126), "faith-breach" (V, ii, 18), and "mouth-honour" (V, iii, 27).

Notes

1. Cf. 6 supra.
2. Cf. Chapters 3, 4, 5 and 7.
3. Hamlet, III, ii, 47.
4. S.D. in 1623 Folio. In modern editions "Sergeant" is generally substituted to accord with Malcolm's "This is the sergeant" (I, ii, 3).
5. He expresses himself in an unconvincing fustian.
6. The 1623 Folio does not localise the scene. Most modern editions give "A camp near Forres".
7. Cf. 9-11 infra.
8. One likely date is 7th August 1606 when the King's Company played at Hampton Court before James and Christian IV of Denmark, two days after James's annual commemoration of his escape from the Gowrie Conspiracy. Cf. 91-93 infra.
9. Hamlet, IV, v, 189.
10. Chambers, ed., 180.
11. D.W., xxvii.
12. Chambers, ed., 161-64, 180-86.

13. Coleridge and others in his wake have questioned the genuineness of the whole speech, with certain reservations. But I am convinced that it is a case of Aut Shakespeare aut diabolus.
14. On which day the King himself attended the trial incognito (D.W., xxviii and G. B. Harrison, A Jacobean Journal, 288).
15. Garnett's use of the pseudonym "Mr. Farmer" may possibly be alluded to by the Porter: "Here's a farmer, that hanged himself on the expectation of plenty" (II, iii, 5-6).
   Still more dubious allusions to topics in 1605-6 have been detected in the Porter's speech.
16. Cf. D.W., xxviii-xxxi.
17. Cf. 19 infra.
18. Cf. 23 infra.
19. Cf. 109-24 infra.
20. Cf. 89 infra.
21. Chambers, Stage, IV, 84, 144-45. Among the properties recorded in the

Court payments for seven plays in the season in question appears the following: "the Pallace of prosperitie Scotlande and a gret Castell one thothere side". The "Pallace" probably pertained to one of the other plays. But "Scotlande" represented by a mountain and "a gret Castell" would be an appropriate setting for the assassination of Darnley at Kirk-o'-Field, which stood about halfway between Arthur's Seat and Edinburgh Castle.

22. The 1598 quarto is the only extant one. But the play was entered in S.R. on 14th May 1594.

23. *Hecatommithi*, III, i.

24. Ed. in *Specimens of the Pre-Shakespearean Drama*. Edited by J. M. Manley. 1897. II, 332.

    I think that Greene's *James IV* might have been the play given by English actors in Edinburgh in 1598 which, according to Elizabeth's agent in Scotland, George Nicolson, scorned the King and the people in a regrettable manner. *Cf.* 138-39 *infra*.

25. D.W., xli. *Cf. ibid.*, xl: "It was the considered opinion of a supreme taster of poetic vintage, George Saintsbury, an opinion twice expressed, that those who believe Shakespeare wrote the whole of *Macbeth* in 1605-6 'must have curious standards of criticism', inasmuch as portions of it, and in particular 'the second scene, are in verse and phrase whole stages older than the bulk of the play' [*Cambridge History of English Literature*, V, 203; *cf. A History of English Prosody*, II, 41-42]. And this verdict Sir Herbert Grierson . . . has endorsed with certain modifications" [*Macbeth*. Edited by Sir Herbert Grierson and J. C. Smith. 1914. xii].

26. Chambers *Stage*, III, 435; *cf.*, II, 179, 330.

27. It can be assumed that Malcolm Canmore (Malcolm III) was the King presented, not Malcolm I or II or IV.

28. William Kempe has a curious passage in his *Kempe's Nine Daies Wonder*, 1600, 21, in which he speaks of "a penny Poet, whose first making was the miserable stolne story of Macdoel, or Macdobeth, or Macsomewhat, for I am sure a Mac it was, though I never had the maw to see it". Kempe could not and would not have written so contemptuously of anything by Shakespeare. J. P. Collier's "discovery" of a S.R. reference to a "ballad of Macdobeth" (his 1858 ed. of Shakespeare) has been dismissed as a forgery.

29. *Cf.* 177 *infra*.

30. *E.g.* John Fordun's Latin *Scotichronicon*, written before 1384 and added to by Walter Bower between 1440 and 1447; Andrew of Wyntoun's *The Orygynale Cronykil*, a metrical history in Scots written between 1420 and 1430; etc.

31. Stopes, 93, 102-3. It has to be admitted that Chambers (*Sh.:* I, 475-76) found little substance in Mrs. Stopes's argument (or in another to the effect that Shakespeare owed something to *The Orygynale Cronykil* of Andrew of Wyntoun). But Dover Wilson (xvii-xix, xlii) accepts Mrs. Stopes's case.

32. Edited by W. B. D. D. Turnbull. 3 vols. Rolls Series.

33. In Cambridge University Library. It had been in the famous collection of Bishop John Moore (1646-1714), bought by George I and presented to the University.

34. The library contained also the Paris edition of Boece, 1527. *Cf.* Dover Wilson, xix and G. F. Warner, *The Library of James VI* in *The Miscellany of the Scottish History Society*, 1893, xxxiv.

35. *Cf.* 13 *supra*.

36. *Cf.* Stopes, 102: "In every case in which Stewart differs from Holinshed, Shakespeare follows Stewart!"

37. I, 340.

38. Stopes, 339.

39. D.W., xix.

40. Stopes, 339.

41. *Cf.* 8-9 *supra.*

42. Stopes, 336-37.

43. *Cf.* 187 *infra.*

44. Stopes, 94. Buchanan has this note: "Milesian or nonsensical, for the inhabitants of Miletus in Ionia were infamous for telling tales so far from being true that they had not the least shadow of truth in them" (*ibid.*, 94-95).

45. In Trinity College Library, Cambridge.

46. I, 344-47.

47. So the Globe edition corrects the Folio S.D.: "*A shew of eight Kings, and Banquo last, with a glass in his hand*".

Chambers (ed. 146) cites, from Cotton Mather's *Magnalia Christi Americana*, 1702, a description of a similar show of the Kings of France made by a magician to Catharine de' Medici.

48. *Cf.* 160 *infra. Cf.* I, iii, 57-69, 86, 118-20; III, i, 3-10, 59-70, 90; III, ii, 37; III, iii, 15-22; III, iv, 12-31; IV, i. 100-24; IV, iii, (for the Stewart descent from Banquo). *Cf.* also I, iv, 35-39, 48-50; II, iii, 72-74, 102-4; II, iv, 25-35; III, vi, 24-49; IV, iii; V, ii, 25-26 (for lineal succession and legitimate kingship).

49. *Cf.* 16 *supra.*

50. I, 340.

51. I, 340-41.

52. *Cf.* 11-13 *supra.*

53. *Cf.* 109-24 *infra.*

54. *Cf.* 96-103 *infra.*

55. D.W., xvi, citing *The Political Works of James I.* Edited by C. H. McIlwain, 1918, 60-61.

56. D.W., xliv.

57. But not to later and more objective students of the period, notably my friend Mr. Nigel Tranter in his *Macbeth the King*, 1978.

58. According to Sir John Harington, the bishops declared that James "spoke by the power of inspiration" (*Nugae Antiquae*. Edited by Thomas Park, 1804, I, 181-82).

59. I, 349.

60. *The Political Works of James I, ed. cit.*, 38.

61. I, 349.

62. Printed in Edinburgh by Robert Waldegrave, the King's printer in Scotland. It was entered in S.R. to John Legatt on 17th March 1598; but no English edition seems to have followed this entry. However, a London edition, which had been entered in S.R. to E. Edgar on 3rd April 1603 (only ten days after Elizabeth's death), was published the same year. It was followed, also in 1603, by another printed by Waldegrave who had just returned to London.

63. Stopes, 104. *Cf.* D.W., xxxix: "Indeed, I cannot believe that this chronicle-play of the house of Stewart, with its witch-scenes full of points likely to be of interest to the author of *Daemonologie*, was written for any eyes but his". I would not myself describe *Macbeth* as a "chronicle-play of the house of Stewart" (*cf.* 13 *supra*); and I think that Shakespeare wrote it for less important eyes as well as for James's.

64. *Cf.* I, iii, 8: "But in a sieve I'll thither sail."

65. James and his Queen landed at Leith on 1st May.

66. *E.g.*: familiars—Graymalkin and Paddock (I, i, 8-9) and Harpier (IV, i, 3); beards, regarded as a mark of a witch (I, iii, 45-47); sailing in a sieve (I, iii, 8); "Posters of the sea and land" (I, iii, 33); killing domestic animals (I, iii, 2); raising storms and tormenting ships (I, iii, 11-17); making victims "dwindle, peak and pine" (I, iii, 23); and concocting magic brews (IV, i, 1-43).

67. *Lamb's Criticism.* Edited by E. M. W. Tillyard, 1923, 22.

68. So it is always called. But in fact the Folio S.D. give no indication of the place. In the non-Shakespearian III, v, 15 it is called "the pit of Acheron".

69. By the mere force of habit Forman gave the year as "1610" (cf. D.W., xxviii, note 1). In his day New Year's Day was generally reckoned to be 25th March.

70. MS. Ashmole 208 in the Bodleian Library, Oxford.

71. Chambers, ed., 161.

72. For "wild", read "ferly" [= wonderful], as in the sixteenth-century editions.

73. I, 339-40. A woodcut on page 243 of the first or 1577 edition of Holinshed shows the three sisters as young and comely women in the height of Elizabethan fashion and the landscape as having one large tree near the figures and others at some distance, as well as other vegetation—by no means a blasted heath.

74. Two other descriptions of the show could have been read by Forman: Anthony Nixon's *Oxford Triumph*, 1605; and Isaac Wake's *Rex Platonicus*, 1607. Cf. Chambers, *Stage*, I, 130 for manuscript accounts and other details of the royal visit.

75. Cf. 11-13 *supra* and Chapter 7.

76. Cf. 185, 187-88 *infra*.

77. I, 347-48.

78. Even if the play was first presented in Scotland.

79. Tubal, another Jew in *The Merchant of Venice*, is a minor figure; and Jessica, though more important, is not specially Jewish.

80. As is also the Moorish Aaron in *Titus Andronicus* (which is included in the Shakespeare canon on very dubious grounds).

81. The phrase "the Celtic temperament" had not yet been coined.

82. *Macbeth*. Edited by Sir Herbert Grierson and J. C. Smith. 1914. xviii-xix.

83. Cf. 182 *infra* and Chapter 4.

84. Dr. Johnson calls this phrase "a natural invective uttered by an inhabitant of a barren country, against those who have more opportunities of luxury" (*Johnson on Shakespeare*. Edited by Sir Walter Raleigh. 1916. 176). Scott speaks of "the proverbial epicurism of the English . . . in Scotland" at the period in which he set *A Legend of Montrose* (chapter 5). Had Shakespeare heard this "proverbial" invective?

85. Chambers, *Stage*, I, 325.

86. Scott, *The Lay of the Last Minstrel*, canto VI, ii.

87. Coleridge quotes:
Into the air; and what seem'd
    corporal melted
As breath into the wind (I, iii, 81-82);
and asks: "Is it too minute to notice the appropriateness of the simile . . . in a cold climate?" (*Coleridge's Shakesperean Criticism*. Edited by T. M. Raysor. 1930. I, 39).

88. How well Macbeth in the first words he utters characterizes so much of the changeable Scottish weather:
So foul and fair a day I have not seen
                    (I, iii, 38).

89. Cf. Stopes, 98: 'as a part of "material", I must consider the strong evidence of Shakespeare's acquaintance with the scenes he described. No Englishman who had not visited Inverness, and experienced the unexpected mildness of its northern climate, would have thought of describing it as "pleasant", "delicate", or of noting the martins and their nests. . . . Nor would he have changed "the green lawn" [*sic*] of Holinshed and "the pleasant wood" of other writers into "the blasted heath" near Forres, as the spot where the witches appeared, unless he had seen some such moors lying gaunt and terrible, as witnesses of past winter storms. . . . It is possible, and even probable that Shakespeare visited Scotland early in the seventeenth century'.

In Chapter 10 I put forward my own case for this possibility, based on many other clues besides the evidence of a familiarity with the locale.

90. Cf. D.W., xlii and 165.

91. I, 351.

92. *Cf.* G. R. French, *Shakespeareana Genealogica*, 1869, 296; F. H. Groome, *Ordnance Gazetteer of Scotland*, n.d., VI, 446; and Sir George Seton, *A History of the Family of Seton*, 1896, I, 337.

93. Chambers, *Stage*, II, 171. Sir W. W. Greg (*Henslowe's Diary*. 1904-8. I, iii) gives 3rd September, instead of 2nd.

94. *Cf.* 5-6 *supra*.

95. *Cf. Henry V*, I, ii, 136-83.

96. For some peculiar and striking parallels between *Macbeth* and Scottish witch-trials in Aberdeen in 1596-7, *cf.* Knight, 431-37.

97. II, iii, 92-99.

98. Bishop Thomas Percy, *Reliques of Ancient English Poetry* (Everyman's Library), n.d., I, 190.

99. IV, vi, 19.

100. *Tragic Drama in Aeschylus, Sophocles, and Shakespeare*, 1904.

101. Sir Walter Scott, *Redgauntlet*, Letter 11.

102. David Masson, *The Life of John Milton*, 7 vols. 1859-94, V, 94.

3

Scots Law in 'Macbeth'

> *Macduff.*   O Banquo, Banquo,
> Our royal master's murder'd!
> *Lady Macbeth.*   Woe, alas!
> What, in our house?
> *Banquo.*   Too cruel any where.
>   *Macbeth*, II, iii, 91-93.

One of the minor ironies of literature is that among the laws recorded by Boece as made by the historical Macbeth is the first known Scottish regulation against unlicensed entertainers.[1] It is thus worded in Holinshed: "Counterfeit fooles, minstrels, jesters, and these kind of juglers, with such like idle persons, that range abroad in the countrie, having no special licence of the king, shall be compelled to learne some science or craft to get their living; if they refuse so to do, they shall be drawn like horses in the plough and harrows".[2]

Shakespeare, who was not ignorant of similar and more recent enactments in England against his quality, has retaliated by raising Macbeth from the obscurity of his not-very-remarkable place in the scanty annals of dark-age Scotland to a tragic eminence in the literature of the world. But I propose to submit some evidence to prove, if I can, that in the drama Shakespeare shows that he had some knowledge of other Scots Law as well.

Macbeth shows Shakespeare's imagination working at its highest intensity. But, at the same time, it proves him, if proof were needed, to have been a most deliberate artificer, a master of the art of making carefully-selected details contribute to and confirm the imaginative effect. We might have expected genius to have ignored these with a divine impatience. Not so the genius of Shakespeare. It remained totally alert in its grandest concentration and actively remembered details in the very height of its creative activity.

There is no more intense passage in the whole play than the opening soliloquy of I, vii:

> If it were done when 'tis done, then 'twere well
> It were done quickly: if the assassination
> Could trammel up the consequence, and catch
> With his surcease success; that but this blow
> Might be the be-all and the end-all here,
> But here, upon this bank and shoal of time,
> We'ld jump the life to come. But in these cases

We still have judgement here; that we but teach
Bloody instructions, which, being taught, return
To plague the inventor: this even-handed justice
Commends the ingredients of our poison'd chalice
To our own lips. He's here in double trust;
First, as I am his kinsman and his subject,
Strong both against the deed; then, as his host,
Who should against his murderer shut the door,
Not bear the knife myself. Besides, this Duncan
Hath borne his faculties so meek, hath been
So clear in his great office, that his virtues
Will plead like angels, trumpet-tongued, against
The deep damnation of his taking-off;
And pity, like a naked new-born babe,
Striding the blast, or heaven's cherubim, horsed
Upon the sightless couriers of the air,
Shall blow the horrid deed in every eye,
That tears shall drown the wind. I have no spur
To prick the sides of my intent, but only
Vaulting ambition, which o'erleaps itself
And falls on the other.

It is for Macbeth the cardinal moment, the moment, not of decision, but of
dreadful negative balance when the good and the bad in him are in the most
dangerous equipoise.[3] The phrasing of Macbeth shows him in the utmost confusion of a double-mindedness that would "not play false" (I, v, 22) but yet
would "wrongly win" (I, v, 23). He looks at the ugliness of a "thought, whose
murder yet is but fantastical" (I, iii, 139), a murder under the most sacred trust,
a "Malice domestic" (III, ii, 25), and a treason in the height. His hyperbolical
imagination trembles on the very brink of incoherence. The imagery in which
it finds utterance is a succession of dissolving views which impress the more
powerfully by their elusive intangibility. Yet into this very swirl of intensity
Shakespeare works some curious features of Scots Law.

The Scotland of the sixteenth and the early seventeenth centuries must
have been one of the most criminous countries in recorded history, particularly
in respect of crimes of violence against the person. The narratives of the
historians, early and late, are bloody enough. But the historians are too selective
and too intent on a generalized narrative to give a picture of such conditions
as can be realized only by adding instance to instance. It is to such records as the
Register of the Privy Council of Scotland, the Books of Adjournal of the High
Court of Justiciary (in longo or as excerpted in Pitcairn's Criminal Trials), the
Acts of the Scottish Parliament, and such anecdotal histories as those of families
and clans that the enquirer should go. The facts, both for the Highlands and for
the Lowlands, are lurid, appalling, and fascinating. Murders of every degree of
atrocity and of every category (slaughter, chaude mele,[4] assassination, parricide,
massacre, and so on), private warfare, family and clan feuds, vendettas, house-
burning, fire-raising, hamesucken,[5] stouthrief,[6] mutilations, lying in wait,[7]

spuilzie,[8] besieging, wearing and shooting of pistolets, umbesetting[9] the high-way, taking prisoner, oppression, inflicting illegal torture, and still other crimes were everyday occurrences with which the authorities were unable to cope.

Individual criminals, if they were persons of middling rank or lower and without the backing of notables, were fairly promptly prosecuted and condemned in sentences of a barbarous *in terrorem* kind. But the prosecution of notables and their humbler accomplices and accessaries limped after the event, *longo intervallo*, if at all; and the chance of such influential criminals and their protégés escaping punishment altogether was more than fifty-fifty.

The impotence of the law and its officers was itself a fruitful cause of crime, for a very large proportion of the crimes is to be attributed to the rough justice of revenge. The legal system gave a sort of sanction to the private pursuit of a criminal or an alleged criminal, and so of anyone against whom a grudge was entertained. By no means all the prosecutions were by dittay, that is, by a charge laid by the Crown. Many were privately instituted. These were mostly, however, in cases involving persons of little importance and residing south of the Highland Line. Members of powerful Lowland families or of Highland clans would in general have scorned legal redress and taken the law into their own hands by way of a private war:

It will have blood; they say, blood will have blood (III, iv, 122).
Yes; and offences far short of blood in the commission were meted blood in the punishment.

The following passage from an anonymous chronicle of the late sixteenth century describes, from a Lowland point of view, the savagery of the North and West; but an impartial researcher to-day in the records of the time will find little to choose between Highlands and Lowlands as regards "Man's inhumanity to man"[10]:

"Trew it is, that thir Ilandish men ar of nature verie prowd, suspicious, avaricious, full of decept, and evill inventioun aganis his nychtbour, be [= by] what way soever he may circumvin him. Besydis all this, they ar sa crewell in taking of revenge, that nather have thay regarde to person, eage, tyme or caus; sa ar they generallie all sa far addictit to thair awin tyrannicall opinions, that in all respects thay exceed in creweltie the maist barbarous people that ever hes bene sen the begynning of the warld."[11]

The authorities, whether the King in Privy Council or the King in Parliament, not to mention his High Court of Justiciary and the General Assemblies of the Church, were continually troubled by news of crime and violence, and as frequently engaged on measures for their better punishment and control, consistent with a politic handling of the greater offenders.

There are two Acts of the Scottish Parliament, with details of which Shakespeare shows his acquaintance in the soliloquy I have already quoted from I, vii of *Macbeth*. The details in question do not figure in Shakespeare's main source, Holinshed's *Chronicles of England, Scotland, and Ireland*, 1577 and 1587,[12] or in any other historical narrative he may have consulted, for the simple reason that they come from what was in his day quite recent legislation. And Shakespeare could have read them, if he did not get them by hearsay, in a

volume published in 1597, *The Lawes and Actes of Parliament, Maid be* [= by]
King Iames the First, and his Successours Kings of Scotland: Visied [= scrutinized],
collected and extracted furth of the Register by Sir John Skene, Lord Curriehill.

The first Act is the 51st of the eleventh or 1587 Parliament of James
VI, which is to the following effect:

"It is statute and ordaned, that the murther or slauchter of quhatsum euer
[= whomsoever] Our Sovereigne Lordis lieges, quhair the partie slaine is vnder
the traist [= trust], credite, assurance and power of the slayer: Al sik murther
and slauchter, to be committed in time cumming, after the daite hereof, the
same being lauchfullie tried, and the person delated found guiltie, be [= by]
an Assise thereof, salbe treason, and the persones found culpable, sall fore-
fault life, landes and gudes."

Scots Law, here as elsewhere, looks back to Roman Law, which classed
such a crime as *proditio* (= treachery or treason) and described it as *homicidium
sub praetextu amicitiae*. Since forfeiture of life, lands, and goods was the regular
punishment for murder in general (as well as for certain other crimes), it might
look as if the Act reflected only too clearly the feebleness of a central government which could think of nothing better in the way of a deterrent than the
giving of the more odious name of treason to murder under trust in particular.
But, as treason, murder under trust involved the additional penalties of the
escheat of heritage and the ignominious treatment of the corpse. Also (and this
is more to the point), the Act, by making murder under trust one of the
varieties[13] of statutory treason,[14] ensured that the crime would be proceeded
against, not in an inferior court of regality in which justice might be wrested
by local influence or prejudice, but with all the formality of a proper assize
before a judge and jury in the High Court of Justiciary.

There was, as I shall try to explain later,[15] a very special reason for the
1587 Act. But I must turn first to the second Act of the Scottish Parliament,
which, I believe, was echoing in Shakespeare's mind when he wrote the already-
quoted soliloquy for Macbeth. It was an Act of 1592, and it was obviously
meant to be a kind of rider to the Act of 1587. The relevant passage is as
follows:

"Because charges of treason, hes not been execute and vsed, with sik
solemnitie & Officiares of Armes, as the weichtines thereof requires: It is
statute and ordaned, that our Soveraigne Lordis Thesaurer [= Treasurer], and
vtheris directers of sik letters, deliuer them in time cumming, to be execute be
[= by] the ordinar Herauldes and Purseuantes, bearand [= bearing] coattes of
armes, or Masers, to bee vsed be them, as of before: And gif [= if] ony execution, vnder the paine of treason, shalbe execute vtherwaies, declaris the execution [*i.e.* the delivery of the aforesaid letters of charge] to be null, and of nane
availe."[16]

Sir George Mackenzie regarded the pomp and circumstance set out in the
Act as a proper "speciality in treason . . . and that for the greater solemnity".[17]

Another "speciality in treason", which originated, not in an Act of Parliament, but in "an express Act of the *Sederunt* of Lords of Session, in *Anno* 1591",[18]
that is to say, by a decision of the Court of Session on a matter of evidence and

procedure, was to this effect: "Women, and others, may be Witnesses in this Crime, though in other Crimes they cannot: and one Witness is sufficient here, and *famosi & impuberes* of what ever age, are receivable as Witnesses".[19] By *famosi* was meant not only persons with disreputable or criminal antecedents, but also *socii criminis* or accomplices.

I submit, then, that Shakespeare, with a liking for legalisms or quasi-legalisms either on the literal or on the figurative level which he frequently manifests in his plays and poems, deliberately worked into his tragedy on a Scottish theme singularities from recent Scots Law and practice.

That he knew of the special category of murder under trust[20] is obvious from the soliloquy in I, vii of *Macbeth*. The fact that none of the commentators has so far found any difficulty in the passage is beside the point. The lines yield an adequate meaning for those who have never heard of murder under trust, whatever extra interest they hold for those who have. After I had recognized the echoes from the 1587 Act, that of 1592, and the Act of Sederunt of 1591 in Macbeth's soliloquy and had done a considerable amount of research on the question, I discussed it with a distinguished Scottish jurist, my friend the late Lord President Cooper (later Lord Cooper of Culross). He was deeply interested in what I had to tell him and followed up our conversation with a long letter in which he wrote as follows:

"I feel strongly that you are on a sound trail. Any dramatist would
be likely to make the point that Macbeth's murder of his King was
treason and a breach of feudal fealty. Any dramatist might have
added the aggravation of kinship, though, I fear, many victims
are kin to the murderer even to-day. But who would have added
as the second branch of the "double trust" the idea of the murderer
being the *host* of the victim, except someone who had heard of
the Maclean murder[21] and of the statute which followed and
which was thereafter sternly enforced? *Ergo* Shakespeare sought
out and then utilised this bit of local colour."[22]

But Shakespeare embodied in the soliloquy many other suggestions from criminal trials, verdicts, judgements, and penalties, *e.g.*:

"surcease" [= the legal stoppage of a suit];
"We'ld jump the life to come" [= We would risk judgement in
the hereafter];
"in these cases We still have judgement here";
"we but teach Bloody instructions" [= we only set in motion
retributive action of a capital kind];
"even-handed justice" [recalling the traditional personification of
Justice with her impartial balance];
"faculties" [= powers as king, prerogatives].

It is true that none of these details, evoking in us images of courts and legal processes, is peculiar to Scots Law. But I can detect in an analysis of the incandescent legalisms in lines 18-25, lines of cloudy magnificence which would have defied even Blake to visualize, echoes of the 1592 Act of Parliament and of the 1591 Act of Sederunt of the Lords of Session:

> his virtues
> Will plead like angels, trumpet-tongued, against
> The deep damnation of his taking-off;
> And pity, like a naked new-born babe,
> Striding the blast, or heaven's cherubim, horsed
> Upon the sightless couriers of the air,
> Shall blow the horrid deed in every eye,
> That tears shall drown the wind.

Not only do the lines conjure up the Grand Assizes of the Last Judgement, its angelic officers, and the ultimate punishment of damnation; but through the swirling and dissolving views run momentary pictures from what Shakespeare knew to be "specialities in treason" in contemporary Scotland: mounted heralds from the Lyon Court in full attire, pompously attended by pursuivants and trumpeters, to proclaim from many market-crosses letters of denunciation and outlawry. And is not Pity the *one* witness judged sufficient in cases of treason, *impubes* indeed, "new-born" at the very instant of the crime and "naked" in the bare simplicity of the fact, crying, not with sentimental compassion for the criminal, but shrilly for the condign punishment of his "horrid deed"?

It will be noticed that Shakespeare underlines the "invitation" of the victim to the murderer's house, which "invitation", as Sir George Mackenzie says, is "one branch of this trust".[23] It is true that, as the play now stands in what is admitted by critics and editors alike to be a shortened and contaminated version,[24] Duncan appears to invite himself to Inverness. But the scene (I, iv) has undoubtedly been cut hereabouts[25]; and I feel sure that Duncan's abrupt and unlikely

> From hence to Inverness
> And bind us further to you. (I, iv, 42-43)

was, not a sudden and unexpected announcement of a royal visit, but the last words of a courteous acceptance (for Duncan is a courteous, expansive, and even effusive monarch) of an explicit invitation from Macbeth, which the unskilful play-reviser has dropped.

In any case, Macbeth's reply carries with it all the *praetextus amicitiae* possible in the hatching of a murder under trust: it has the very note of an eager invitation from a host to a guest:

> The rest is labour,[26] which is not used for you;
> I'll be myself the harbinger and make joyful
> The hearing of my wife with your approach;
> So humbly take my leave.   (I, iv, 44-47).

It calls forth from the affectionate and admiring Duncan "My worthy Cawdor" (I, iv, 47), an appropriate phrase from an invited guest to a trusted host (whatever ironic overtones it holds for the audience of the play); and Duncan, in a remark to Banquo immediately after Macbeth's departure, obviously considers himself as going to Inverness in consequence of an invitation:

> Let's after him,
> Whose care is gone before to bid us welcome.
> (I, iv, 56-57).

Macbeth's sinister aside as he goes from the royal presence sharply contrasts with his laboured and hypocritical professions of loyalty and hospitality in it, and shows him as realizing, from Duncan's acceptance of his invitation, the longed-for opportunity to fulfil his murderous schemes:

> The Prince of Cumberland![27] that is a step
> On which I must fall down, or else o'er-leap,
> For in my way it lies. Stars, hide your fires;
> Let not light see my black and deep desires:
> The eye wink at the hand; yet let that be
> Which the eye fears, when it is done, to see.
> (I, iv, 48-53).

As the murder under trust of Duncan involves two partners in crime, the second as well as the first has to make a *praetextus amicitiae* to the victim. This is effected by Lady Macbeth in welcoming Duncan at the Castle Gate (I, vi). Shakespeare keeps Macbeth (a little improbably) off-stage, to allow Lady Macbeth to make her professions alone. They cannot, of course, include an actual invitation; but they do express loyalty and pleasure with, as Coleridge notes, a "laboured rhythm and hypocritical over-much":[28]

> All our service
> In every point twice done and then done double
> Were poor and single business to contend
> Against those honours deep and broad wherewith
> Your majesty loads our house: for those of old,
> And the late dignities heap'd up to them,
> We rest your hermits.   (I, vi, 14-20).

The same exaggeration runs on into her next speech:

> Your servants ever
> Have theirs, themselves and what is theirs, in compt,
> To make their audit at your highness' pleasure,
> Still to return your own.   (I, vi, 25-28).[29]

Duncan himself uses the significant words, "hostess", "guest", and "host", as if to make the situation and relationship quite clear:

> See, see, our honour'd hostess! (I, vi, 10).

> Fair and noble hostess,
> We are your guest to-night. (I, vi, 24-25).

> Give me your hand;
> Conduct me to mine host. (I, vi, 28-29).

Dover Wilson, while admitting the underlying hypocrisy and guile of both Macbeth and Lady Macbeth, nevertheless stresses their courtesy and fine manners: "They make, in fact, the perfect host and hostess; and the lovely sunlit scene in which she welcomes Duncan under her battlements is, for all the irony that mocks it, none the less a thing of sheer delight in its display of beautiful courtesy on both sides".[30] Even so I would rather insist that the polite and mannerly professions of loyalty, service, devotion, and welcome all add up to an elaborated *praetextus amicitiae*: they all contribute, and are meant to contribute, to the invitation, trust, and assurance by which the intended victim is lured to the slaughter.

It is perhaps worth adding that Lady Macbeth's nervous and blundering attempt at exculpation, on the discovery of the murder of Duncan:

Woe, alas!

What, in our house? (II, iii, 92-93),

which shocks Banquo into his curt rebuke:

Too cruel any where (II, iii, 93),

is also a kind of allusion to murder under trust.

In planning the murder of Banquo, Macbeth proceeds more deliberately and cunningly than in the case of Duncan, to avoid altogether the suspicion which the first crime had aroused. Once again what he plans is a *homicidium sub praetextu amicitiae*. He makes a show of special friendship to Banquo, greeting him as "our chief guest" (III, i, 11) and passing Lennox, Ross, and other lords and their ladies without a word to them as likewise guests. He still more explicitly invites Banquo:

To-night we hold a solemn supper, sir,

And I'll request your presence.

(III, i, 14-15);

and a little later, with unnecessary empressement he adds:

Fail not our feast. (III, i, 28).

Moreover, in an apparently casual way, he elicits from Banquo how he will spend the time till supper, when he will return from his ride, and whether he will be accompanied by Fleance whose death also is necessary for Macbeth's full satisfaction. But in addition, the better to avoid the slightest doubt of his guilt, Macbeth secures two or, as it turns out, three murderers to strike the fatal blows and ensures that the double crime will be perpetrated "something from the palace" (III, i, 132) and in his own absence from the locus.[31] He requires "a clearness" (III, i, 133), as he says:

Within this hour at most

I will advise you where to plant yourselves;

Acquaint you with the perfect spy o' the time,

The moment on 't; for 't must be done to-night,

And something from the palace; always thought

That I require a clearness: and with him—

To leave no rubs nor botches in the work—

Fleance his son, that keeps him company,

Whose absence is no less material to me

Than is his father's, must embrace the fate

Of that dark hour. (III, i, 128-38).

So he naively blusters in the banquet scene to Banquo's accusing ghost:

Thou canst not say I did it: never shake

Thy gory locks at me. (III, iv, 50-51.)[32]

But in fact, and despite his contrivances, he has made himself, up to the hilt, what Scots Law calls "art and part" of the crime; by originating the very conception of it; by working on the two men he had secured with lying misrepresentations to the effect that Banquo, not himself, had been their enemy and oppressor; by taunting them with unmanliness if they did not resent their wrongs even to the length of murder; by praising their courage when they consent to act; by assuring them of his royal favour; and by counselling them as to place where, time when, and the favouring circumstances. By "*Art*", says Sir George Mackenzie, "is meant, that the crime was contrived by their art or skill, *eorum arte*; by *part* is meant that they were sharers in the crime committed, when it was committed, *& quorum pars magna*. The Civilians used in place of *Art and part, ope & consilio*".[33]

A later Scottish jurist, David Hume, in writing the section "Of Art and Part by hiring to kill" in his *Commentaries on the Law of Scotland, Respecting the Description and Punishment of Crimes*, describes this criminal relationship almost as if he had Shakespeare's tragedy before him:

"He . . . who not only exhorts and urges in general to do the slaughter, but proceeds to show how easily and how safely it may be done in a certain way, or at a certain time and place, and opens the detail of a contrivance for execution of the purpose, which plan is accordingly followed, may justly be accounted one of the most important persons in the story, though he leaves the entire execution to his associates. An address of this kind is not a naked advice, which has no effect on the person to whom it is given, farther than as a coincidence of wishes, but is in truth a most substantial assistance, which may be of as much service towards the perpetration of the deed, and may as much determine the actor to the attempt, as even the promise of presence at the fact. The adviser here equips the actor for the business; *instruit consilio*; and is the life and soul of the enterprise. . . . In short, the only counsel which can plausibly be maintained to come under the intendment of the law in this matter is a direct and special counsel; a persuasion to kill by use of the topics calculated to work on the particular man, and relative, more or less, to some near occasion of doing the deed; whereby to excite him to an immediate course of measures towards the slaughter."[34]

There are, as might be expected, other phrases in *Macbeth* of a legal or semi-legal quality. But only two of them seem to me to have a distinguishably Scottish flavour. One of them, "bond" as used in III, ii, 49 and IV, i, 84, will be noticed later in an account of the incidents which led to the 1587 Act declaring murder under trust to be treason.[35] The other is "interdiction", which comes in Macduff's despairing exclamation:

> Fit to govern!
> No, not to live. O nation miserable,
> With an untitled tyrant bloody-scepter'd,
> When shalt thou see thy wholesome days again,
> Since that the truest issue of thy throne
> By his own interdiction stands accursed
> And does blaspheme his breed?   (IV, iii, 102-8).

Dr. Johnson in his *Dictionary* takes the word in this context to mean "curse" and pronounces it "An improper use of the word", deriving it "from the papal *interdict*". But "judicial interdiction" in Scots Law means "a restraint imposed by the Court of Session upon a person incapable of managing his own affairs"; and a man, realizing his own weakness of character, may resign the conduct of his affairs to others by a "voluntary interdiction". Macduff metaphorically stretches the term to cover a disabling self-accusation by Malcolm (IV, iii, 44-102), to which he has resorted in his uncertainty as to Macduff's trustworthiness.

When Shakespeare wrote *King Lear*, after *Macbeth*, he seemed to recall the notion of a felony aggravated by being committed under trust. The felony in this instance is not a murder, but an act of atrocious violence against the person, the blinding of Gloucester by Cornwall, in the presence and with the approval of Goneril and Regan. The pinioned Gloucester in his own castle appeals to his captors by reminding them of the relationship of guest to host:

> What mean your graces? Good my friends, consider
> You are my guests: do me no foul play, friends.
>
> (III, vii, 30-31).

> I am your host:
> With robbers' hands my hospitable favours
> You should not ruffle thus. (III, vii, 39-41).

In Scots Law it was just as much a murder under trust for the guest to murder the host as for the host to murder the guest. But since Gloucester was not in fact killed, the crime committed against him was what Scots Law designated hame-sucken, *i.e.* the felonious seeking of a man out and assaulting him in his own house.

Notes

1. *Scotorum Historiae*, 1574, 251.
2. I, 343.
3. *Cf. Julius Caesar*, II, i, 63-69:
   Between the acting of a dreadful
      thing
   And the first motion, all the interim is
   Like a phantasma, or a hideous dream:
   The Genius and the mortal
      instruments
   Are then in council; and the state of
      man,
   Like to a little kingdom, suffers then
   The nature of an insurrection.
4. A homicide committed on a sudden and in heat of blood.
5. The felonious seeking of a man out and assaulting him in his own house.
6. A violent and masterful theft, generally as committed in the victim's house.

7. *I.e.* in order to kill or plunder.
8. The taking away of moveables belonging to another without his consent or legal justification.
9. Completely blocking.
10. Robert Burns, *Man was made to Mourn*.
11. *The Historie and Life of King James the Sext*, Bannatyne Club, 1825, 217. *Cf.* Sir Robert Gordon, *Genealogical History of the Earldom of Sutherland*, Edited by John Colwin, 1813, 188.
12. The two editions published in Shakespeare's lifetime.
13. For others, *cf.* Mackenzie, *Laws*, 50; and *Institutions*, 293-94.
14. A peculiarity of Scots Law at the time. *Cf.* Mackenzie, *Institutions*, 293-94: "We have a Kind of *Treason* in

Scotland, which we call *Statutory Treason*, because it is meerly introduced by Statute, and not by common Law, [a typical instance being] *Murder under Trust*, as if one Man should Kill another, when he invites him to his House." In the course of time other varieties of murder under trust came to be recognised by the courts and by the Scottish jurists: a husband killing his wife, a father his child, a master his servant, a tutor his pupil, or *vice versa*. Cf. Mackenzie, *Laws*, 128-30, *Institutions*, 293-94, and *Observations*, 21, 243; and Hume, *Commentaries*, I, 452-55.

The most notorious murder under trust in Scottish annals was the Massacre of Glencoe in 1692. In it the roles of murderer and murdered were reversed, since it was the guests who turned on their hosts. *Cf.* Hume Brown, III, 17-21; and Sir W. F. Arbuckle's contribution on *History and Traditions* to the National Trust for Scotland's Guide Book to *Glencoe and Dalness*, 1949, 38.

Sir Walter Scott, who was a devotee of Scots Law with all its idiosyncrasies and quiddities and a keen student of criminology, refers at least thrice to murder under trust. In *The Heart of Midlothian*, chapter 5, the sapient Mr. Saddletree thus expounds: "Whoy, there are two sorts of *murdrum*, or *murdragium*, or what you *populariter et vulgariter* call murther. I mean there are many sorts; for there's your *murthrum per vigilias et insidias*, and your *murthrum* under trust." In *Redgauntlet*, chapter 12, the young advocate Alan Fairford warns Provost Crosbie that he "may be an accomplice to murder before the fact, and that under circumstances which may bring it near to murder under trust". And in *The Abbot*, chapter 33, the Lady of Lochleven rebukes her steward, Jasper Dryfesdale, for having "attempted a deadly crime—poison under trust" on

the imprisoned Queen Mary; and for being "fool as well as villain, who could not even execute the crime he had planned". Scott, too, has these moving lines *On the Massacre of Glencoe*:

> The hand that mingled in the meal
> At midnight drew the felon steel,
> And gave the host's kind breast to
>   feel
> Meed for his hospitality!
> The friendly hearth, which warm'd
>   that hand,
> At midnight arm'd it with the brand
> And bade destruction's flames
>   expand
> Their red and fearful blazonry.

After the Union of the Scottish and English Parliaments in 1707, an Act of 1709 made the law in respect of treason uniform for the two countries; and, in the process, murder under trust was reduced "to its natural and proper rank, of an aggravated murder" (Hume, *Commentaries*, I, 452).

15. *Cf.* 55 *infra*.
16. Sir John Skene, Lord Curriehill, *The Lawes and Actes of Parliament, Maid be King Iames the First, and his Successours Kings of Scotland*, 1597.
17. Mackenzie, *Laws*, 52.
18. *Ibid.*, 52.
19. *Ibid.*, 52.
20. The same crime, still in association with treason, is alluded to later by Macbeth:

> Treason has done his worst: nor
>   steel, nor poison,
> Malice domestic, foreign levy,
>   nothing,
> Can touch him further.
>   (III, ii, 24-26).

No poison was in fact employed against "the gracious Duncan" (III, i, 66). But in Scots Law the buying or bringing home of poison was declared a statutory treason by an Act of 1450.
21. *Cf.* Chapter 4.
22. Letter of 24th January, 1951.
23. Mackenzie, *Laws*, 129.

E

24. D.W., xxvi. *Cf.* A. C. Bradley, *Shakespearean Tragedy*, 1922, 468.
25. D.W., 13, prints Duncan's speech (I, iv, 33-43) with two breaks.
26. An obscure phrase. The "rest" of what? I suggest that the phrase once was a perfectly natural sequel to something which the reviser has cut out, with blunt shears.
27. Duncan has just announced the bestowal of this honour on his elder son, Malcolm (I, iv, 35-39), which was tantamount to naming Malcolm heir-apparent.
28. *Coleridge's Shakespearean Criticism*, Edited by T. M. Raysor. 1930. I, 73.
29. *Cf.* I. *Chronicles*, xxix, 14: "all things come of Thee, and of Thine own have we given Thee".
30. D.W., liii. *Cf.* John Masefield, *A 'Macbeth' Production*, 1945, 38.
31. The surprise appearance of a third murderer (III, iii) has been variously explained. Some have thought that he was Macbeth himself disguised and that his going in person to participate in the crime is indicative of his growing distrust of all about him. He does not take even his wife into his confidence in the matter of Banquo, being sure of her approval later:
    Be innocent of the knowledge, dearest chuck,

Till thou applaud the deed.
                              (III, ii, 45-46).
But Macbeth's behaviour in the banquet scene (III, iv, 12-32 and 50-51) negatives the possibility of his having been present at Banquo's death. I think that an obscure sentence, "I will . . . Acquaint you with the perfect spy o' the time" (III, i, 129-30), when Macbeth is briefing the two murderers, may be a deliberately mysterious promise to send them a partner. After all, he lets drop the statement that he has other hirelings:
    There's not a one of them but in his house
    I keep a servant fee'd.
                              (III, iv, 131-32).
32. *Cf.* A. C. Bradley, *op. cit.*, 360-61: "some strange idea is in his mind that the thought of the dead man will not haunt him, like the memory of Duncan, if the deed is done by other hands".
33. Mackenzie, *Laws*, 331-32. In English Law an accessary before the fact is not, I think, regarded as a principal in a felony, but only as a subordinate. *Cf.* Dr. Johnson's *Dictionary*, *sub* "accessary" and "accessory".
34. Hume, *Commentaries*, I, 434-35.
35. *Cf.* 58-59 *infra*.

4

Echoes of a Clan Feud in 'Macbeth'

> It will have blood; they say, blood will have blood.
>
> *Macbeth*, III, iv, 122.

The special reason for the Scottish Parliament in 1587 passing the Act which distinguished murder under trust as a statutory treason was a series of treacherous and atrocious incidents of 1586 in the long feud between Clandonald of Islay and Kintyre and Clanlean of Duart in Mull. The 1591 Act of Sederunt of the Lords of Session, which allowed as witnesses in treason trials women, disreputable persons including accomplices in the treason, and children of any age, and which accepted the evidence of a single witness as sufficient, and the 1592 Act of Parliament, which required charges of treason to be formally proclaimed by heralds accompanied by pursuivants or macers with coats of arms so as to signalize the seriousness of the crime, were relevant sequels to the 1587 Act.

Before I try to narrate the main episodes in the feud, I should explain why I bring it into a book about *Macbeth*. Shakespeare was, I submit, anxious not to treat his Scottish theme from a distance, so to speak, and merely in the routine manner of the journeyman playwrights. He wanted to make his tragedy, although about eleventh-century persons and incidents, an interpretation of the Scottish ethos. It is an interpretation of a very favourable kind with which not even the most sensitive Scot could quarrel, on the ground of anti-Scottish bias or of any cheapening or detraction. On the contrary, Shakespeare's Scots (with the single exception of the Porter) are all dignified characters, not least the criminal hero and heroine themselves and the witches; and the whole circumstances and way of life of the characters have an austere simplicity and grandeur. At the same time, Shakespeare shows an awareness of the wilder and more turbulent conditions that still prevailed in sixteenth- and seventeenth-century Scotland and made it a very different milieu from that of contemporary England. But he wanted to suggest the difference without exaggerating it or making his drama appear to have been written mainly to illustrate it.

In trying to catch the appropriate colour, he took such hints and telling details as he encountered in the sources from which he drew his plot, especially of course Holinshed. He knew, too, something about alleged witches in Scotland and about recent witch-trials there.

As for the clan feud which has never before been referred to with reference to Shakespeare, one narrative of it contains details of things done or things said which strangely recall parallels in *Macbeth*. The feud itself has long since faded into a historical limbo. But for years on both sides of 1600 it was an exciting topic for gossip and comment, and, in the opinion of Lowlanders, the latest proof of the barbarous wickedness of those who lived beyond the Highland Line. This was just the sort of hot news in which Shakespeare would be interested as qualifying the atmosphere and background of a Scottish tragedy.

The clan feud may be said to have begun in 1562, though there had been still earlier bickerings, as a quarrel about the right to occupy certain Crown lands in the Rhinns of Islay. The records of the Privy Council point to the Macleans as the first aggressors, at least in the judgement of the authorities. From a minor affair, like dozens of others in the Highlands and Islands, it became a fierce and protracted warfare, punctuated by some of the worst treacheries and the bloodiest atrocities in the grim annals of the clans; and in the end, which did not come till 1615, it brought utter ruin to the once-powerful Macdonalds of Islay and Kintyre.

It is unnecessary to trace the earlier course of the feud during the fifteen or sixteen years after 1562. But by 1578 the two clans were under young, active, and high-handed chiefs who were not inclined to let wounds heal or wrongs be forgotten, Angus Macdonald of Dunnivaig and the Glens[1] and Lachlan Maclean of Duart. They actively prosecuted the feud, until in January 1579 the Privy Council ordered them, by a given date, to exchange assurances of indemnity, under the penalty of a declaration of treason against a defaulter. This move produced a détente in the hostile relations between the two chiefs, and led to the marriage of Macdonald and Maclean's sister.

Despite this brothership-in-law and the assurances of indemnity, the hostilities were not suspended for long; and the feud broke out again, provoked to some extent perhaps by the Privy Council's greater indulgence to Macdonald than to Maclean. So things continued in an intermittent war with no significant change during the rest of James VI's minority. But in 1585, after James had taken the reins of government into his own hands, he felt compelled to interfere, the feud raging with greater fury than ever and spreading to involve other clans.

The immediate cause of the explosion was Maclean's massacre of sixty Macdonalds, not clansmen of Angus Macdonald himself, but of his namesake Donald Gorm Macdonald of Sleat. This latter chief, with his numerous retinue, was going on or returning from a visit to Angus Macdonald. But he was forced by the weather to seek an anchorage for his galleys off Maclean's part of Jura. As it happened, two members of Macdonald of Sleat's clan with whom he had quarrelled had been compelled to do likewise. In pursuance of their quarrel, the two malcontents carried off some of the cattle on the island, in order to embroil their own chief with Maclean. They succeeded only too well. Maclean at the head of a superior force fell without warning on the Sleat Macdonalds, killing the sixty already referred to. Only the chief himself, who was sleeping in his galley, is said to have escaped, though presumably the men sailing the vessel likewise got away.

Naturally, the whole Clandonald tribe in all its branches and their allies in other clans were roused to retaliate. So violent was their reaction against the aggressors that the King had to weigh in on the side of Maclean in September

1585, though only to the extent of asking Macleod of Harris to help him. James's usual policy with regard to the turbulent Highlands and Islands was to tolerate a great deal in the way of strife and feuding between the clans; to allow the cauldron, as it were, to simmer and bubble until it boiled over; and then to exercise such authority as he had or as the chiefs would recognize, in a temporizing and moderating way.

Whether because of James's policy or not, Macdonald appeared to have been in a conciliatory mood. On returning from a conference in Skye with Macdonald of Sleat, he determined, against the advice of his counsellors and in spite of the fears of his brothers who refused to accompany him, to visit Maclean and try to reach an acceptable settlement. He was, at first and to all appearance, well received by Maclean. But the latter could not forgo his grand opportunity. On the day after Macdonald and his retinue had arrived, Maclean ordered all of them but one, perhaps too old to matter, to be imprisoned. They were kept in strict confinement until, to save his own life and the lives of his followers, Macdonald renounced the long-disputed lands in Islay and surrendered his young son James and his brother Ranald as hostages. But Macdonald, on securing his release, was all the more determined to have his revenge on Maclean when a good opportunity offered itself.

In July 1586 Maclean went to Islay for the fulfilment by Macdonald of his undertaking regarding the area in dispute. He took with him the boy hostage, but left the other at Duart. On the ground of its greater convenience and better supply of food and drink, Macdonald invited Maclean to his house at Mull-intrea. The very suspicious Maclean agreed to go only after demanding and receiving the most solemn and repeated assurances of good faith. He and eighty-six of his clansmen were lavishly entertained to begin with. Then Macdonald with between three and four hundred of his men surrounded the house where the Macleans were lodged and made them all prisoners, except two who were refused quarter and were burnt to death in the ensuing blaze.

It is probable that Macdonald had intended to wade no further in blood, but to extort a rescinding of the agreement he had been forced to make concerning the lands in Islay. But at this juncture occurred a Machiavellian treachery within Clanlean. Allan Maclean, who was nearly related to his chief, spread the false rumour that Ranald Macdonald, the hostage left at Duart, had been put to death there. Allan Maclean's hope was that Macdonald, on hearing the false report, would kill all his Maclean prisoners and that he (i.e. Allan) would get the guardianship of his chief's children and the management of his lands.

He did not in fact bring about Maclean's death. But Macdonald, believing his brother Ranald to have been killed, let loose his vengeance on the rest of the prisoners in his hands. On his orders, two Macleans were executed every day until only the chief himself remained; and he was saved only by Macdonald's breaking his leg in mounting his horse to see the last execution.

By this time the news of the protracted butchery reached James in Edinburgh. He did not try to exercise his royal authority in a direct way, but asked the chieftains of the Campbells (their over-all chief, the Earl of Argyle, being then a minor) to mediate. But so strong was the position of a Highland chief and so weak the arm of the law and the executive that Macdonald got off on very easy terms indeed. He agreed to free Maclean on condition that he himself received a pardon from the Crown and that eight Maclean hostages of rank were placed in his hands to ensure the carrying-out by Maclean of certain engagements which he had to subscribe.

Soon after the armistice (for it was no more than that), Macdonald went off to take part in hostilities in Ireland, presumably anticipating no immediate retaliation from Maclean. However, Macdonald's absence was Maclean's opportunity. Ignoring his own pledges and obligations and with no regard for the safety of the eight Maclean hostages, he laid waste a great part of Islay with fire and sword.

News of the devastation recalled Macdonald from Ireland. He took no revenge, such as might have been expected, on the eight hostages in his hands, but instead invaded in force Mull and Tiree, killing indiscriminately all the inhabitants he could lay his hands on and every kind of domestic animal. At the same time Maclean ravaged and plundered a great part of Kintyre. Nor were the effects of this civil war confined to the two opposed clans. The Macdonalds of Islay had the support of their kinsmen of Clanranald and Clanian, and of Clanleod from Lewis, the Macneills of Gigha, the Macallasters of Loup, the Macfies of Colonsay, and other smaller septs, besides entering into an offensive-defensive alliance with Lachlan Macintosh, Captain of the confederacy of Clanchattan. The Macleans had with them Clanleod of Harris, the Macneills of Barra, the Mackinnons, and the Macquarries.

So desperate was the state of affairs and so threatening the possibility of things even worse that the King and his Privy Council had to make some move, even if it only further manifested the weakness of the royal government. Nothing was done to qualify or countermand the pardon granted to Macdonald for all the atrocities committed by him; but the King and his Council reversed their sanction of the delivery of eight hostages by Maclean to Macdonald and issued a proclamation ordering the hostages to be surrendered to the young Earl of Argyle and his tutors or guardians, by whom they were to be brought to royal custody. They would then remain wherever the King decided until a final settlement was reached of all the issues in dispute between the two clans. And in the meantime Macdonald and Maclean and their supporters and allies were to keep the peace and to abstain from all armed assembly and all hostile acts, so as not to thwart the King's endeavours. About the same time James wrote in his own hand a letter, dated 20th April 1587, to the Earl of Huntly expressing his intention to take some special pains for the pacification of the Western Isles, as he had lately done for his scarcely less turbulent Borders, and urging Huntly to do his utmost to prevent the Islanders from convening under arms and from committing acts of aggression. It is probable that James addressed similar letters to other influential persons in the Highland area.

The eleventh Parliament of James's reign, as has been stated,[2] passed as its 51st enactment the statute which raised murder under trust to the bad eminence of treason, as a direct result of Macdonald's massacre of the Macleans when he was their host and they were his guests. The same Parliament passed eighteen other Acts, more or less specifically designed to establish and maintain good order in the Borders and in the Highlands and Islands and to improve the administration of justice in both areas. The first of them, numbered 92, has this title: "*Anent the quieting of disordered subiectes, inhabitants of the* Bordours, Hielandes, *and* Iles". It has this revealing preamble:

"Our Soueraine Lord, and his three Estaites convened in this present Parliament, considering the wicked inclination of the disordired subjects, inhabitants, on sum partes of the bordures fore-anent *England,* and in the *Hie-landes* and *Iles,* deliting in all mischieues, and maist vnnaturallie and cruellie waistand [= wasting], harriand [= harrying], flayand [= pillaging], and destroyand [= destroying] their awen [= own] nichtboures, and native Countrie people, takand occasion [= taking advantage] of the least trouble that may occurre in the inner partes of the Realme, quhen they thinke that care and thocht of the repressing of their insolence, is ony waies forzet [= forgotten]: to renew their maist barbarous cruelties, and godlesse oppressiones. For remeid quhairof, attour [= in addition to] and beside the lovable lawes and constitutions alreadie maid, in this behalfe: Quhilk Ovr Soveraine Lord, with advice of his three Estaites, ratifies and appreuis [= approves] be [= by] thir [= these] presentis. It is statute and ordaned . . ."³

One is tempted to murmur in comment the words of Macbeth:

Blood hath been shed ere now, i' the olden time,
Ere humane statute purged the gentle weal;
Ay, and since too, murders have been perform'd
Too terrible for the ear.   (III, iv, 75-78).

The purpose of Act 92, supported as it was in various ways by most of the others, was to make it imperative for all landlords, bailies, and chiefs of clans to find large sureties, in proportion to their wealth and the number of their vassals or clansmen, for the good behaviour of all those under them. If a superior failed to make immediate reparation of any injury or damage committed by persons for whom he was responsible, the wronged party could sue the superior himself; and, in addition, the superior would have to pay a heavy fine to the Crown.

This scheme of sureties and pledges came to be known as the General Bond or General Band.⁴ Is there an echo of this in *Macbeth*?

Come, seeling night,
Scarf up the tender eye of pitiful day;
And with thy bloody and invisible hand
Cancel and tear to pieces that great bond
Which keeps me pale!   (III, ii, 46-50).

The word *bond* may be another echo in:

Then live, Macduff: what need I fear of thee?
But yet I'll make assurance double sure,
And take a bond of fate: thou shalt not live;
That I may tell pale-hearted fear it lies,
And sleep in spite of thunder.
(IV, i, 82-86).

King James's attempt at a composition of the clan feud was thwarted by Macdonald's refusal to surrender the eight Maclean hostages, as he had been ordered to do by a royal proclamation. In consequence he was outlawed. Maclean, on the other hand, having declared himself a loyal subject, was received into the royal favour, though his record was not one whit the cleaner. Instead of trying to consolidate his position, however, by a new discretion of life and conduct, Maclean seemed to think that he had received a licence for further revenge and outrage.

His victims this time were not Macdonalds of Islay and Kintyre, but another branch of the Macdonalds, Clanian of Ardnamurchan, who had been among Angus Macdonald's allies in the recent hostilities. As it happened, John Macian had proposed marriage to Maclean's widowed mother. She was a daughter of one Earl of Argyle and aunt of another, the one who was the already-mentioned minor. Maclean had at first opposed his mother's intended marriage with Macian; but then, with a treacherous purpose, he gave his approval. Macian, accordingly, came with his principal clansmen to Maclean's house at Torloisk in Mull. They were welcomed as honoured guests with all the traditional hospitality and every appearance of friendship. After the marriage ceremony and the wedding banquet, the bride and bridegroom retired to a room in the mansion; and the gentry of Clanian and their servants were accommodated in a near-by barn. There, in the middle of the night, they were massacred, except two who managed to escape. Macian, roused by the uproar and the cries of his clansmen, tried to defend himself against Maclean who had burst into the bridal chamber, and was saved only by the entreaties of his wife. Along with the two of his retinue who had escaped the general slaughter, he was cast into a dungeon where he was daily tortured.

Then, with the help of about a hundred Spaniards from an Armada ship which had been forced to shelter in Tobermory Bay, Maclean waged war in the Macdonald islands of Rum, Eigg, Canna, and Muck, burning every homestead and sparing neither age nor sex. On the mainland of Ardnamurchan he laid waste the whole district round Macian's castle at Mingary. But he met a superior force made up from neighbouring clans which the King and his Council had ordered to oppose him; and he withdrew to his own island of Mull.

Angus Macdonald was just as busy and warlike as his rival. He added a body of English mercenaries to his clan strength and devastated large tracts of Kintyre, Mull, Tiree, and Coll, harrying and slaughtering as indiscriminately as ever Maclean did.

But at last both sides, having "supp'd full with horrors" (V, v, 13), came to a composition by which the eight Maclean hostages in Macdonald's hands were exchanged for Macian and the other prisoners taken by Maclean. It could only have been an uneasy and precarious peace, with both sides waiting for the first favourable opportunity to take the enemy by surprise. Nevertheless, the breathing-space gave the King and his Council time for politic action or, as James would have called it, kingcraft. No attempt was made to force the rival clans into obedience. A more cautious and cunning policy was pursued. To Maclean, Macdonald, and their principal supporters remissions under the Privy Seal were granted in 1590 for all the outrages committed by either side in the course of the feud. By these means, Maclean, Macdonald, and Macdonald of Sleat, under a promise of a freedom to come and go without damage to themselves or to their property, were lured to Edinburgh, on the pretext of consulting with the King on the good government of the whole battle-area. Then, in spite of the safe-conducts, James had all three chiefs seized and imprisoned in Edinburgh Castle.

Macdonald and Maclean were indicted for all their crimes, as if no pardons in respect of them had ever been granted. Macdonald "Refusit to pass to ane Assyis"[5] (i.e., he pleaded guilty). It is not precisely stated that Maclean likewise pleaded guilty.; but it is clear that he did so. Both chiefs, too, "become in our soverane lordis will"[6] (i.e. they submitted themselves and their property to the King's disposal).

The dittays or indictments against the two chiefs are appalling documents. Macdonald's dittay of 19th January 1591 covers a greater variety of indictable offences than it would be worth while to rehearse at length.[7] But they can be given more compendiously: [1] treason by the raising and paying of bands of men, including strangers (i.e. others than his own clansmen) and Englishmen, and with those bands waging a private war on Maclean from September to December 1587, with "sindrie slauchteris, byrningis [= acts of arson], heir-schippis [= plunderings] and vthir notorious murthouris and oppressiounes"; [2] treasonable fire-raising, burning, and harrying, also in 1587, in the course of which he "vnmercifullie slew, brynt to deid [= burnt to death] and murdreist twa hundreth persounes, . . . men, wyffes and bairnis . . . . . . committand [= committing] thairbye maist wyild, barberous and tressonabill creweltie"; [3] being "airt, pairt, red [= advice] and counsall, of the tres-sonabill ffyre-rasing and burning" of a town in Mull in June 1590 and of "resset [= receiving stolen goods] and ratihabitioune" [= approval of the theft], not to mention one murder; [4] the murder under trust, in the same month and year, of two of Maclean's men, "takyn vnder assurance betwix him and his partie Lauchlane McClane", by having them beheaded before him; and [5] treason, "Forsamekill [= for as much] as [he] being ane landit gentle-man, has in all the depredatiounes, ffyre-rasingis, murthouris and heirschips aboue writtin, and in the executing of everie ane of thame, committit manifest thift and stouth reif [= violent and masterful theft] of cattell, insycht [= farming gear] and pleneissing [= equipment], stollin, resset and reft" by him or his associates. I would draw particular attention to [4]. The dittay actually cites at some length Act 51 of James's 1587 Parliament which Macdonald's treacherous massacre in 1586 had provoked.[8] This was in fact the first recorded prosecution under the Act. It should be noted that the dittay goes no further back in Macdonald's criminal record than 1587 and does not include any reference to the 1586 massacre.

The dittay against Maclean, delivered on the same day as Macdonald's, was even longer, but in similar terms.[9] Maclean had an army of "men of weir [= armed men], strangearis, Spanzertis [= Spaniards], quha were ane pairt of the armie, callit 'THE HALIE LYG',[10] destinat for suppressioun of all that professit the trew and Cristian Religioune". With this host, raised in November 1588, he carried fire and sword into Macdonald's territory. The words *treason*, *slaughter*, *burnings*, *depredations*, *oppressions*, and so on are monotonously reiterated. On one occasion the number massacred by Maclean and his army was "about aucht [= eight] or nyne scoir [= score] of sawles", to say nothing of those killed in the widespread fire-raising. On another occasion (and here again, in Maclean's dittay, the Act determining murder under trust as treason is cited at length), three score of men and boys were killed, the retinue of the man who that very day had married Maclean's mother. On a third occasion he and his followers slew another large but unspecified number of men, women, and children, who were all likewise "vnder traist and assurance" because of a composition into which he and Macdonald had entered at the instance of the Earl of Argyle and his surrogates and which was guaranteed to last from July 1589 to the following May. In July 1589 he caused to be killed at least "fourscoir gentilmen, besyde ane multitude of wemen, bairnis and puir laboureris of the ground".

Though Macdonald and Maclean had merited death over and over again as principals in treason by murder under trust and in other flagrant ways, and though Macdonald of Sleat was at least involved as accessary, art and part, in many of the crimes, yet all three were pardoned for all the offences they had committed; but on strict conditions, the King retaining the power to pronounce sentences of death and forfeiture in the event of a failure to carry out the terms to the letter.

One condition, which was in part probably dictated by James's chronic impecuniosity, was the payment of heavy fines, £20,000 by each of the two great rivals and £4,000 by Macdonald of Sleat. Angus Macdonald had to arrange the surrender of his two sons and one of his nearest relatives as hostages for his own re-appearance before the Privy Council on a day fixed; and even if he did appear on the stated day, his hostages were to remain in ward till Macdonald of Sleat provided other hostages from his own kin for the performance of the conditions for his release. Maclean, who seems to have been treated more favourably by James, was not required to give hostages before being set free, but only to promise them by a certain date. All three chiefs were to return to custody in Edinburgh Castle on twenty days' warning, whenever they were summoned, so that the Privy Council might be assured of their obedience. The last condition of the pardons was that John Campbell of Calder, guardian of the young Earl of Argyle, became surety for the two Macdonalds, and John Campbell of Ardkinglass for Maclean. Before the release of the three chiefs in the summer of 1591, the Macdonalds, at the instance of the English Ambassador, Robert Bowes, were compelled to find further securities for their decorum in Ireland; and through Bowes, Maclean offered to serve Queen Elizabeth in the same country against the two Macdonalds, if necessary, as well as against the rebellious Sir Brian O'Rourke.

But in spite of all the conditions and sureties Macdonald and Maclean continued to be bad neighbours and unruly subjects to the ends of their lives; and their sons were as troublesome, especially Macdonald's eldest son Sir James. The story of their misconduct after the period I have tried to cover lies beyond my present concern. All that I need add is that by 1615, after many abortive attempts and many devious schemes, James and the Scottish Privy Council succeeded in bringing the Isles where the feuding had raged so long to something like peace. The Macleans settled down and remained in possession of their ancient territory or most of it. But the Macdonald lands in Islay and Kintyre were granted to Campbells; Sir James Macdonald, who had been imprisoned in Edinburgh Castle, had to flee to a precarious existence in Ireland; and other ringleaders of the broken clan took to piracy among the Western Isles.

No contemporary of the events, however, had more than an incomplete and scrappy knowledge of the facts. One person at the time did collect the floating rumours and included them in *The Historie and Life of King James the Sext*, which covers the years from 1566 to 1596, with a short continuation to 1617. It is an anonymous work, written within the period of which it treats (perhaps by more than one author, though only one is likely to have been responsible for the account of the clan feud). It was not published till it was edited for the Bannatyne Club by Thomas Thomson in 1825.[11] It has come down in at least six, more or less complete manuscripts, all apparently dating from the late nineties of the sixteenth century and the first two decades of the seventeenth. There may well have been others; but in any case the existence of as many as half a dozen copies of a manuscript of such length bears witness to its having aroused a considerable contemporary interest. That it was not printed in Scotland may have been due to a fear of offending the authorities or influential individuals mentioned in it; and in England, where the printing presses were much more numerous and active, it would not have interested either publishers or readers unless it had been translated into the Southern idiom. As its editor says: "like the narrative of every contemporaneous chronicler, it is visibly tinged with the colours of passion and party spirit; . . . apparently it is not the composition of a person actually concerned in the great events which he commemorates, or even very closely allied to the great actors in this eventful period of our annals".[12] In fact, the chronicler was something of a gossip, inclining to the anecdotal and including in his narrative of the feud allegedly verbatim remarks and exchanges. I shall give his narrative[13] without drawing attention to the discrepancies between it and the actual facts.

The anonymous chronicler cuts into the clan feud as if it had begun in 1586, with no reference to any antecedents except distrust and coldness: "althoght thay war brether in law, yit the ane was alwayis in sik suspicioun with the uther, that of ather [= either] syde thair was sa litle traist, that almaist sendle [= seldom] or never did thay meit in amitie, lyk unto the common sort of people, bot rather as barbaris upoun thair awin [= own] guairde, or ather [= else] be [= by] thair messingeris". But he makes no mention of Lachlan Maclean's massacre of the Macdonalds of Sleat in 1586. In fact, the chronicler, though he writes with a Lowlander's reprobation of all Highland barbarism, is rather more favourable to the Macleans than the sum-total of the facts warrants. He makes the immediate cause of the trouble in 1586 (which was to call forth the 1587 Act concerning murder under trust) Angus Macdonald's "understanding, be [= by] dyverse reportis, the gude behavior of Maclayne to be sa

famous, that almaist he was recommendit and praysit be [= by] the haill
newtrall people of thais partis above him self; whilk ingendrit sik rancor in
his hart, that he pretermittit na inventioun how he mycht destroy the said
Maclayne".

[*Cf.*:—

He hath honour'd me of late; and I have bought
Golden opinions from all sorts of people,
Which would be worn now in their newest gloss,
Not cast aside so soon.   (I, vii, 32-35).

To be thus is nothing;
But to be safely thus.—Our fears in Banquo
Stick deep; and in his royalty of nature
Reigns that which would be fear'd . . .
There is none but he
Whose being I do fear; and, under him,
My Genius is rebuked; as, it is said,
Mark Antony's was by Caesar.
(III, i, 48-51, 54-57)].

The better to effect the purpose he had in mind Macdonald made a show
of friendship. He "devysit to draw on a familiaritie amang thayme, and inveitit
[= invited] himself to be bancattit [= feasted] be [= by] Maclayne; and that
the rather, that Maclayne sould be the reddier to cum over to his Ile with him
the mair glaidlie, ather [= either] being requyrit, or upon set purpose, as best
sould pleas him. And when Angus had sent adverteisment to Maclayne, that he
[*i.e.* Angus Macdonald] was to cum and mak gude cheir, and to be mirrie with
him certayne dayis, Maclayne was verie glaid thareof, and ansuerit to the
messinger,—my brother salbe welcome to me, sayd he, cum when he list. The
messinger ansuerit, it wald be to morrow."

[*Cf.*:

Macbeth.   My dearest love,
Duncan comes here to-night.
Lady Macbeth.   And when goes hence?
Macbeth. To-morrow, as he purposes.
Lady Macbeth.   O, never
Shall sun that morrow see!
(I, v, 59-62).

Away, and mock the time with fairest show:
False face must hide what the false heart doth know.
(I, vii, 81-82).

Lady Macbeth.   Come on;
Gentle my lord, sleek o'er your rugged looks;
Be bright and jovial among your guests to-night.
Macbeth. So shall I, love; and so, I pray, be you:
Let your remembrance apply to Banquo;
Present him eminence, both with eye and tongue:

Unsafe the while, that we
Must lave our honours in these flattering streams,
And make our faces vizards to our hearts,
Disguising what they are.   (III, ii, 26-35)].

Accordingly Macdonald arrived with his retinue on the day he had chosen and was made welcome. The entertainment was of a protracted kind. "And when it was persavit [= realized] that Maclaynis provision was almaist spent, Angus thocht it then tyme to remove. Indeid the custome of that people is sa gevin to gluttonie, and drinking without all measure, that as ane is invetit [= invited] to another, thay never sinder [= part] sa lang as the vivers [= victuals] do lest."

[Cf.:

                his two chamberlains
Will I with wine and wassail so convince
That memory, the warder of the brain,
Shall be a fume, and the receipt of reason
A limbeck only: when in swinish sleep
Their drenched natures lie as in a death,
What cannot you and I perform upon
The unguarded Duncan? what not put upon
His spongy officers, who shall bear the guilt
Of our great quell?   (I, vii, 63-72).

What, sir, not yet at rest? The king's a-bed:
He hath been in unusual pleasure, and
Sent forth great largess to your offices.
This diamond he greets your wife withal,
By the name of most kind hostess; and shut up
In measureless content.   (II, i, 12-17).

That which hath made them drunk hath made me bold;
What hath quench'd them hath given me fire.
                                        (II, ii, 1-2).

Macduff. Was it so late, friend, ere you went to bed,
    That you do lie so late?
Porter. 'Faith, sir, we were carousing till the second cock.
                                        (II, iii, 24-27)].

The time had now come for Macdonald to extend a treacherous invitation to Maclean to pay him a return visit. His words of invitation sub praetextu amicitiae are thus reported by the chronicler: "becaus I have maid the first obedience unto you, it will pleas you cum over to my Ile, that ye may ressave als gude treatment with me as I have done with you". Nevertheless Maclean was cautious in consequence of Macdonald's record, and "ansuerit that he durst not adventure to cum to him for mistrust; and Angus said,—God forbid that evir I sould intend or pretend any evill aganis you; bot yit, to remove all doubt and suspicion fra your mynd, I will geve you tua pledges, whilkis [= which] salbe sent unto you with diligence; to wit, my eldest sone, and my awin [= own] onlie brother germain: These tua may be keapit heir be your freyndis, till ye cum saiflie bak agayne".

At this Maclean agreed to go; "and forder [= further] to testefie that bayth he simplie belevit all to be trew, and that upoun hoip [= hope] of gude freyndship to continew, he thocht expedient to retene à [= one] onlie pledge, and that was Angus his brother [*i.e.* Angus's brother], and wald cary with himself his awin [= own] nevoy [= nephew] the sone of Angus". His motives in so doing were probably, as the chronicler suggests, somewhat mixed.

In any event, he and forty-five "men of his kynnisfolk, and stowt servands" made up the party which sailed from Duart in Mull in July 1586. On their arrival in Kintyre "thay war maid welcome, with all humanitie, and war sumptuoslie bancattit [= feasted] all that day".

Macdonald, however, had warned "all his freynds and weillwillers within his Ile[14] of Kintyre, to be at his hous that same nycht, at nyne of the clock, and nather [= neither] to cum soner nor laitter; for he had concludit with himself to kill thayme all the verie first nycht of their arryvall, fearing that geve [= if] he sould delay any langar tyme, it mycht be that ather [= either] he sould alter his malicious intentioun, or els that Maclayne wald send for sum greater forces of men for his awin [= own] defence. Thus he concelit his intent still, till bayth he fand the tyme commodious, and the verie place proper".

[*Cf.*:
> If it were done when 'tis done, then 'twere well
> It were done quickly, etc.   (I, vii, 1-2, etc.).

> Nor time nor place
> Did then adhere, and yet you would make both:
> They have made themselves, and that their fitness now
> Does unmake you.   (I, vii, 51-54).

> Whiles I threat, he lives:
> Words to the heat of deeds too cold breath gives.
>   (II, i, 60-61).

> Time, thou anticipatest my dread exploits:
> The flighty purpose never is o'ertook
> Unless the deed go with it: from this moment
> The very firstlings of my heart shall be
> The firstlings of my hand. And even now,
> To crown my thoughts with acts, be it thought and done:
> The castle of Macduff I will surprise;
> Seize upon Fife; give to the edge o' the sword
> His wife, his babes, and all unfortunate souls
> That trace him in his line. No boasting like a fool:
> This deed I'll do before this purpose cool.
>   (IV, i, 144-54)].

Accommodation for Maclean and his followers had been provided in "a lang hous, that was sumthing distant fra uther howsing".

[*Cf.*:
> for't must be done to-night,
> And something from the palace.
> (III, i, 131-32)].

Thither they retired, Maclean being suspicious enough to take the nephew who was his hostage into bed with him.

Within an hour Macdonald had posted two hundred men about the building. "Tharefter he came him self, and callit at the dure upon Maclayne, offring to him his reposing drink, whilk [= which] was forgottin to be gevin to him before he went to bed."

[*Cf.*:
> Go bid thy mistress, when my drink is ready,
> She strike upon the bell.   (II, i, 31-32).

> the surfeited grooms
> Do mock their charge with snores: I have drugg'd their possets,
> That death and nature do contend about them,
> Whether they live or die.   (II, ii, 6-9)].

"Maclayne ansuerit, that he desyrit na drink for that tyme. Althoght [= nevertheless], so be, said the uther, it is my will that thou arryse and cum furth to ressave it. Then began Maclayne to suspect the falset [= deceit], and so arraise with his nevoy [= nephew] betuix his shoulders, thinking that geve [= if] present killing was intentit agains him, he sould save him self salang [= so long] as he could, be [= by] the boy; and the boy persaving his father with a naiked sworde, and a nomber of his men in lykmanner about, cryit with a lowd voyce mearcie to his uncle for Gods saik; whilk was grantit, and immediatlie Maclayne was removit to a secret chalmer [= chamber] till the morrow."

Macdonald then cried to the rest of the Macleans to come out of the long house if they wanted to save their lives, two mentioned by name being excluded from the apparent amnesty. The remainder having obeyed the summons, the excepted pair refused and were by Macdonald's immediate order "cruallie and unmearcefullie brynt [= burnt] to the death [in the blazing long house]. These tua war verie nar [= near] kynnismen to Maclayne, and of the eldest of his clan, renownit bayth for counsall and manheid".

[*Cf.*:
> 'tis much he dares;
> And, to that dauntless temper of his mind,
> He hath a wisdom that doth guide his valour
> To act in safety.   (III, i, 51-54)].

"The rest that war preasoners, of the haill nomber aforetauld, war ilk ane [= each one] beheadit the dayis following, ane for ilk day, till the haill nomber was endit; yea, and that in Maclaynis awin [= own] sight, being constraynit thareunto with a dolorous adverteisment, to prepare himself for the lyk tragicall end, howsone [= as soon as] thay sould be all killit. And when the day came that Maclayne sould have bene brocht furth, miserablie to have maid his tragicall end, lyk unto the rest, it pleasit Angus [Macdonald] to lowp

[= leap] upon his horse, and to cum furth for joy and contentatioun of mynd, evin to se and behauld the tyrannicall fact with his awin [= own] eyis. Bot it pleasit God, wha mearcifullie deilis with all man, and disappoyntis the decrees of the wicked, to disapoynt his intent for that day also, for he was not sa sone on horse, but the horse stumblit, and Angus fell of him and brak his leg, and so was careit hayme."

[*Cf.*

I have no spur
To prick the sides of my intent, but only
Vaulting ambition, which o'erleaps itself
And falls on the other.   (I, vii, 25-28)].

By this time news of the massacre had reached the Lord Justice General, the Earl of Argyle, "wha immediatlie assemblit his freyndis, and thay thoght necessar to compleyne to the King for revenge". The King responded by sending "an herauld at armes callit Ormond"[15] with letters to Macdonald commanding him to hand Maclean over to the Earl of Argyle. But the herald "was interruptit at the heavening port [= entrance to the harbour] . . . and so returnit". However, "be [= by] exceiding travell [= endeavours] maid be Argyllis freynds, and many unreasonable strait conditions grantit to Angus, at the last, Maclayne was randrit" [= set free].

But Maclean was not content with his release. "[W]ithin few moneths tharefter, Maclayne maid . . . preparatioun of armit men, and assemblit a great nomber of weill disposit persons, wha came with him to Kintyre for revenge of the former injurie; whare, what be [= by] fyre, what be sworde, and what be watter, he destroyit all mankynd, nayne except [= without any exceptions] that came in his way, and all sort of beast that servit for any domestik use or pleasure of man: And finallie, he came to the verie place whare Angus was mirrelie camping, luiking for na sik suddan invasioun for the tyme; geve [= if] he had not bene horsit incontinent, and withdrawin him self to a strang castell whilk was nar by, he had bene weill recompanceit for his former traitorie."

The sage chronicler adds at this point a comment which implies a rebuke of the authorities: "It is a certayne rewll, that all fault growis greater be oversight and forgevenes; for geve [= if] transgressions be puneist in dew tyme, the prence not onlie dois his dewtie in executing of justice, to the great contentatioun of the offendit person, and gude example to the posteritie, as a mirror of his gude lyf, bot also he gevis a terror to all offendors weill to behave thayme selfis, for feare of regorous puneishment."

Cf.:

But in these cases
We still have judgement here; that we but teach
Bloody instructions, which, being taught, return
To plague the inventor; this even-handed justice
Commends the ingredients of our poison'd chalice
To our own lips.   (I, vii, 7-12)].

The chronicler thus concludes his narrative of the feud: "I have tauld you at lenth the barbarous proceidings of these Ilandishmen, wha althoght thay war writtin for be [= by] the King, and subtellie traynit in to Edinburgh in the yeir of God 1591, with promeis of the King saiflie to pas and repas, unhurt or molestit in thair body or guddis, yit thay war bayth committit to warde within the castell of Edinburgh, whare the King, according to equitie, reason, justice and gude policie, sould have put thayme to a tryall, and had thayme convict for sik odious unmearcefull crymes committit be [= by] thayme, bayth aganis the law of God and man, war notwithstanding demittit [= allowed to depart] frie to repas hame agayne, for a small pecuniall sowme, and a shaymefull remission grantit to ather [= each] of thayme."

Notes

1. Often referred to as Angus McConneil, the surname or patronymic being very variously spelt. *Cf.* 194, note A *infra*.
2. *Cf.* 45-46 *supra*.
3. *Cf.* Skene, *op. cit.* on 46 and 53, note 16 *supra*.
4. Probably so called to distinguish it from the many other bonds or bands entered into by individuals or groups in the later sixteenth century. Similar contracts continued to be made in the seventeenth century, *e.g.* the Bond or Band and Statutes of Icolmkill in 1609 to which the principal chiefs gave assent and which began a new phase in the history of the Western Isles.
5. Pitcairn, I, part ii, 228.
6. *Ibid.*, I, part ii, 228, 230.
7. *Ibid.*, I, part ii, 226-28.
8. *Ibid.*, I, part ii, 227: "ITEM, Forsamekill [= for as much] as, be [= by] Act of Parliament, it is statute and ordanit, that in caise ony of our souerane lordis liegis wer slayne or murdreist, being vnder the credeit and power of the slayer, the committer of sik slauchter suld be declarit tratour; and the deid to be Tressoune, with foirfaltour [= forfeiture] of lyffe, landis and guidis: And trew it is and of veritie, that in the moneth of Junij lastwes . . . McIlheynych and . . . McIlheynych, being captiues and presoneris, detenit be [= by] him be the space of dyuerse dayis, and takyn vnder assurance betwix him and his partie Lauchlane McClane; he, in the said moneth, causit bring thame out of pressoune, and in his awin [= own] presence causit stryke of thair heidis without ony dome [= trial], and by [= beyond] all ordour of law, vsurping his gracis auctoritie; quhairthrow he hes incurrit the cryme of Tressoune and panes [= penalties] thairof."
9. *Ibid.*, I, part ii, 228-30.
10. The Holy League began in the fifteen-seventies under Henry, Duke of Guise as a faction to prevent Henry of Navarre, who was a Hugenot, from succeeding to the French throne after Henry III. It grew to include Henry III himself, Philip II of Spain, the Pope, and others as a confederacy for the destruction of Protestantism in general.
11. In 1706 David Crawford published as "from an authentic MS" *Memoirs of the Affairs of Scotland*, which is a very corrupt, doctored, and manipulated version of *The Historie*, etc.
12. xviii.
13. 217-23.
14. Kintyre, like the Isle of Whithorn, is a peninsula.
15. Not a surname, but the official title of one of the pursuivants of the Lyon Court.

F

5

The Gowrie Conspiracy

Away, and mock the time with fairest show:
False face must hide what the false heart doth know.
Macbeth, I, vii, 81-82.

The feud between Angus Macdonald of Dunnivaig and Lachlan Maclean of
Duart, each with the full support of his clan, was a purely Scottish sensation;
and neither the clan war itself nor the ultimate legal consequences would rouse
any interest south of the Border or be even reported there. If, as I have suggested, Shakespeare had some knowledge of the feud and of Scots Law, he
must have had access to it by means at which we can only guess.

But a far more resounding Scottish sensation was the extraordinary case
which is known as "the Gowrie Conspiracy". Unlike the clan feud, it was fully
publicised, as I shall indicate later, and that not only in Scotland, but in England
as well and indeed all over Europe. Shakespeare could not possibly have escaped
the noise and notoriety of it, any more than he could have remained unaware
of the Gunpowder Plot. Moreover, as a recent attempt, according to the
official version, on the life of an anointed King of Scotland, it was as certain to
have been in Shakespeare's mind when working on a plot about the treasonable
murder of an earlier Scottish King, especially as he deliberately introduced for
King James's gratification plenty of witchcraft and pointed references to undis-
puted lineal succession, the descent of the House of Stewart from Banquo and
prophecies of its perpetuity, the establishment of the United Kingdom, James's
policy of peace, and his inheritance from his royal predecessors of the miraculous
gift of healing.

There is no more perplexing historical mystery than the Gowrie Conspiracy:

A gulf profound as that Serbonian bog
Betwixt Damiata and mount Casius old,
Where armies whole have sunk.[1]

As Robert Pitcairn, who knew the relevant documents as no other student has
done, said: It "has long been reckoned as one of the darkest pages of Scottish
History; and the subject has, perhaps, given rise to a greater profusion of controversial tracts, and to more difference in opinion among historians, than
almost any other passage in our Annals".[2] It has fascinated historians, antiquaries,
and researchers, both professional and amateur, not to mention partisans and
cranks of all kinds and degrees. The innumerable books, pamphlets, and articles

written since the event are of very variable quality and reliability. Many of them, both early and late, have been biased in favour either of the King or of the Ruthvens; and most, if not all, of these partisan examinations have been written by persons who reached their dogmatic conclusions by the easy method of burking inconvenient facts. By far the best monograph on the subject was written by my life-long friend, the late Sir William Arbuckle. His painstaking and masterly piece of research, The 'Gowrie Conspiracy',[3] was written out of as complete a knowledge of the facts as can now be obtained and of all the hypotheses and theories put forward since 1600, with no attempt to evade difficulties or suppress awkward details. It is to be hoped that it will be read in heaven by "the old Scots lady who said that one of the few satisfactions we might expect on the Day of Judgment would be to learn the truth about the 'Gowrie Conspiracy' ".[4]

The stoutly Presbyterian David Calderwood, who had been a man of twenty-five when the Gowrie Conspiracy occurred, expressed in his exhaustive History of the Kirk of Scotland a like hope that time would ultimately bring a solution of the mysteries and recalled the rhyming distich painted above a chimney brace in Ruthven Castle:

> Vera diu latitant, sed longo temporis usu,
> Emergunt tandem, quae latuere diu.[4]

However, my own concern is not the elucidation of the Gowrie affair itself. Though I have had to read not a little of the literature, early and late, which it has begotten, what interests me is the certainty of Shakespeare's knowledge of the sensation and the consequent reverberations thereof in his Macbeth. He is unlikely to have had access to any of the official dispatches or records or to unofficial private letters; and he probably was as ignorant of the many sermons, printed as well as delivered, which either supported or mistrusted the royal account. But he was certain to have read one or more of the pamphlets printed for general circulation, on such a news item as would nowadays be carried on banner-headlines in the Press and blared forth by radio and television; and he could not have escaped the rumours, gossip, and guesses of all kinds which were as rife in England and on the continent as in Scotland itself.

It is appropriate now to give the version of the Gowrie affair which would be known to Shakespeare from the officially inspired pamphlet of 1600. Whatever else he may have heard or read is more problematical; and in any case, as a member of a profession harassed by Puritanical clergy and laity in England, he would be but little disposed to hearken to the doubts and insinuations of similar voices in Scotland, besides being too liege a monarchist and too shrewd a man of business. I tell the story below in as close a paraphrase as possible of the 1600 pamphlet, with many quotations of the very words of the quaint original, in the hope that the phraseology will not be too difficult to understand.[5]

On Tuesday, 5th August 1600, King James was preparing, between five and seven on a fine morning, to go buck-hunting, as was his frequent custom when in residence at Falkland Palace at that time of year. He would be accompanied by gentlemen of the Court, attendants, and huntsmen. But before he could mount, Alexander Ruthven (the oldest surviving brother and so heir-presumptive of John, Earl of Gowrie and generally known by the courtesy title of the Master of Ruthven), "being then lighted in the town of Falkland, hasted him fast downe to owertake his Maiestie before his on-leaping, as hee did. Where meeting his Highnesse, after a very lowe curtesie, bowing his head vnder his Majesties knee, (although hee was neuer wont to make so lowe courtesie) drawing his Maiestie aparte, hee beginnes to discourse vnto him (but with a very deiected countenaunce, his eies euer fixed vpon the earth) howe that it chaunced him, in the euening before, to be walking . . .without the towne of Saint Johnstoun [= Perth] . . ., and there, by accident, affirmed to have rencountred a base like fellow, vnknowne to him, with a cloke cast about his mouth; whom, as hee inquired his name, and what his errand was, to be passing in so solitarie a part . . . the fellow became on a sodaine so amazed, and his tongue so faultered in his mouth, that, vppon his suspitious behaviour, hee begonne more narrowly to look unto him and examine him; and perceiving that there appeared something to be hid under his cloke, hee did cast by the lappes of it, and so finds a great wide pot to be under his arme, all full of coyned gold in great peeces; assuring his Majestie, that it was in very great quantity. Upon the sight whereof . . . hee tooke backe the felow, with his burthen, to the towne, where hee, priuatly, without the knowledge of any man, tooke the fellow, and bound him in a priuy derned [= concealed] house; and after locked many doores vpon him, and left him there and his pot with him, and had hasted himselfe out of Saint Johnstoun that day, by foure howers in the morning, to make his Maiestie advertised thereof, according to his bound dutie; earnestly requesting his Majestie, with all diligence and secresie, that his Majestie might take order therewith, before any know therof; swearing and protesting that he had yet concealed it from all men, yea from the Earle his own brother."

Thanking Alexander for his good will, the King said that it would not become him to meddle in the matter, since no treasure of a free subject could be his unless it was found hidden in the earth.[6] The fellow's mere declaration of his intention to have hidden it, as he had told Alexander, made no difference. Alexander, then, ventured the opinion that the King was too scrupulous and, if he did not meddle, the Earl and other great men might do so, "and make his Maiestie the more adoe". At this the King began to suspect that the gold had been brought by Jesuits from abroad "for practising Papistes, (therewith to stirre up some new sedition, as they haue oftentimes done before)". Alexander's reply to questions about the kind of coin and the kind of man carrying it confirmed the King in his surmise and led him to conclude that the bearer of the treasure was "some Scots Priest, or Seminarie so disguised, for the more sure transporting thereof".

The King resolved to send one of his own servants with Alexander to Perth, in order to make the Provost[7] and Bailies hold both the man and the treasure until the royal decision in the matter was taken.

This proposal "stirred maruelously" Alexander, who declared that, if either the Earl or the Perth Bailies were let into the secret, the King "would gette a verie badde count made to him of that treasure". It had been Alexander's "great loue and affection" which had brought him on his errand and made him prefer the King's interest both to his own and to his brother's. He humbly craved that in return the King would ride to Perth and be the first to see the treasure, anything further in the way of reward being left to "his Majesties owne honourable discretion".

The King was astonished, "both of the vncouthnesse of the tale, and of the strange and stupide behauiour of the reporter". But, as the morning was fine, the game already located, and the courtiers mounted with the huntsmen in attendance, the King felt forced to cut short his interview with Alexander, saying that he could not delay longer, but that he would bear the matter in mind and give a determinate answer at the end of the chase.

Alexander was very "miscontent" at the King's declining to ride forthwith to Perth. It was, he said, not every day that the King would find "such a choise of hunting as he had offered him". Besides, the fellow in ward might cause such a din that the secret would be out and the treasure tampered with before any word had been received from the King; and also the Earl would miss his brother "in respect of his absence that morning". Whereas if the King came away at once to Perth, the Earl and the whole town would be "at the sermon", and the King could take such secret action in the matter as he pleased.

The King, however, rode off to join the hunt; while Alexander remained behind, having two men with him, Andrew Henderson and Andrew Ruthven, "appointed by the Earle his brother, to carry backe vnto him the certayne newes, in all haste, of his Majesties comming". Assuming that the King would in the end decide to make the journey, Alexander sent Andrew Henderson, the Earl's chamberlain,[8] back to Perth with all speed to advise the Earl of a possible visit by the King in about three hours, "adding these wordes, 'Pray my Lorde my brother to prepare the dinner for us' ".

The King, though he had joined the hunt, "could not stay from musing and wondering vpon the news". He sent one of the party, the surgeon John Nesmith, to fetch Alexander. On his coming the King told him that, after consideration and in view of Alexander's last earnest argument, he had decided to go in person to Perth as soon as the chase ended. In the meantime the King rode off to catch up on his party and Alexander followed, the only other person near them being John Hamilton of Grange, one of the royal master-stablers.

The chase, "one of the greatest and sorest . . . that euer his Maiesty was at", did not end till eleven or later. During it, at any stop or delay, Alexander earnestly whispered to the King to hasten the end of the chase so as to ride the sooner to Perth. At the end, the King, "not staying upon the curry [= dressing, preparation] of the diere (as his use is) scarcely took time to alight, awayting vpon the comming of a fresh horse to ride on". But Alexander "would not suffer the King to stay in the parke . . . while his fresh horse . . . was brought" from the near-by stables, "but with very importunity forced his Majestie to leap on agayne upon that same horse, that he had hunted all the day vpon, his fresh horse being made to gallop a mile of the way to ouertake him; his Maiestie not staying so much as vpon his sword,[9] nor while the Duke [of Lennox] and the Earle of Mar, with diuerse other Gentlemen in his company, had changed their horse". The King merely said that he was going to see the Earl of Gowrie and would return before the evening.

Some of the Court, after hurrying back for remounts, were unable to make up on the King till within four miles of Perth. Others rode forward on their wearied beasts, "whereof some were compelled to alight by the way: and, had they not both refreshed their horses, fed them, and given them some grasse by the way, they had not carried them to S. Johnstoun". The reason for this breathless pursuit of the King had no better ground than a suspicion that the King had gone to apprehend the Master of Oliphant, "who had late laid downe [= exercised] a vile and prowd oppression in Angus".

Meanwhile Alexander, seeing the Duke of Lennox, the Earl of Mar, and others getting fresh horses, besought the King to tell them that, as he would return the same evening, there was no need for any but three or four of his own servants to follow him; and especially the Duke of Lennox and the Earl of Mar should not come, for otherwise the presence of a nobleman would mar the whole purpose of the expedition. "Whereuppon his Maiestie, halfe angry, replied, that hee would not mistrust the Duke nor the Earl of Mar in a greater purpose than that, and that hee could not vnderstand what hinderance any man could make in that errand."

Alexander's last remarks raised suspicions and "many and sundry thoughts" in the King's mind. But he was unable to believe that any harm to himself was intended by the young man, with whom he was well acquainted through Alexander's recent suit to be one of the Gentlemen of the Bedchamber. The utmost of the King's suspicion was that the Earl of Gowrie had dealt so harshly with his high-spirited young brother "as hee was become somewhat beside himselfe". And such a surmise was supported by Alexander's "raised and vncouth staring, and continual pensiuenes all the time of the hunting", as well as by his strange and unlikely communication and discourse.

Accordingly the King acquainted the Duke of Lennox with all that had passed between him and Alexander. He earnestly asked what the Duke knew of the character of the young man who was in fact his brother-in-law[10] and whether the Duke "had perceiued him to be subiect to any high apprehension", the King declaring plainly that he thought Alexander "not well setled in his wits". The Duke was also told by the King to be sure to accompany him into the house where "the alleadged fellow and treasure was". The Duke wondered greatly at Alexander's story "and thought it very vnlikely". But he had never noticed any sign of derangement in the young man.

The private conferring of the King and the Duke made Alexander suspect its purport. He accordingly urged the King to tell the matter to nobody and to let nobody except himself go with the King to see the prisoner and the treasure. The King, "half laughing, gaue answere, that he was no good teller of money, and behooued therefore to have some to helpe him in that errand". But Alexander's "reply was, that he would suffer none to see it but his Maiesties self at the first, but afterwardes he might call in whom hee pleased".

The King now began "directly to suspect some treasonable deuise". Suspicious thoughts swirled through his mind, but he could reach no definite conclusion. So he rode on "betwixt trust and distrust, being ashamed to seem to suspect, in respect of the cleannesse of his Maiesties own conscience, except he had found some greater ground".

Alexander continued to urge the King to ride faster, even though his own spent horse was scarcely able to maintain the pace. When they were two miles on their way, Alexander let the King go a little ahead and sent on his other attendant, Andrew Ruthven, to let the Earl of Gowrie know how far they had then ridden. When the company were within a mile of Perth, Alexander told the King that he would post to the town to inform the Earl of the imminent royal arrival.

[Alexander Ruthven's repeated appeals to the King to make haste, his sending first Andrew Henderson and then Andrew Ruthven back to Gowrie House with news of the King's movements, and finally his posting ahead himself to acquaint the Earl of the King's near approach recall at least, if they do no more, Macbeth's similar urgency to get to Lady Macbeth the momentous tidings of Duncan's coming to Inverness Castle:

> *Macbeth.* The rest is labour, which is not used for you:
> I'll be myself the harbinger and make joyful
> The hearing of my wife with your approach;
> So humbly take my leave.   (I, iv, 44-47).

> *Lady Macbeth.*   What is your tidings?
> Is not thy master? who, were't so,
> Would have inform'd for preparation.
> *Messenger.* The king comes here to-night.
> *Lady Macbeth.*   Thou 'rt mad to say it:
> Is not thy master with him? who, were't so,
> Would have inform'd for preparation.
> *Messenger.* So please you, it is true: our thane is coming:
> One of my fellows had the speed of him,
> Who, almost dead for breath, had scarcely more
> Than would make up his message.
> *Lady Macbeth.*   Give him tending;
> He brings great news.   (I, v, 31-39).

> *Duncan.*   Where's the thane of Cawdor?
> We coursed him at the heels, and had a purpose
> To be his purveyor: but he rides well;
> And his great love, sharp as his spur, hath holp him
> To his home before us.   (I, vi, 20-24).

It is to be noted that Macbeth makes no mention of the king's coming in his letter to Lady Macbeth (I, v, 1-15).]

But, in spite of having been twice advised beforehand of the royal party's being on the way, the Earl was found by his brother on his arrival "sitting at the midst of his dinner, neuer seeming to take knowledge of the Kings comming". As soon as Alexandar made his report, the Earl rose hastily from the table and summoned all his servants and friends to accompany him. Some three or four score in number, they met the King with a train not exceeding fifteen persons in all, at the end of the South Inch. The King's party wore no "kinde of armour, except swordes, no not so much as daggers or whingears" [= knives carried on the person for use at table or for defence at need].

On arriving at Gowrie House, the King had to wait an hour before his dinner was served, "The longsomenes of preparing the same, and badnes of the cheere, being excused vpone the sodaine comming of his Maiestie, vnlooked for there". While waiting, the King asked Alexander when it would be time for him to go to the "priuate house" where the prisoner and the treasure were. All was "sure enough", replied Alexander, and there was no reason to go for an hour while the King dined at his leisure. He also asked the King to pay no attention to him and not to be seen whispering to him before the Earl, who, having missed his brother that morning, might begin to suspect "what the matter should meane".

The King accordingly began to converse on "sundry matters" with the Earl, from whom, however, he could get "no direct answer . . ., but halfe wordes, and imperfect sentences". When the King was actually dining, the Earl stood at the foot of the table very pensive and dejected, often whispering to one or other of his servants over his shoulder, and often going out of the room and returning, just as he had done before the King began his meal, all "without any welcoming . . ., or any other hearty forme of entertainement". The lords and gentlemen of the Court stood about the table and were not invited to dine "(as the use is when his Majesty is once set downe, and his first seruice brought up)", until the King had almost finished.[11] The Earl conducted the lords and gentlemen to their dinner in another room, but, again departing from custom, did not himself sit down.[12] He went instead back to the King and stood silent as before at the end of the table. Seeing this, the King began "to entertayne the Earle in a homely manner, wondring hee had not remayned to dyne with his ghests, and entertayne them there".

When the King was about to rise from the table, all the rest of his party being still at their dinner in the next room, Alexander, who was standing behind the King, "pulled quietly vppon him, rounding in his Majesties eare, that it was time to goe, but that he would faine haue beene quit of the Earle his brother, wishing the King to send him out into the hall to entertayne his ghests. Whereupon the King called for drinke, and, in a merie and homely maner, sayd to the Earle, that although the Earle had seene the fashion of entertainement in other countries, yet he would teach him the Scottish fashion . . .; and therefore, since he had forgotten to drinke to his Maiesty, or sit with his ghests and entertayne them, his Maiesty would drinke to him his owne welcome, desiring him to take it foorth and drinke to the rest of the company, and in his Majesties name, to make them welcome."[13]

[Cf.:
Macbeth. You know your own degrees; sit down: at first
    And last the hearty welcome.
Lords.   Thanks to your majesty.
Macbeth. Ourself will mingle with society,

And play the humble host.
Our hostess keeps her state, but in best time
We will require her welcome.
Lady Macbeth. Pronounce it for me, sir, to all our friends;
For my heart speaks they are welcome.
            First Murderer *appears at the door*.
Macbeth. See, they encounter thee with their hearts' thanks.
Both sides are even: here I'll sit i' the midst:
Be large in mirth; anon we'll drink a measure
The table round.   (III, iv, 1-12).

Lady Macbeth.   My royal lord,
You do not give the cheer: the feast is sold
That is not often vouch'd, while 'tis a-making,
'Tis given with welcome: to feed were best at home;
From thence the sauce to meat is ceremony;
Meeting were bare without it.
Macbeth.   Sweet remembrancer!
Now, good digestion wait on appetite,
And health on both!   (III, iv, 32-39).

Lady Macbeth.   My worthy lord,
Your noble friends do lack you.
Macbeth.   I do forget.
Do not muse at me, my most worthy friends;
I have a strange infirmity, which is nothing
To those that know me. Come, love and health to all;
Then I'll sit down. Give me some wine; fill full.
I drink to the general joy o' the whole table,
And to our dear friend Banquo, whom we miss;
Would he were here! to all, and him, we thirst,
And all to all.
Lords.   Our duties, and the pledge.
                (III, iv, 83-92)].

On the Earl's going away as directed, the King rose and asked Alexander
to bring Sir Thomas Erskine with him. Alexander promised that he would get
any one or two of the royal party to follow the King, but at the same time
desired the King "to commaund publikely that none should followe him". So,
accompanied only by Alexander, the King left the room where he had dined,
passed through the end of the hall where the lords and others were sitting at
their dinner, went up a turnpike stair, and walked through three or four rooms,
the doors of all of which Alexander locked behind them. Then, with a more
smiling face than he had shown all day before, and "euer saying he had hym
[*i.e.* his prisoner] sure and safe enough kept", Alexander ushered the King into
a little study in a projecting turret of Gowrie House, in which stood "wyth a
very abased countenance, not a bondman, but a freeman, with a dagger at his
girdle". Alexander immediately locked the study door, changed his smiling

expression, put on his hat, drew the dagger from the "freeman's" girdle, and held the point of it at the King's breast, avowing that the King was in his power to do with as he pleased, "swearing many bloody oths, that if the King cryed one word, or opened a window to look out, that dagger should presently go to his heart", and declaring his certainty that the King's conscience was burdened for murdering Alexander's father.[14] Astonished at so sudden a change, the King stood "naked, wythout any kinde of armour but his hunting horne, which he had not gotten leysure to lay from him, betwixt these two traytors"— Alexander with the dagger in his hand and a sword at his side and the "free-man" trembling and quaking like one condemned rather than like "an execu-tioner of such an enterprise".

The King then began to "dilate" on the horrible crime of shedding his royal and innocent blood. Such an act would not go unavenged, for God had given him children and good subjects; and if they did nothing, "yet God woulde raise vppe stocks and stones to punish so vile a deede". The execution of Alexander's father [William Ruthven, Earl of Gowrie] was no burden on the King's conscience, for at the time of it he was a minor and dominated, as was the whole country, by a ruling faction. Moreover, the father's execution was carried out in the normal course of law and justice.[14] The King appealed to Alexander to remember how well James had ever deserved of the whole Ruthven family by restoring all their lands and dignities[14] and by nourishing and bringing up two or three of his sisters "as it were in his owne bosome, by a continual attendance vpon his Maiesties deerest bedfelow in her priuy-chamber".[15] James also spoke of the terrors of conscience Alexander would suffer, especially since he had been educated in and professed the same religion as the King. The soul of the holy Master Robert Rollock,[16] whose pupil the young man had been, would denounce him for learning from another source the practice of such unnatural cruelty. James then gave his word as a Prince that, if his life was spared and he could go free again, he would never reveal to a living soul what had passed between them and would never allow Alex-ander to be harmed or punished for it.

The King was by no means hopeful of the outcome of his plea, so cruel did his captor look and so disrespectful was he in standing covered. Such behaviour seemed to forebode an immediate extremity. But Alexander appeared to be "somewhat amazed" by the King's persuasive language. He removed his hat and protested with oaths that the King's life would be safe, provided that he made no noise or outcry; and Alexander added that he would only bring the Earl of Gowrie in to speak with the King. On the King's asking what the Earl would do with him, since they would gain little by holding such a prisoner, Alexander would say only that the King's life would be safe if he kept quiet and that the Earl himself would tell the rest. As Alexander was leaving the study, he said to the "freeman", "I make you here the Kings keeper till I come backe agayne"; and to the King himself, "You must content yourselfe to haue this man now your keeper, vntill my comming backe". He then departed, locking the door after him.

The King, now alone with the man, asked if he was to be murdered by him, and to what extent he was a party to the conspiracy. Trembling and astonished in voice and bearing, the man declared that "as the Lord should judge him, he was neuer made acquaynted with that purpose, but that he was put in there perforce, and the doore lockt vpon him, a little space before his Maiesties comming". And indeed, all the time Alexander was threatening the King, the man was atremble, praying his young master for God's sake and many other adjurations not to touch the King or do him any harm. Though the King had been made by Alexander to swear that he would not cry out or open any of the windows, he now commanded his keeper to open the window on his right hand, which the man readily did; so that, though he was stationed there "to use violence on the King, yet God so turnd his heart, as he became a slaue to his prisoner".

None of the King's party knew of his dangerous situation. When they were rising from dinner, the Earl of Gowrie being in the hall with them, one of Gowrie's servants entered in a hurry and assured his master that the King was gone and riding across the Inch. When the others heard of this sudden departure, they rushed in a body to the gate of the courtyard. To some of them who enquired of him, the porter [Robert Christie] declared that the King had not yet gone. But, with a very angry look at him, the Earl said that the porter was nothing but a liar. And Gowrie told the Duke of Lennox and the Earl of Mar that he would soon ascertain where the King actually was. Having so spoken, he ran across the courtyard and up a staircase. But his real purpose was to talk to his brother, who had at the same time left the King in the study and hurried downstairs.

Very soon the Earl came running back to the gate where the lords and the others were waiting in a maze. He assured them that the King was indeed long since gone away by the back exit and that, if they did not follow at once, they would not overtake him. With that, the Earl called for his horse; and the rest ran together out of the gate towards the Inch, shouting for their horses to be brought and "passing all (as it was the prouidence of God) vnder one of the windows of that study wherein his Maiesty was".

Back into the same study Alexander soon returned. He threw up his hands as if in desperation and said that he could not mend things and the King must die. Also he produced a garter, swearing that he would have to bind the King's hands. At the word "bind", James declared that "he was borne a frie King, and should die a free King". Alexander gripped the King's wrist as a first step. But the King suddenly broke loose. When Alexander put his right hand to his sword, the King with his right hand seized both hand and sword, and with his left hand clutched the other by the throat, just as Alexander gripped at the King's throat, with two or three fingers in the King's mouth, to prevent his crying out. In the struggle the King forced Alexander to the already-opened window, under which at the very moment were passing the King's train and Gowrie. Leaning out his head and elbow to the right, the King shouted out that he was about to be murdered by traitors. Lennox, Mar, and the rest of the royal party heard and recognized the voice. But Gowrie kept asking "what it meant?" and seemed never to have seen the King or heard him. They all dashed in at the gate together. Lennox and Mar ran to the main staircase up which the King had gone earlier. But Gowrie and his men made for another "quiet turnepeck, which was euer condemned before, and was only then left open, (as appeared) for that purpose".

Meanwhile the struggling King had dragged Alexander through the now-open door of the study. He had at last got his assailant to his knees with his head under the royal arm. James then forced Alexander right to the door leading to the top of the "quiet turnepeck". Wresting Alexander's sword from him, the King intended to strike the young man with it and throw him down the stair. All this time, the third man of the trio was standing behind the King and doing nothing but tremble.

One of the King's Gentlemen, John Ramsay, looking for a way to reach the King from the courtyard, found the "quiet turnepeck" and ran up to the top of it. In the room there next to the study, he twice or thrice stabbed Alexander with his dagger, the King maintaining his grip, holding his opponent close, and finally pitching him down the stairs. During this brief encounter, the trembler withdrew from the room and disappeared. On Alexander's way down, Sir Thomas Erskine and Sir Hew Herries met him and finished him off. His last words were: "Alas! I had not the weight of it".[17]

To explain a point here: When the King's cry from the turret window was heard by the group at the gate of Gowrie House, Erskine had been behind the rest in their rush forward, and had seized the Earl of Gowrie and thrown him to the ground. But as Erskine had no dagger to strike Gowrie with, the latter's servants rescued their master. So Erskine, separated from the rest of the King's train who had gone up the main staircase, heard Ramsay's voice at the top of the "quiet turnepeck" and ran up it, calling on Herries and another man, one Wilson (a servant of Erskine's brother James), to follow him.

As soon as Erskine, Herries, and Wilson reached the room where the King was and before the door to the stair could be shut, Gowrie followed them in, having himself come up by the same turnpike. He had a drawn sword in each hand and a steel bonnet on his head.[18] With him were seven of his servants, each like their master carrying a sword. With a great oath, Gowrie cried "that they should al die as traitors!"

All this time the King was still in the room. He was quite unarmed himself and, seeing Gowrie with two swords, looked about for Alexander's sword, which had been dropped by him when he was thrust down the stair. The King's servants, however, got him out of the room into the study and shut the door between for safety. The four of them, Ramsay, Erskine, Herries, and Wilson, re-engaged Gowrie and his seven retainers; and "it pleased God, after many strokes on all handes, to giue his Maiesties seruants the victorie", Gowrie being run through the heart by Ramsay and dying "without once crying vpon God", and his servants being "dung over the staires with many hurtes". Ramsay, Erskine, and Herries were badly injured and wounded.

Throughout the fracas, Lennox, Mar, and the rest of the royal party were trying with heavy hammers to break into the room through another of the locked doors, which they had reached by coming up the main staircase. It took them half an hour or more to break open the double doors and enter. Beyond their expectation they found the King delivered from the imminent danger he had been in, and Gowrie lying dead at his feet. The King at once knelt down, all the rest likewise kneeling about him; and James "out of his owne mouth, thanked God of that miraculous deliuerance and victory, assuring himselfe, that God had preserued him from so dispaired a perill, for the perfiting of some greater work behind, to his glorie, and for procuring by him the weale of his people, that God had committed to his charge".

The news of the killing of Gowrie, who was the Provost of Perth, shortly came to the ears of "the tumult of the towne". Knowing nothing of his treasonable design, they continued in a mob for two or three hours, until the King pacified them by often speaking and beckoning to them from the windows of Gowrie House. He ordered the Bailies and the other good citizens to be brought to him. When they came, he related to them the whole strange episode and committed to their keeping the corpses of the two traitors until his further pleasure should be made known to them.

Before leaving Perth, James had Gowrie's pockets searched for letters that might throw light on the conspiracy. But all that was found in them was a small parchment bag drawn tight, "full of magicall characters, and wordes of inchantment, wherein it seemed that hee had put his confidence, thinking himselfe neuer safe without them, and therefore euer caried them about with him". It was noticed that his wound did not bleed so long as the talismans were on his person, but that immediately on their removal the blood gushed out in great abundance, to the amazement of all who saw it. This was "an infamy which hath followed and spotted the race of this house for many discents, as is notoriously knowne to the whole cuntrie".[19]

It was nearly eight o'clock in the evening before the King could leave the town, so great was the tumult. But by the time he had ridden four miles towards Falkland, the whole way, despite the darkness and the rain, was beset with people of all ranks, on foot or mounted, receiving him with great joy and acclaim. "The frequencie and concourse of personnes of all degrees to Falkland the rest of the weeke, and to Edenburgh the next, from all the quarters of the countrie, the testimony of the subiectes hearty affection and ioy for his Maiesties deliuerie, expressed every where, by ringing of bels, bonefiers, shooting off guns of all sorts, both by sea and land, &c. with all other things ensuing thereupon, I haue," says the author of the pamphlet, "of set purpose pretermitted, as well knowne to all men, and impertinent to this discourse; contenting myselfe with this plaine and simple narration." But the author adds, "for explanation and confirmation thereof, the Depositions of certaine persons, who were either actors and eie-witnesses, or immediate hearers of those thinges that they declare and testifie". If any difference in substance or circumstance from the printed narrative appears in them, the reader "may vnderstand the same to be vttered by the deponer in his owne behoofe, for obtaining of his Maiesties princely grace and fauor".

The deposition given first is that of James Wemyss of Bogie,[20] made and signed by him at Falkland on 9th August 1600. Its insertion was with a view to prove, not the treasonable intentions of Gowrie, but his dabbling in forbidden arts, an allegation which had a special importance in the mind of the King. Wemyss deponed, in the terminology of Scots Law, that on a recent occasion in Strathbraan Gowrie had claimed to be able to stop an adder in its track by pronouncing a Hebrew word "which in Scottish is called 'holinesse'; but the Hebrew word the deponer remembers not of". Gowrie had told Wemyss of using the word often before for the aforesaid purpose and said that he had got the word "In a cabbalist of the Jewes, and that it was by tradition". To Wemyss's question " ' what a cabbalist meaned?' The Earle answered, 'It was some wordes which the Jewes had by tradition, which wordes were spoken by God to Adam in Paradise; and therefore, were of greater efficacie and force than any wordes which were excogitate since, by Prophets and Apostles' ". In addition to knowing the word of power, the utterer of it must have a firm faith in God; and Gowrie added "that this was no matter of maruel amongst schollers, but that al these things were naturall". In Italy he had conversed with a necromancer, who was very learned and "a deep theologue", about "the curiositie of nature". Once at a concert, a man, staring in the Earl's face, told the company "thinges of him, which he could neuer attaine unto, nor be worthy of". The Earl reproached the man and asked him to forbear further remarks of the same kind. When the same man began again on another occasion, the Earl said that, if the man continued with his lies, then he, the Earl, would tell truth of the man, namely that "within such a space he should be hanged for such a crime; and so it came to pass". But in fact the Earl "spake it by guesse, and it fell out so". The Earl also maintained that "it was nothing to make an herbe fleshe, which would dissolve into flies". Again, said the Earl, the seed of man and woman might be brought to perfection otherwise than in the womb. On being advised by Wemyss to be careful about the persons to whom he made such communications, the Earl said that he would speak them to none but great scholars, and that he had told them to Wemyss only because he knew him to be "a fauorer of him, and a friend of his house, [who] would not reveale the same againe, seeing hee knewe they would be euill interpreted amongst the common sorte".[21]

The second deponer, who testified at Falkland on 20th August 1600, was William Rynd. The "Maister", prefixed to his name at the head of the document, indicates that he was a university graduate. He was attached to Gowrie's household and had been abroad with him in the capacity of a travelling tutor. His deposition begins with the mysterious characters found on the Earl's dead body. Rynd had first seen them at Padua, when he found them in Gowrie's pocket. On being asked where he had got them, Gowrie replied that "by chance he had copied them himselfe". Rynd recognized Gowrie's hand in the Latin characters, but could not say whether the Hebrew ones were his also. He vouched for their being the same as those shown to him at Falkland by Master Patrick Galloway.[22] When the Earl would change his clothes, Rynd would take the characters out of the pocket and ask " 'Wherefore serves these?' And my lord would answer, 'Can you not let them be? they do you no evill' ". If the Earl left his chamber without the characters, he would turn back as in anger till he found them and put them in his pocket. On several occasions Rynd would have burned the characters, had he not feared the Earl's wrath. If Rynd purposely left them out of the Earl's pocket, "my lord would be in such anger with the deponer, that for a certayne space he woulde not speake with hym, nor coulde not finde his good countenaunce". In short, the Earl "would neuer be content to want the characters off hymselfe, from the first time that the deponer sawe them in Padua, to the houre of my lords death". In Rynd's opinion, the Earl kept the characters so carefully on his person "for no good; because he heard, that, in those partes where my lord was, they would give sundry folkes breeues" [= magical writings or amulets].

The testimony of Rynd then turns to the events at Gowrie House on Monday and Tuesday, 4th and 5th August 1600. From it, it is clear that the Earl and his brother Alexander had kept their design entirely to themselves. Though Rynd knew of various comings and goings related to the King's visit, he knew no more than that. But he surmised that the Earl "had dissembled with him" in saying that "hee knew not how he [*i.e.* the King] came". And Rynd's opinion was that Alexander "could not have drawne the King to my lordes house, without my lordes knowledge; and that, when hee heard the tumult, he was resolued in his heart the Maister [*i.e.* Alexander] had done his Maiestie wrong; and that no true Christian can thinke otherwise, but that it was an high treason, attempted against his Highnesse by the Master and the Lord".

Two days after his main deposition, Rynd was re-examined at Falkland.[23] In reply to a question, he said that, when they were abroad together, he had several times heard the Earl reason "anent the duetie of a wise man in the execution of an high enterprise . . . and that he was euer of that opinion, that 'he was not a wise man, that hauing intended the execution of a high and dangerous purpose, communicate the same to any but to himselfe' ".[24]

The third deponer was Andrew Henderson, Gowrie's chamberlain.[25] In his deposition, made at Falkland on 20th August 1600, Henderson identified himself as the man already in the study to which Alexander had taken the King on the fatal 5th August. His evidence is, therefore, very material and has to be summarized fairly fully, even at the cost of some repetition. On the evening of 4th August, Gowrie told Henderson that, instead of going to Ruthven Castle on the morrow according to a previous arrangement, he was to accompany the Earl's brother Alexander and Andrew Ruthven to Falkland and, when directed to return to Perth, to do so "with all diligence, if he [*i.e.* Alexander] send a letter or any other advertisement with you". Also Alexander told him to warn Andrew Ruthven to be ready to accompany them at 4 o'clock on the morning of 5th August. At Falkland which the trio reached about 7 o'clock, Alexander, as soon as he had heard from Henderson where the King was to be found, went there and spoke with the King "a good space". When this first interview had taken place, Alexander, to begin with, was minded to send Henderson off posthaste to Perth to "aduertise my lord, that his Maiestie and he [*i.e.* Alexander] would be there incontinent, and that his Maiestie would be quiet". But Alexander soon bade Henderson follow him and not leave until Alexander had spoken again to the King, which he did at a break in the Park wall. This time Henderson was ordered to make for Perth. He did so with all possible speed.

At Gowrie House, apparently before he saw the Earl, he put off John Moncrief, who wanted to know where he had been, by saying he had been "beyond the bridge of Erne",[26] because the Earl had ordered him to "let no man know that he was to ride to Falkland". Then he informed the Earl of the imminent arrival of the King and desired that orders be given for dinner to be prepared. To the Earl's question about "how his Maiestie took with the Master his brother?", Henderson replied "Very well! and that his Majestie laide his hand ouer the Maisters shoulder". Henderson had taken no heed of how many were in the royal party, beyond the fact that they were the customary retinue and included some Englishmen. The only person of special note that Henderson recalled was the Duke of Lennox. An hour later Henderson, as directed by the Earl, "putte on his secret, and plaitte sleeues" (= body armour under his outer garments). The reason given by the Earl for this precaution was that "he had an Hyland man to take". As the usual server of the Earl's meals, his majordomo George Craigengelt, was ill, Henderson was asked by the steward about noon to deputize; and about half-past twelve the Earl called for the first service to be brought in. It was at this stage that Andrew Ruthven arrived back from Falkland and spoke quietly to the seated Earl; but Henderson did not get the purport of their talk. When Henderson was commanded to bring in the second service, Alexander and a certain William Blair came to the Earl in the hall. The Earl and those dining with him immediately rose from the table. Henderson assumed that they were going to take the aforesaid Highlander. However, instead of going in the appropriate direction, the Earl and his company went towards the South Inch. Henderson followed, was present when the King's party met the Earl's, and returned with the combined trains to Gowrie House, where Henderson was "directed to get drinke". Alexander then came to Henderson and ordered him to make William Rynd "sende him [i.e. Alexander] vp the keye of the galerie chamber", which was in the top storey of Gowrie House. The key was indeed delivered to Alexander somewhere in the upper part of the House, where he was immediately joined by the Earl. They conversed there; and the Earl came down to the ground level again and sent Thomas Cranston to summon Henderson to the room where the King was dining. From it Gowrie sent Henderson up to Alexander in the gallery and immediately followed up himself. He told Henderson to remain in the gallery and do whatever Alexander ordered him to do. This was to go into the study "and tarry untill I come backe; for I will take the key with me". So it was done, and in a short time Alexander returned, bringing the King with him. "And, at his verie entrie, couering his head, [Alexander] pulled out the deponers dagger, and held the same to his Majesties breast, saying, 'Remember ye of my fathers Murder? Yee shall now die for it.' " But Henderson "threw [the dagger] out of the Masters hand". And in his deposition he "swore, that as God shall iudge his soule, if the Maister had retained the dagger in his hand the space that a man may goe sixe steps, he would have stricken the King to the hiltes with it: But wanting the dagger, and the Kinges Majestie giuing him a gentle answere, he said to the Kinges Majestie, with abominable oathes, that, if he would keepe silence, nothing shoulde aile him, if he would make such promise to his brother, as they would craue of him". What promise? asked the King. But Alexander's only reply was that he would bring his brother. Then, "hauing first taken oath of the King, that he should not crie, nor open the windowe", Alexander withdrew, locking the study door on the King and Henderson. In Alexander's absence, the King asked Henderson who he was and whether the Earl would "doe any evill" to the King. "The deponer answered, 'As God shal iudge my soul, I shal die first'. And the deponer pressing to haue opened the windoe, the Maister entred, and said, 'Sir, there is no remedie; by God, you must die': and having a loose garter in his hand, pressed to have bound his Maiesties hands; and the deponer pulled the garter out of Maister Alexander his hand. And then the Maister did put one of his hands in his Majesties mouth, to haue stayed him to speake, and helde his other arme about his Highnesse necke: and that this deponer pulled the Maisters hand from his Highnesse mouth, and opened the windowe." When Henderson was opening the window, Alexander said "Wilt thou not helpe? Woe betyde thee, thou wilt make vs all die!" The King's cry from the window brought his train from the street through the gate to the courtyard. Henderson ran and opened the door at the top of the turnpike, through which door John Ramsay entered. Henderson remained long enough to see Ramsay stab Alexander and "thereafter priuily conueyed him-selfe downe the turnepecke to his owne house", where he explained to his wife "That the Kings Majestie would have beene twice sticked, had not hee releeued him".

In the course of this Chapter, I have drawn attention to one or two points of resemblance between incidents in the Gowrie episode and incidents in *Macbeth*. But I have reserved for Chapter 7 a fuller treatment of the parallelism between the historical events and the play.[27]

Notes

1. *Paradise Lost*, II, 592–94.
2. Pitcairn, II, 146.
3. *The Scottish Historical Review*, XXXVI, 1957.
4. Arbuckle, 110.
5. The quotations are from Pitcairn, II, 210–23.
6. *I.e.* was treasure-trove.
7. The Earl of Gowrie was himself the Provost.
8. At least for the lands of Scone Abbey, which had become Ruthven property after the Reformation. William Ruthven, fourth Lord Ruthven, was created the first Earl of Gowrie in 1581, the Earldom being erected out of the lands of Scone Abbey. He was the principal actor in the Ruthven Raid of 1582, which took the young James out of the power of the first Duke of Lennox and the Earl of Arran. In 1583 James freed himself and pardoned the actors in the Raid. But, when the pardon was reversed by the Scottish Parliament, the first Earl of Gowrie engaged in a new plot to seize Stirling Castle. He was arrested, tried, and beheaded at Stirling in 1584; and his property and titles were for-feited. In 1586–87 the estates and

G

honours were restored in favour of his eldest son James, who became the second Earl of Gowrie but died in 1588 at the age of thirteen. James was succeeded by his younger brother John, born about 1577, as the third Earl of Gowrie, who was the Earl of the Gowrie Conspiracy.

9. *I.e.* till the sword could be brought from the Palace.

10. The Duke's wife was Lady Sophia Ruthven, sister of Gowrie and Alexander. She had died before 1592.

11. Pitcairn, II, 172, note 5: "According to usual etiquette, the King dined apart from the rest of the guests, and was waited upon by his entertainer, though this appears to have been done in an ungracious manner".

12. Gowrie had himself dined at half past twelve, as soon as he had heard of the King's having consented to come to Perth. *Cf.* Pitcairn, II, 176, 222.

13. Pitcairn, II, 172, note 6: "This ancient custom was, in some measure, equivalent to the modern practice of drinking healths. The King's *scoll* was drank [*sic*] by deputy on this occasion, Gowrie, in his Majesty's name, drinking 'to my Lord Duik', &c. Frequent allusions are made to a similar custom in Shakspeare, &c".

14. *Cf.* 85–86, note 8 *supra*.

15. The Ladies Beatrix and Barbara Ruthven and one of their other sisters.

16. Robert Rollock (?1555–1599) was the first Regent or Principal of Edinburgh University.

17. Or in the vernacular: "Allace! I had na wyte of it!", which can be rendered in modern English by: "Alas! I am not to blame for it!".

18. Two such swords, according to the Italian fashion, were carried in one scabbard and served for a double defence as sword and dagger. The Earl was a singularly skilful swordsman.

19. Gowrie's father and grandfather, at least, had been suspected of practising necromancy and witchcraft.

20. He was one of Gowrie's cousins. His estate may have been Bogie, near Kirkcaldy in Fife.

21. It appears, not from Wemyss's deposition but from a letter of George Nicolson, Elizabeth's Ambassador in Scotland, to Sir Robert Cecil, dated 12th November 1600, that the King had received from one Colvil "the collection of the fortune to befall Gowrye, upon his nativity, written with the Earl's hand, in French, at Orleans, and there found, containing that he should return, be in great credit, seek for a wife, and yet dye with his sword in his hand, before he should be married" (Pitcairn, II, 219, note 1).

22. One of the King's Chaplains. *Cf.* 88 *infra*.

23. George Nicolson on 21st August 1600 reported to Sir Robert Cecil: "Mr William Rynd, the pedagogue, *hath been extremely booted*, but confesseth nothing of that matter against the Earl or his brother" (Pitcairn, II, 220, note 2). The same news was sent in a letter from Dover to an unknown correspondent on 28th September; the writer was either Patrick, fifth Lord Gray or, more probably, his son, the intriguing Patrick, Master of Gray (sixth Lord Gray from 1609). The Ruthven and Gray families were nearly related by marriage (*ibid.*, II, 319, note 1).

The instrument of torture, known as the boots, was borrowed from the Edinburgh City authorities for use at Falkland. On 3rd October 1600 the lokman (= public executioner) was paid sixteen shillings and eightpence for bringing it back to Edinburgh (*ibid.*, II, 245).

24. *Cf.* 121 *infra*.

25. *Cf.* 85–86, note 8 *supra*.

26. Bridge of Earn is about three miles from Perth on the road to Falkland.

27. *Cf.* 109–24 *infra*.

6

The Sequels of the Gowrie Conspiracy

> *Macduff.* Hail, king! for so thou art: behold, where stands
> The usurper's cursed head: the time is free:
> I see thee compass'd with thy kingdom's pearl,
> That speak my salutation in their minds;
> Whose voices I desire aloud with mine:
> Hail, King of Scotland!
>
> *Macbeth*, V, viii, 54-59.

King James was understandably thankful for having escaped unscathed on 5th August 1600 from a very ugly situation. He reacted in what might be called an extravagant way, along three lines: [1] the publication and confirmation of the events of the day in his own words or by the mouths or pens of others acting under his inspiration; [2] the proclamation of public thanksgivings and holidays and the bestowal of honours and rewards; and [3] relentless legal processes against the dead Earl, his brother Alexander, and the very house and name of Ruthven, and against other persons arraigned on suspicion of complicity.

The King himself was the first to give something in the nature of a public account of the affair. This he did in improvised speeches from the windows of Gowrie House immediately after his escape, to pacify the mob of Perth which had riotously besieged the House at the news of the violent deaths of their Provost and his brother.[1] And he followed this up by sending for the Bailies and other respectable inhabitants to brief them.

But more important and considered was the first account committed to paper. It, too, was James's own work. It says much for his stamina and resilience that he began it in a dispatch to his Privy Council not before ten o'clock at night and possibly later on the very day of his delivery, after hunting strenuously for some hours in the morning, riding about fifteen miles to Perth, enduring the strain of exciting and exhausting events there for six or seven hours, and riding another fifteen miles back to Falkland. This dispatch was completed in time to reach the Privy Council in Edinburgh by 9 o'clock in the morning of the next day. The Lord Provost and the Town Council of Edinburgh were also informed the same day, by a letter from Falkland to the Lord Provost "be [= by] Dauid Moyses, writter [= solicitor or scrivener], declayring, at lenth, the forme and maner [of] the tressonabill Conspiracie",[2] and also by the King's dispatch "presentet be Sir Patrik Mvrray".[2]

87

The dispatch has not survived. But its contents were communicated at once orally and fully to George Nicolson, the English Ambassador, who, still on the same 6th August, wrote his report to Sir Robert Cecil.[3] James himself, during the same month, sent James Hamilton[4] to be his agent or Ambassador in London and "to deliuer to the Queen the maner of the Conspiracie against his Master".[5] A little later James sent the Captain of his Footguard, Preston by name, "a very proper and discret Gentleman, . . . to deliuer more matter discouered of the Treason intended".[6]

James returned from Falkland to Holyroodhouse on 11th August. He landed at Leith. According to the consistently unfriendly and anti-prelatical David Calderwood: "The citizens of Edinburgh were attending upon him in their armes. Mr David Lindsay, minister at Leith, takes him to the kirk, ex-horteth him after thanksgiving to performe his vow, made before times, of performance of justice; at which words he smyled, and talked with these that were about him, after his unreverent manner of behaviour at sermons. There-after, he went up to Edinburgh, and sat upon the merkat-croce, cloathed with tapestry, accompanyed with some of the Nobility, where Mr Patrick Galloway[7] made a sermon to the people conveened."[8] The occasion was much more impressive, as it was meant to be, than the belittling Calderwood's description of it. Galloway's sermon included a long narrative, no doubt inspired by James himself, giving "the haill circumstance of the Tresone proposit",[9] very much on the lines of Nicolson's report to Cecil, but with some added details, especially as to how Gowrie was killed. Galloway denounced the Earl as a dealer in magic and a concealed Papist who had tried to induce the King to subvert the Pro-testant establishment. Galloway concluded with the dramatic disclosure of the name of the man in the turret study, Andrew Henderson, Gowrie's chamberlain, and with the reading of a letter from him to Galloway describing his share in the events of 5th August and confirming Galloway's own account. King James sat nodding his head in agreement; and, in addition, he testified "be [= by] hes awine [= own] mouth"[10] as to the truth of Galloway's narrative. Thereafter the congregation sang the hundred and twenty-fourth Psalm, "Now Israel may say, and that truly", which is still the regular Scottish song of deliverance.

Another sermon, going over again the events of 5th August, was preached in St. Giles', Edinburgh, on 24th August. It was by William Cowper, one of the ministers of Perth, who had been specially summoned to preach because he was well acquainted with the Ruthven family and because, after being at first unwilling to believe anything discreditable of Gowrie and his brother, had later come completely round to accept the official account. Whether James heard Cowper's sermon is not clear; but he was probably present for its delivery.

He was certainly present when Galloway preached again on the Gowrie affair in Glasgow on 31st August. On the same day, probably before the service, James listened to an oration by "one, in the name of the Towne; congratulating him for the delivery out of the late danger; with a commemoration of their service to him and his progenitors".[11]

These seem to be the only recorded examples of sermons on the Gowrie Conspiracy preached soon after the event. But there were certainly a great many more, probably at least one in every parish church in the country at a conservative estimate. It is quite certain, therefore, that the dramatic events of 5th August received a publicity unparalleled by anything before in Scotland. I should add that, as I shall explain later,[12] not a few of the clergy professed scepticism as to the official version and no doubt preached it as well, until silenced by the royal authority.[13]

But James wanted to give all and sundry of his subjects (and others in England whom he expected soon to be his subjects) a more detailed account than could be delivered orally in sermons to comparatively small audiences; "in order to quiet, as well as to satisfy, the public mind, which had been much inflamed by Mr Robert Bruce and the other refractory Ministers of Edinburgh; who greedily availed themselves of this opportunity of expressing their incredulity, by way of avenging themselves against the King, for his obstinate adherence to Episcopacy, &c."[14] Accordingly he caused to be printed "ane lytil buik",[15] giving the official version of the events of 5th August, together with the depositions of James Wemyss of Bogie, William Rynd, and Andrew Henderson who, as the "lytil buik" itself says, were "either actors and eie-witnesses, or immediate hearers of those thinges that they declare and testifie".[16]

"The King's Narrative" or "The Account published by Authority", as it has been called, appeared "cum privilegio Regio". It has all the circumstantiality and quality of an eye-witness account. But, while many persons could have reported this or that incident in the affair, the only one who could have provided an eye-witness account of everything, first and last, that happened on 5th August 1600 was James himself. It is pretty certain that he did not actually write the pamphlet; but it must have been written virtually at his dictation. And I guess that the amanuensis was the loyal Patrick Galloway, who dutifully sprinkled his pages with pious ejaculations and congratulatory phrases.

The pamphlet was ready for printing in Edinburgh about the beginning of September, or even earlier.[17] For on 3rd September George Nicolson sent a copy to Sir Robert Cecil. It probably appeared in at least two Edinburgh editions, one printed by Robert Waldegrave, an Englishman who had been appointed the King's Printer in Scotland in 1591, and the other by Robert Charteris, a member of a Scottish printing family.

No exemplar of either of the Edinburgh editions is known to have survived. Most of the copies were probably thumbed out of existence by curious contemporaries. But, as it happened, William Oldys, the editor of the *Harleian Miscellany*, had access to a copy and in 1745 printed from it in his third volume with this title: *Gowrie's Conspiracie. A Discovery of the unnaturall and vyle Conspiracie, attempted against the King's Maiesties Person, at Sanct-Johnstoun, upon Twysday the Fifth of August, 1600.*[18]

An English version of the Scottish original was printed in black-letter in London in 1600 by Valentine Simmes, with the following title: *The Earle of Gowries Conspiracie against the Kingis Maiestie of Scotland, At Saint John-stoun, vpon Tuesday the fift of August, 1600.*[19] Simmes published another edition in 1603 after James's accession to the English throne.[20]

I have more or less implied that *Gowrie's Conspiracie* was the first published

account of the sensation. But it may have been beaten by a short head to the
printing press, by a tract of a very different character. For it was an attempt,
apparently by one of James's clerical opponents, to vindicate the Earl of Gowrie
and to disseminate incredulity about the official version of the events. The knowledge that such a treatise had been at least written and possibly published had
reached Berwick-on-Tweed by 4th September, on which day Sir John Carey,
the Deputy Governor, wrote to inform Sir Robert Cecil of it.[21] Pitcairn says:
"This . . . Treatise must have been privately circulated in MS., or, if printed,
the impression had been seized at press. Not a vestige of the Tract remains. Even
the Title, or an abstract of the facts and arguments, is unnoticed by any of the
numerous contemporaneous writers who profess to espouse the cause of the
Earl of Gowrie."[22] On the other hand, the Rev. James Scott, who was a Perth
minister, quotes from a manuscript which he called "Stewart's Collections",[23]
to this effect: "After the Earl of Gowrie's death, a small treatise was published
in his vindication, but was suppressed. Some copies of it were, however, pre-
served; and Sir Robert Douglas has said, that his brother Sir William had seen
one of these vindications, and that also several old gentlemen in Perthshire
owned that they had seen it."[24] What appears to be a copy of the anti-James
and pro-Gowrie tract was found by Andrew Lang among the State Papers[25]
and used by him in his *James VI and the Gowrie Mystery*.[26] The tract almost
certainly never fell into Shakespeare's hands, and apparently, in consequence of
its suppression, into so few other hands that it left practically no trail behind it.[27]

As for Shakespeare's knowledge of the Gowrie Conspiracy, I am as certain
that he read at least the official version of such a first-class sensation as that, let
us say, Sir Walter Scott read the news of the Battle of Waterloo. On the other
hand, it is unlikely that Shakespeare ever saw such of the sermons as were
printed soon after the affair. But he may have read an interesting tract of a
sermonizing kind which was printed in Edinburgh by Robert Waldegrave in
1600. Its title is: *A Short Discourse of the good ends of the higher Prouidence, in the
late attempt against his Maiesties person.* It is anonymous; but it is likely to have
been another of the loyal compositions of Patrick Galloway.[28] It has some noteworthy phrases and overtones. The writer believed: "The Eternall Prouidence
[had] giuen many markes, euen from the firste conception of his Majestie, that
he is appoynted for great thinges: and [willed] at last, before his approches to
his destined right, now in the good age of his sister of England (whom he
hartilye wisheth long to liue, and who hath euer had him in the deare account
of hir owne sonne) that he should be incouraged, be [= by] a speciall signe of
his high protection and hand with him, and therewith also, haue a further triall,
both of his owne and his peoples hearts."[29] This meant, among other things,
that he was "invred [= accustomed, habituated] first with a dangerous (I must
say it) excesse in a Prince", namely and actually, too much "clemencie, goodnes
and truste".[30] These gracious and kingly qualities were manifested in the high
favour James extended to the Ruthvens, which was so wickedly repaid. "Yea,"
the panegyrist goes on, "and in these essayes, that we heere speake of (so little
commerce haue sick designes with God's assistance, or their own wit) their hart
may fayle them, their resolution may wauer, the partie [= intended victim] may

dash them, or his humanity mease [= maze, bewilder] them: a dread, a suspect, a word, or a looke may alter the case: and finally, the protection of God may intercede, withstand, or confounde them."[31]

It is not impossible that Shakespeare may also have seen a more pretentious and sonorous effusion in Latin, printed in Edinburgh by Robert Charteris in 1601 "Cum privilegio Regio": *De Execrabili et Nefanda Fratrvm Rvvenorvm in serenis- simi Scotorum Regis caput Conjuratione, apud Perthum, Augusto mense, an. 1600, Vera ac dilucida Narratio. Cui praemissa est, Prefationis loco, velitatio cum Lectore in fide et assensu commodando paulo religiosiore. His accessere ad Regem Soteria Carmine Heroico.*[32] The author, if all the items in the tract were by the same person, seems to have been a Mr. Thomas Cargill who was rewarded with twenty pounds by the Aberdeen Town Council in 1601 "for his Latin Treatise, congratulating the King on his deliverance from Gowrie's Conspiracy".[33]

I have already mentioned *The Historie and Life of King James the Sext* in discussing the Maclean-Macdonald feud.[34] This anonymous chronicle contains, in the pages added later to the narrative, a brief summary of the Gowrie affair which appears to follow the official account but gives also some details gleaned from the news and rumours of the day.

Two other chroniclers were contemporaneously at work on the period and narrate the Gowrie episode at some length and with some important variations and additions, in their manuscript Histories of Scotland.[35] Robert Johnston was the name of one chronicler: the name of the other is unknown. But since their works were not published, they presumably yielded nothing to Shakespeare.

The public thanksgivings for the King's escape from treason began spon- taneously, without any prompting from the authorities, as James made his way back from Perth to Falkland on the evening of 5th August, through cheering crowds of happy people.[36] But James wanted to extract as much acclaim and to promote as much nation-wide joy and relief as possible and to spread the celebrations from 1600 on to many anniversaries of his great day.

The Privy Council in Edinburgh understood well enough on 6th August what was required of them by the King's dispatch.[37] They rose to the occasion with a Proclamation, in an inappropriately involved style, to this effect: "and becaus his heynes, praisit be God, be [= by] his mychtie hand, by [= beyond, contrary to] all expectatioun, is sauit [= saved] and preseruit: THAIRFOIR, willing that thankis be gevin to Almichtie God, the onlie instrument of that preserva- tioun: And in consideratioun of the small boundis of any of the Perroche Kirkis, within this burgh, to notifie the said happie deliuerance of oure souerane lord fra the said perrill and danger, with the death of the saidis traitouris, sua [= so] worthelie deseruit: And thairfore, requireing thame, as it is the pairt of all his deutifull subiectis, to rander thankis to God, for his said deliuerie; and in taikin [= token] of thair joy, caus the haill bellis [= all the bells] within the burgh to be rung; and at nycht caus mak banefyreis, alsweill within this burgh as within the Cannoin-gate and village of Leyth, efter the accustumat forme obseruit in the lyke caissis, for the vttering [= expression] of the joy of his Maiesties happie deliuerance: And hes Ordanit Mr. Dauid Lindsay to prais God, within the Kirk for the same; and Ordainis the people to accumpany him to that effect."[38]

The Lord Provost and Town Council of Edinburgh had the same information from Falkland before them, at the two meetings held on 6th August to
discuss how best to manage the City's celebrations, by having the Edinburgh
ministers convene their flocks for thanksgiving services, by having all the
cannon of the Castle shoot salutes, by ringing all the bells, and by lighting
bonfires.[39] They also deputed two of their number to carry a congratulatory
letter to the King at Falkland, inviting him to come to Edinburgh and offering
him the Town's service.[40]

Robert Birrel, the homely and loyal diarist, records with approval the
Edinburgh celebrations: the service at the Market Cross, attended by the Privy
Council and members of the nobility, as well as by a great crowd of lesser
mortals, when "the haill peiple sett doune on thair kneis, gifing thankis to God
for the Kingis deliuerance out of sic ane grait danger";[41] and the more secular
manifestations of joy by a general assumption of arms, the firing of cannon and
muskets, the din of bells, trumpets, and drums, and the lighting of fireworks
and bonfires "in sic maner, the lyik was nevir sene in Scotland, ther wes sic
daunceing and mirines all the nicht".[42]

But this was only the beginning. The Town Council of Edinburgh,
apprised on 8th August of the King's coming on 11th August, "fyndis expedient, that the haill Counsall meitt his Maiestie the said day, in thair best
armour; and ordainis at [= that] the nichtbouris [= citizens] be wayrnet
[= warned] to that effect, ilk persoun vnder the payne of xx li".[43] So James's
arrival in Leith and his triumphal progress up to Edinburgh, which I have
already described,[44] made 11th August as festive a holiday as 6th August had
been.

The celebrations not only spread to "all pairtis of the cuntrie"[45] but extended over at least August and September. The enthusiasm of Dundee was
such that, in the ardour of local patriotism and rivalry, the townsfolk "come all
wp in armes to haive spoilzeit [= despoiled, pillaged] the burch of Perth; bot
praisit be God, the King knew the toun of Perthis part to be frie" [i.e. of blame
or guilt].[46]

The royal, and consequently the official, intention was to make the celebrations more than a once-for-all event. On 12th August the Privy Council at
Holyroodhouse, in pursuit of a policy of forfeiture, passed an Act "mortifeing
[= setting aside] L.1000 yeirlie to the Puir [= poor], furth of [= out of] the
reddiest of the fruitis, rentis and dewteis of the Abbay of Scone;[47] in perpetuall
memorie of the said happie deliuerie".[48] On 21st August the Privy Council,
sitting at Falkland, passed an Act "*anent ane solempne* THANKISGEVING *for his
Maiesteis delyuerie*"; with "aduyse of the Commissioneris of the Generall
Assemblie, to be maid and keipit, in all the Kirkis of this realme, vpoun the last
Tuysday of September nixt, and the Sabbothe nixt and immediatlie following
thairefter".[48] Not content with even those arrangements for due celebration and
thanksgiving, the King sent from Stirling on 24th August a letter to such of the
Edinburgh ministers as were his "Trustie Freindis" and not opposed to his
wishes. It went beyond the Act of Council to say: "And in respect of our said
happy deliverie upon a Twisday, We have, by the advice [of the Commissioners

of the General Assembly], appointed that every Twisday heerafter sall be a day of ordinar preaching, within every burgh within the boundis of the Synods."[49] Another important Act of the Privy Council in the matter came nearly a year later, on 16th June 1601, in view no doubt of the approaching first anniversary of the Gowrie Conspiracy. By it the lieges were commanded "to keip the said fyft of August zeirlie [= yearly], solemne fra all sort of handy labour, wark, and serious occupatioun, quhilk onnywyise [= which in any way] may distract thame fra the . . . exercise of thankisgeving to God . . . and reioysing for his hienes happie preseruatioun, wrocht [= wrought] sa meraculouslie be [= by] Goddis divyne Prouidence".[50]

So, to take an example or two, the Town Council of Aberdeen ordered the inhabitants to accompany the Magistrates through the streets, singing psalms and praising God, on the first anniversary. The Market Cross was to be decked out; wine with spiceries was to be drunk; and the glasses used were to be ritually broken.[51] And, as has already been noticed,[52] the Town Council on the same occasion rewarded Mr. Thomas Cargill for his Latin treatise congratulating the King. Orders were given, certainly as late as 1619, for other anniversary celebrations in Aberdeen.[51]

The Town Council of Perth, whose Bailies had been summoned to appear before the Privy Council at Linlithgow on 16th September 1600 to answer for the misbehaviour of their fellow-townsmen on 5th August,[53] was specially anxious to manifest their joy. On 15th April 1601 the King visited Perth as a sign of his restored favour. He was made a burgess at the Market Cross. Eight puncheons of wine were set there and were "all druckin out. He ressauit [= received] the banquet fra the toun, and subscriuit the Gilde-buik, with his awin [= own] hande 'JACOBUS REX' ",[54] to which he added a not insignificant Virgilian tag, *parcere subiectis et debellare superbos*.[55] Nor did Perth soon let the custom drop. There are several orders in the Records for celebrations of the anniversary in the decade following the Conspiracy; notably one on 4th August 1608 in which the Town Council, to honour King James's two miraculous escapes from treason, ordained "that the fyft day of August and the fyft day of November, be perpetualie kepit heireftir, for his Maiesteis preseruation, according to his Maiesteis desire; because thir tua dayis are preceislie keipit in England and Scotland".[56] In 1611 the Town Council, well ahead of the anniversary in that year, ordained on 23rd July that, for the fit and solemn keeping of the great day, a Proclamation be sent round to announce that it became the Town Council and all good subjects in the burgh where the treason was committed to rejoice and be thankful "by resorting to the hering of Godis word, at the ringing of bellis, by setting out of bonfyris, and all wther godlie declaratioun of thair willing and contentit hartis".[56]

There was another side to all the celebrations, the stubborn non-compliance and more or less openly expressed incredulity of a party among the clergy, including several of great influence and authority. This was in the main a somewhat disingenuous attempt to thwart and pester the King in a long-continuing wrangle that involved many issues. One of the issues was James's interest in the theatre and his patronage of players, which will be discussed later, in Chapter 8;[57]

and in the discussion I shall raise again the subject of the scepticism of the clerical opposition to the official story of the Gowrie Conspiracy.

Like Duncan near the beginning of *Macbeth* (I, ii, 63-67; I, iii, 89-109; I, iv, 14-42) and Malcolm at the end (V, viii, 60-75), James was generous in his immediate rewards to the most active of his rescuers at Perth, to a large extent out of the forfeited Gowrie estates and offices.[58] Nor did he ever forget their services, as is evident from the many favours extended to them long after 1600. It is not clear whether any of the vast domains and resources of the Ruthvens remained, at the end of the day, in the possession of the Crown. But James was himself made at least negatively richer by the fact that his debt of £40,000 was extinguished by Gowrie's death and forfeiture.

Such advancement or recompense as was granted to the Duke of Lennox will be noted later.[59]

John Erskine, Earl of Mar, who had been one of Gowrie's godparents, and his near relative Sir Thomas Erskine belonged to a family for all of whom James had a warm affection. Mar was older than James by four years or more. But the two and also Sir Thomas Erskine had been brought up and indeed educated together. In his characteristic way of bestowing affectionate nick-names, James called Mar "Jocky o' Sclaittis", because when they played a boyish game together Mar had "slated" (= outwitted) him. Mar had at one period been in James's bad graces for joining the party of the Earls of Morton and Angus about 1580 and for siding two years later with the Ruthven Raiders. But James and Mar were soon reconciled. Mar was restored as Keeper of Stirling Castle and was appointed a Privy Councillor and the Great Master of the House-hold. His most important charge, however, was the guardianship of the young Prince Henry from 1594, with special instructions from the King. This appoint-ment led to quarrels and intrigues at Court; but James resisted all the efforts of Queen Anne and her allies to withdraw the Prince from Mar's care. In 1601, soon after the Gowrie Conspiracy, the King entrusted him and another as joint-Ambassadors with the delicate task of furthering James's claim to the English throne. After James's accession, Mar soon followed him to London, where he was at once made an English Privy Councillor and a Knight of the Garter. As he fell ill several times in England and attributed those attacks to the English air's not suiting him, he spent most of the rest of his life in Scotland, returning south of the Border only for one or two brief visits. But James continued to bestow favours. The lands of the secularized Abbeys of Dryburgh and Cambus-kenneth and the Priory of Inchmahome were erected into the Lordship of Cardross for Mar in 1606 and in 1608 he was created Lord Cardross. From 1610 till he resigned in 1630, he was Lord High Treasurer of Scotland. He died in 1634.

Sir Thomas Erskine was the same age as the King,[60] and, educated together, they remained lifelong friends and intimates. Erskine was always about the Court, becoming a Gentleman of the Bedchamber in 1586 and receiving valu-able grants of land in the fifteen-nineties. For his part at Gowrie House he was rewarded with Dirleton Castle and extensive estates in East Lothian and the shires of Berwick, Perth, and Kinross. In 1601 he was admitted to the Privy

Council and was commissioned with the Duke of Lennox in an embassy to France. After James's accession to the English throne, Erskine went to England, where he received a series of royal awards: Captain of the Yeomen of the Guard in 1603, an office which he held till 1632; Baron Dirleton or Baron Erskine of Dirleton in 1604;[61] Groom of the Stole in 1605; Viscount of Fenton in 1606; an English Privy Councillor in 1611, with a re-admission to the Scottish Privy Council; a Knight of the Garter in 1615; and Earl of Kellie in 1619. He died twenty years later in 1639.

According to the diarist Robert Birrel, Erskine's man, whose name was Wilson, was "made gentleman" on 15th November 1600.[62]

John Ramsay, second son of Robert Ramsay of Wyliecleugh in the Merse of Berwickshire, was about twenty-three at the time of the Gowrie Conspiracy and a Page of Honour or a Gentleman in Waiting to the King. He received the accolade of knighthood on 15th November 1600[63] as Sir John Ramsay of East Barns,[64] which had been Gowrie property in East Lothian. He was also assigned the special honour "that upon the 5th of August annually . . . he, and his Heirs-male, for ever should bear the Sword of State before the King and his Successors".[65] Ramsay accompanied James to England and remained high in his favour. In 1606 he was created Viscount of Haddington and Lord Ramsay of Barns. At the magnificent celebration of his marriage in 1608 to Lady Elizabeth Ratcliffe, daughter of the Earl of Sussex, "The King drunke a health to the Bridegrome and his Bryde in a cuppe of gould and when he had donne sent it by my Lord of Fenton [= Sir Thomas Erskine] and therein a pension out of the Exchequer of 600 pounds a yeare to him and to her and to the longer lyver of them".[66] The following year Ramsay received a grant of the lands of the former Melrose Abbey and in 1615 the additional title of Lord Ramsay of Melrose.[67] In 1621 he was created Earl of Holderness and Baron of Kingston-upon-Thames. He died in 1626, the year after King James.

Dr. Hugh Herries, of a cadet branch of the house of Lord Herries, was knighted at the same time as Ramsay.[68] His more tangible reward for his part in rescuing the King was the Cousland estates of the Gowrie Earldom in Midlothian.

Erskine, Ramsay, and Herries were also heraldically honoured by additions to their arms, all emblematic of their activity in sword-play at Gowrie House.[69]

William Murray younger of Tullibardine in Perthshire, who had been in the King's retinue on 5th August but who does not seem to have played an important role in the events of that day, received Gowrie's office of Sheriff of Perthshire. It was Murray who performed the gruesome task of transporting to Edinburgh the long-unburied bodies of Gowrie and his brother Alexander for public hanging, drawing and quartering as declared traitors.[70]

Another who was generously rewarded, for his special activity in extricating James from Gowrie House and the Perth mob, was Sir David Murray of Gospertie in Perthshire. About the same age as James, he had been brought up at Court and was very much a King's man. The year before the Gowrie Conspiracy he was knighted, admitted to the Privy Council, and made Comptroller of the Treasury. In 1600, immediately after the Conspiracy, he received the office of Provost of Perth which had been held by Gowrie. In 1602 some of the Gowrie estates in Perthshire and Fife were granted to him. In 1603 he was appointed Captain of the King's Horse Guards in Scotland and accompanied James to England. At an uncertain date, but probably in 1604 or 1605, Murray received the Scone Abbey estates of Gowrie and with them the title of Lord Scone. He was also nominated one of the Commissioners for the proposed constitutional Union of the two Kingdoms. After remaining for some years in England, he returned to Scotland and was active there on James's behalf in many ecclesiastical negotiations. In 1621 he was advanced in the peerage as Viscount Stormont, taking his title from a district in Perthshire which had been Gowrie property. He died in 1631.

But perhaps the most unexpected of James's beneficiaries was Andrew Henderson, the man in the turret study at Gowrie House. Though he had been more involved in the treasonable affair, however innocently and reluctantly, than several others who paid for their minor parts in it with their lives, Henderson was for politic reasons spared as the only witness who could confirm the King's account of the events in the turret, and spared also because he had tried to dissuade Alexander Ruthven and to help James. After being charged with complicity and then having the charge dropped at the command of the King,[71] Henderson was allowed to retain his chamberlainship of the Scone Abbey estates, at first under the Crown and then under Lord Scone. About a week before James set out for London to receive his second Crown, he granted Henderson a tack [= lease] of the teind [= tithe] sheaves of Kinnochtry, four miles from Cupar Angus in Perthshire, for two periods of nineteen years each. Henderson visited London in 1604 and got the further reward from James of a pension of 500 marks. He began to buy and build and become litigious, but by no means popular or admired. He soon quarrelled with Lord Scone and made accusations against him, especially over the non-payment of his pension, carrying his grievances in 1612 to James in London. The King gave instructions for the pension to be regularly paid in future, but dismissed the accusations against Lord Scone and ordered Henderson to be confined to the house and lands he had already purchased at Lawton in the neighbourhood of the already-mentioned Kinnochtry.

Of course the legal processes were set agoing immediately after the abortive plot at Gowrie House; and they were remorselessly pursued for months,[72] with all the formality and ceremony considered proper to such a case of high treason, and indeed with more elaboration than in any other on record. The procedure followed was of ancient date, but as modified and fortified by the 1587 and 1592 Acts of Parliament and the 1591 Act of Sederunt of the Court of Session, which were discussed in Chapter 3.[73]

The King's dispatch, written at Falkland Palace on the night of 5th-6th August and received by the Privy Council in Edinburgh on 6th August, set the ball rolling; unless we regard as the very first motion the probably antecedent dismissal by James of his Queen's Gentlewoman, Lady Beatrice or Beatrix Ruthven, Gowrie's sister.[74]

This move against one of the Ruthvens was followed on 6th August by the sending of a party to seize at Dirleton Castle Gowrie's two youngest brothers, William and Patrick. But having been forewarned, they slipped over the Border into England.[75] On the same 6th August, at Perth, the first of many depositions was taken, that of Thomas Cranston. He is described as "swmtyme seruitour" of the Earl of Gowrie.[76] But since he was accorded and used the addition of "Mr." and was a brother of Sir John Cranston of Cranston in Midlothian, his position in Gowrie's great household was not that of a menial. The accusation against him was that he was one of the Gowrie retainers who had drawn their swords during the tumult on 5th August.[77]

On 7th August the King in Council at Falkland ordered "officeris of airmes, shereffis in that pairt" to charge the Bailies of Perth to keep unburied the bodies of Gowrie and his brother Alexander until "they vnderstand forder [= further] of his heynes will and pleasour thairanent".[78] Other letters were issued for the arrestment of rents from Gowrie estates; and various charges were published: to repel all persons named Ruthven from approaching the King and Queen;[79] to render up all Gowrie's castles and other buildings with their contents to the Lord High Treasurer; and to prevent the disposal of anything pertaining to the Earldom without the Privy Council's instructions.[80]

On 9th August at Falkland a deposition was taken from James Wemyss of Bogie. It was considered of particular importance because of its references to Gowrie's interest in the occult and his claim to magical power; and in consequence it was one of the three depositions added to and published along with the official account of the Conspiracy.

On 12th August, the day after James's triumphal return to his Capital, he and the Privy Council at Holyroodhouse, not content with what had already been done to seize all Gowrie property, forbade "the passing of Giftis of the Erldome of Gowrie",[81] presumably to prevent the transfer of Gowrie goods from hand to hand and so their escaping the net of forfeiture.

On the same day in August and by the same authority orders were issued for George Craigengelt, Hugh Moncreiffe, Andrew Henderson, Patrick Eviot and Harry and Alexander Ruthven to be denounced rebels for non-appearance to answer such things "as sould haue bene inquirit of thame . . . and layd to thair charge".[82] The calls to compear, as the Scots Law term is, must have gone out earlier, probably very soon after 5th August.[83] The first four of the persons mentioned above were attached to the Gowrie household in various capacities. Harry and Alexander Ruthven may have been also; but their kinship with the Earl and his brother Alexander was the likelier reason for their denunciation. They were brothers of William Ruthven of Freeland, an estate a few miles south-west of Perth.[84] Hugh Moncreiffe was a brother of William Moncreiffe of Moncreiffe in Perthshire; and Patrick Eviot a brother of Colin Eviot of Balhousie, near Perth. George Craigengelt had the position, as already noted,[85] of majordomo at Gowrie House; he responded to the denunciation by compearing and making a deposition at Falkland on 16th August.[86] Andrew Henderson, chamberlain of the Scone Abbey estates of Gowrie, was of course a key figure, having been the man stationed by Alexander Ruthven in the turret study on 5th August.[87] Apparently he came out of hiding and got in

touch with the royal Chaplain, Patrick Galloway. His deposition, made at
Falkland on 20th August, was one of the three published along with the official
account.[88] A sixth person, Andrew Johnstoun, a burgess of Perth, was added to
the list of denounced rebels on 19th August;[89] but no more is heard of him
and it is possible that the charge was dropped because he had died.

On 20th August, William Rynd, who had been Gowrie's travelling tutor
on the continent and had continued in his household, perhaps to instruct the
younger brothers of the Earl, made his deposition at Falkland, with an addition
two days later.[90] It, too, was regarded as important and was published with the
official account, probably because it mentioned Gowrie's solicitude for the
cabbalistic characters he always carried on his person.[90]

On 21st August James sent from Falkland, by Thomas Hamilton of Drum-
cairn,[91] the King's Advocate, his warrant for the trial at Perth of Thomas
Cranston, George Craigengelt, and John McDuff "alias Barroune, in Stra-
brand"[92] (= baron bailie of the Gowrie estates in Strathbraan, Perthshire). It is
a curious document to modern eyes, for it requires not only that the three
should be tried, but "thay being convict, that ye cause dome [= sentence] to be
pronunceit aganis [th]ame, to hang [th]ame to deid; And that ye sie the same
dome put to executioune, without delay".[93]

Nor was there any delay. For the very next day Hamilton produced, before
the High Court of Justiciary sitting at Perth, the three dittays or indictments
charging Cranston, Craigengelt, and McDuff with being "airt and pairt of the
Treasonable crymes vnderwritten".[94] The dittays are long, explicit, and re-
petitive.[95] They add many details to the story that are not incorporated in the
official narrative, though none perhaps is specially significant. As they were
read out in court at Perth, they would of course become matter for discussion
outside; and their additions, more or less garbled, would be caught up in the
spate of rumours and gossip. There is really nothing in the dittays to show that
the panels (= the three persons arraigned) had any foreknowledge of the
Conspiracy. But they, along with others of Gowrie's household and retainers,
had drawn their swords in the near proximity of the King and been active in
some of the scuffling in and about Gowrie House on 5th August.

The dittays were verified or confirmed by the Advocate's submission of
the depositions of the three accused themselves,[96] and the depositions of Andrew
Henderson, a Perth Bailie Oliver Young, James Drummond of Pitcairns near
Dunning in Perthshire, and David Rynd, flesher in Perth. The Advocate also
cited divers Acts of Parliament relating to treason, including without a doubt
the recent two which I have mentioned several times, those of 1587 and 1592.[97]
Moreover, he "Repetis the notorietie of the fact, and the knawledge of the
Assyis [= jurors[98]] thame selffis".[99] Finally he added, perhaps in a conventional
formula: "and gif [= if] thay clange [= acquit], Protestis (for) Wilfull and
manifest Errour".[100]

The jury, it is hardly necessary to say, "eftir longe ressoning and consulta-
tioune", found all three panels "Fylit, Culpabill and Convict of airt and pairt
of the maist crewall, abhominabill and tressonabill Conspiracie".[101] The sentence
was death by hanging at Perth and the forfeiture of all the possessions of any

kind belonging to the panels; and no time was lost in implementing it, for the next day, 23rd August, all three were hanged—and, no doubt, drawn and quartered as well.[102] They had confessed nothing and had denied all knowledge of any conspiracy.

On 26th August summonses of treason were issued against the following persons: William Ruthven, Gowrie's eldest surviving brother and, since the death of Alexander Ruthven, his presumptive heir; William Ruthven's tutors and curators "gif [= if] he ony hes";[103] Hugh Moncreiffe; Andrew Henderson; Patrick Eviot; Harry and Alexander Ruthven; "and all vtheris haveand [= having] or pretendand [= pretending] to haue enteres [= interest] in the foirsaid actioun and cause of Treassoun".[104] They were required to compear, not before the High Court of Justiciary, but before the King in Parliament on 4th November.

The two summonses[105] were executed on 28th and 30th August with pomp and circumstance, as will be gathered from the testimony in writing handed in at the trial by John Blinschell, Islay Herald, who was the most important of the officials concerned. He was accompanied on his missions by a trumpeter to "blow the horrid deed in every eye" as Macbeth says (I, vii, 24), a messenger-at-arms, and four lesser functionaries; and on every occasion, in Edinburgh and Leith and in Kinross, Perth, and its neighbourhood and in Dirleton and East Lothian, there was a great display of heraldry.[106]

Both of Blinschell's certificates of his executions of the two summonses were read at the trial. The following passage from one of them will suffice to show the elaboration and formality of the procedure:

"Vpoun the xxviij day of August, the zeir [= year] of God J^m and sex hundreth zeiris, I Johne Blinschell, Ilay Herauld, ane of the schireffis in that pairt within constitute, past [= went], at command of thir [= these] our souerane lordis lettres and summondis of Treassoun, to the duelling hous of Alexander Adamesoun in Edinburgh, in vmq^{le} [= late, deceased] Mr Thomas McCalzeans close, quhair [= where] Williame Ruthven, brother and apperant air or successour to vmq^{le} Johne Erle of Gowrie, and vmq^{le} Maister Alexander Ruthven, his brother, maid residence;[107] and lykwayes, to the Castell of Dirltowne, quhair [= where] the said Williame resortit and maid sumtyme residence with Dame Dorathie Stewart, Countes of Gowrie, his mother, becaus I culd nocht apprehend him personalie; and at euerie ane of the saidis duelling housses rex^{ue} [= respectively], with my displayit coitt [= coat] of armes and sound of trumpett, eftir I had knokit sex seuerall knokis at euerie ane of the saidis duelling housses rex^{ue} be [= by] vertew of the saidis lettres, in his hienes name and authoritie, I summond, warnit, and chargit the said William Ruthvene, &c."[108]

The authorities were mindful of even those on the periphery of the Gowrie affair, as can be seen from the Privy Council's order of 10th September from Stirling to the Bailies of Perth, as representing the whole body of townsfolk, to compear before the King and Council at Linlithgow, and answer for the contempt and indignity done to the King after his delivery, by many, all armed, who surrounded Gowrie House, "vttering maist irreuerent and vndeutifull speiches" and who "could nawayis [= in no wise] be moved to forbeir thair tumultuous and insolent behauiour; but did quhat [= what] in them lay, be [= by] crying for fyre and poulder, and rynning with jestis [= joists, beams] at the zettis [= gates] of the said hous, to haue blawin [= blown] vp the zettis of the said house, and to haue exponed in hasard the lyfes of his Maiestie and his guid subiectis".[109]

In consequence of their non-compliance with the summonses to render themselves up to justice, William Ruthven and the others cited were "put to the horn"[110] by the issue at a date unknown of a Letter of Horning[111] which declared them outlawed. But on 3rd October, by a Letter of Relaxation under the King's seal, William Ruthven, Hugh Moncreiffe, Andrew Henderson, Patrick Eviot, and Harry and Alexander Ruthven were released from "all Horningis execute aganis thame at the instance of quhatsumeuir persones"[112] [= any persons whatsoever]. The purpose of this relaxation is not clear: it certainly did not lift the accusations.

The Scots Parliament began a session on 1st November 1600. It was a busy time, before and during it, for Blinschell and other officers of the Lord Lyon's Court, to judge by the expenses noted in the Lord High Treasurer's Accounts.[113] According to normal practice, Andrew Home, messenger-at-arms, at the Market Cross in Edinburgh, after the inevitable fanfare of trumpets, commanded and charged all "Erlis, Lordis, Prelattis, Commissioneris of barrones and burrowis [= burghs] . . . ryding on horsbak, cled with fute mantillis, and vther abuilzementis [= habiliments], requisit for the honour of the present Parliament, repair, attend and accompanie his Maiestie, everie ane in thair awin [= own] rankis, at lenth set doun in the saidis Lettres".[114] Certain other measures may have been taken in view of the special interest of the coming trial for treason. Thus no noblemen or barons attending the Parliament were to "resort within the Palice, with ony ma [= greater] companie nor [= than] is particularlie prescryuit to thame".[114] None of the lieges was to repair to any places of his Majesty's residence "armit with secreitis, jakis, plait-slevis [= kinds of protective wear under outer garments], or ony vther hid armour".[115] Only such persons "as salbe appointit to await vpoun his hienes Nobilitie and estaitis" were to pass the guard at the High Street and the Canongate[115] "vnder the pain of deid". And all "ressett [= reception], supplie or intercommoning with Jesuittis" was prohibited.[115]

To begin with, various preliminary items of business occupied the assembly's attention and were transacted. But the one item bulking largest in everybody's mind was the treason trial before the King and Parliament sitting as a Court of Justice. On 4th November, Thomas Hamilton as the King's Advocate produced the "Summondis of Treassoun, dewlie execute and in-dorsat"[116] against William Ruthven, his tutors and curators (if he had any), and all others having or claiming to have interest in "the mater of Treassoun vnderwrittin".[117] The inclusion of references to tutors, curators, and others unnamed was a piece of legal verbiage. The summons was thrice formally called at the bar. But William Ruthven did not compear; nor had anyone expected him to do so. As already noticed,[118] he and his younger brother

Patrick had escaped in early August to England.[119] On William Ruthven's non-appearance, John Blinschell, Islay Herald, testified, as already noted,[120] that he had duly executed the summons; and the King's Advocate "askit instrumentis",[121] that is to say, a formal warrant from Parliament authorizing him to take such further action as was appropriate.

More or less the same procedure was gone through in respect of the second summons, which was directed against Hugh Moncreiffe, Andrew Henderson, Patrick Eviot, and Harry and Alexander Ruthven. But in this case, the procedure required the thrice calling of the summons "at the tolbuth [= jail] window".[121] Except Henderson, none of the named persons appeared, which is not surprising for they were not in the jail. Henderson, who had been in the Tolbooth since 28th August or earlier, was accordingly brought to the bar by one of the Edinburgh Bailies. As before, Blinschell testified that he had executed the summons;[122] and, as only Henderson "comperit to defend in the said mater",[123] the King's Advocate "askit instrumentis".[123] He also produced the already-mentioned Letter of Relaxation.[124] Whereupon the Court ordered Henderson to be returned to the Tolbooth.[123]

On 11th November the proceedings of the 4th were repeated. But on this occasion Henderson's name was, by the King's command, deleted from the summons.[125]

On the same 11th November the Lords of Articles were chosen from the House as a committee for verifying the execution of the summonses of treason.[126] It was the business of the Lords of Articles, says William Robertson, "As far back as our records enable us to trace the constitution of our Parliaments . . . to prepare, and to digest all matters which were to be laid before the Parliament. There was rarely any business introduced into Parliament, but what had passed through the channel of this committee."[127]

On 15th November the King and the Lords of Articles heard or re-heard the two summonses of treason, together with "ressones and causes thairin contenit",[126] and found them relevant. The same day the entire Parliament went through the same process of hearing and finding relevant; "and thairfoir they admittit the samyn [= same] to the said Aduocattis probatioun"[126] [= proving his case by leading evidence].

The Advocate at once produced the Letter of Horning duly executed against Hugh Moncreiffe, Patrick Eviot, and Harry and Alexander Ruthven. Nothing was apparently said at this stage about a similar Letter against William Ruthven, though such a missive must have been issued.[128] The Advocate then read "the haill Depositiounis of the witnesses examinat befoir the Lordis of Articlis" between 11th and 15th November.[129] There were no less than thirty-two of them. The deponers included the following gentlemen of the Court who had been in the King's hunting party: the Duke of Lennox; the Earl of Mar; the Abbot of Inchaffray (Drummond); the Abbot of Lindores (Leslie);[130] Sir Thomas Erskine; Sir John Ramsay; John Graham of Orchil, near Ardoch in Perthshire; and John Graham of Balgowan, near Methven in Perthshire. Other deponers were: members of Gowrie's household, Andrew Henderson being the most important in respect of his evidence;[131] citizens of Perth; landed

H

gentlemen in the Perth neighbourhood; and servants of the King. It is probable
that the depositions of James Wemyss of Bogie and William Rynd were
read,[132] though there is no record to confirm this surmise; and it is as probable
that the report by the Bailies and Town Council of Perth on the examination
and depositions of three hundred and fifty-five "Induelleris of Perth", which
had been taken during September by order of the King and Privy Council, was
submitted by the Advocate, but not read *in extenso*.[133] He did read, however, the
depositions of Thomas Cranston and George Craigengelt; and he reported
their condemnation and their execution at Perth on 23rd August. He apparently
said nothing about the deposition of John M'Duff who was condemned and
hanged with them, or about the depositions of Oliver Young, James Drummond of Pitcairns, and David Rynd submitted at the trial on 22nd August.[134]
"And last, the said Aduocat repetit the notorietie of the deid of the said Treassoun, togidder with the haill circumstances of the said mater; and renuncit
forder [= further] probatioun for preving [= proving] of the pointtis of baith
the saidis summondis of Treassoun; and desyrit the said proces to be advysit
[= deliberated on]. And thairvpoun the said Aduocat askit instrumentis."[135]

It might appear from my narrative that John Earl of Gowrie and Alexander
his brother had been displaced in the concern of Parliament by the parties against
whom the often-mentioned summonses of treason were directed, William
Ruthven and others unnamed on the one hand, and Hugh Moncreiffe, Patrick
Eviot, and Harry and Alexander Ruthven on the other. But it was not so. The
dead Earl and his dead brother were still the prime targets. Accordingly, after
all the legal rigmarole and repetition, "the haill Estaitis of Parliament, in presens
of the Kingis Maiestie, . . . being ryplie advysit . . . findis, decernis and declaris"
that Gowrie and Alexander "committit and did oppin and manefest Treassoun
aganis oure said souerane lord, in all pointis, articles and maner contenit in the
said summondis".[136]

And so the sentence was pronounced by David Lyndesay, the Dempster
of the Parliamentary Court. The name, memory, and dignity of Gowrie and
Alexander Ruthven were to be extinguished; and their arms were to be can-
celled and deleted from the books of arms and nobility,[137] "sua [= so] that thair
posteritie sall be vnabill and incapabill in all tyme cumming to bruik [= use],
posses or inioy ony offices, honouris, digniteis, successionis, possessionis, and all
gudis, moveable and immoveable, richtis, titillis, hope of successioun, and
vtheris quhatsumeuir [= whatsoever], within this realme".[138] Everything,
actually or potentially belonging to either of the traitors, was to be forfeited
to the King for ever. Besides all that, in order further to manifest detestation of
the treason, the bodies of the traitors were to be "caryit vpoun Moninday nixt
[17th November] to the mercat croce of Edinburcht, and thair to be hangit,
quarterit and drawin, in presens of the haill peopill; and thaireftir the heidis and
quarteris of their carcages to be affixit vpoun the maist patent pairtis and places
of the burrowis [= burghs] of Edinburcht, Perth, Dundee and Striviling"
[= Stirling].[139] Moreover, the turret, which was the scene of the drama of
treason, was to be cast down.[140]

As for the alleged accessaries who were still alive, William Ruthven was

safe for the time being in England.[141] and the case against other persons unnamed in the first summons was virtually dropped; but the four (Hugh Moncreiffe, Patrick Eviot, and Harry and Alexander Ruthven), against whom the
second summons of treason stood, were, in spite of being *non inventi*, unani-
mously sentenced by a Parliamentary doom "to vnderly the panis [= pains] of
Treassoun and Lesemajestie, and last punischement prescryvit be [= by] the
the lawis of this realme".[142] Also everything of any kind, actual or potential,
real or notional, belonging to them was forfeited to the King for ever; and their
posterity in all time coming was to be incapable and unable to enjoy and possess
any honours, dignities, benefices, successions, or other goods or gear.

It is not clear whether the four accused in the second summons were ever
executed, though no doubt the forfeitures were thorough and their posterity
disabled. My surmise is that the four escaped first to England and then to the
Continent. The wording of the sentence quoted above is a pronouncement of
guilt, not an indication of how a capital punishment was to be inflicted.

Notes

1. *Cf.* 81 *supra.*
2. Pitcairn, II, 244. Robert Bruce and other Edinburgh ministers heard the letter and the dispatch read.
3. *Ibid.*, II, 313-15.
4. Knighted in 1605 and created Viscount Claneboye in 1622. He received grants of large estates in Ulster.
5. Letter of Rowland Whyte, dated 26th August 1600, to Sir Robert Sidney, Lord Governor of Flushing (Pitcairn, II, 318).
6. Letter of Whyte to Sidney, dated 12th September 1600 (*ibid.*, II, 318).
7. *Cf.* 82 *supra.*
8. Pitcairn, II, 248 from Calderwood. The sermon is printed in Pitcairn, II, 248-51.
9. *Ibid.*, II, 246 from Robert Birrel's "Diarey".
10. *Ibid.*, II, 246 from Birrel.
11. *Ibid.*, II, 255 from Calderwood.
12. *Cf.* 149-56 *infra.*
13. Pitcairn, II, 247, notes that a great variety of orations, etc. have been printed, both in Scotland and in England, on the anniversaries of the Conspiracy.
14. *Ibid.*, II, 209.
15. *Ibid.*, II, 297 from Robert Johnston's MS. History of Scotland.
16. *Ibid.*, II, 218.
17. Pitcairn, II, 209, says "immediately after the Trials for the Conspiracy took place". But his conjecture is manifestly wrong, for trials ran on to the middle of November. *Cf.* 96-103 *infra.*
18. Sir David Dalrymple, Lord Hailes printed the tract, *c.* 1760, as the first number of an intended but never completed series of papers relating to the Gowrie Conspiracy.
19. Pitcairn printed from this London version (II, 208-23). He heads his reprint thus: *A Discourse of the vnnaturall and vile Conspiracie, attempted against his Maiesties person, at Saint Johnstoun, vpon the fift day of August, being Tuesday, 1600.* As already noted (71 *supra*), I followed this, the most readily accessible reprint, in my paraphrase (71-85 *supra*).
20. Simmes also printed nine quartos of plays by Shakespeare between 1597 and 1604. They show him to have

been the best printer of Shakespeare
quartos, his *Much Ado* of 1600, for
example, being in R. B. McKerrow's
opinion "one of the few Shakespeare
play books that was decently printed"
(Halliday, 598). But Simmes was
frequently in trouble for printing
unauthorised books, and at last, in
1622, he was forbidden to work as a
master printer. *The Earle of Gowries
Conspiracie* was not entered in the S.R.

21. Pitcairn, II, 209; and *Border Calendar*,
II, no. 1235. Lord Hailes, who knew
of Carey's letter, assumed that the
treatise had actually been printed
(Pitcairn, II, 209).

22. II, 209.

23. When Scott was writing (1818), the
MS. was in the library of the Perth
Society of Antiquaries.

24. *A History of the Life and Death of John,
Earl of Gowrie*, 1818, 5.

25. *Calendar of State Papers*, Scotland
(Elizabeth), lxvi, no. 52.

26. 252-56.

27. Its bias and venom will be clear from
this summary of it by Arbuckle, 92-93:
"The anonymous writer, who says
that his information came from some
of the King's followers who had been
present, and from the depositions of
Cranstoun, Craigengelt and Barron
[= McDuff], claims that the Ruthvens
were the victims of a royal plot.
Gowrie, it is said, was on the point of
removing to Lothian, presumably to
Dirleton, on 5 August, when his
brother went that morning to Falkland with Andrew Ruthven and
Andrew Henderson in response to a
summons from the King, intending
thereafter to go on and meet the Earl
next morning on the shore of the
Firth of Forth After talking with the
King, however, Alexander sent Henderson to inform the Earl that the
King was coming to visit him for
some purpose unknown. Then follows
an account of the events in Gowrie
House which is palpably inaccurate.

It implies a carefully planned royal
plot to kill the brothers, involving a
reconnaisance of the house by Dr
Herries three days before and the
taking over of the keys of the house
from the Earl's porter when the King
arrived. The writer finds the motive
in James's dislike of Gowrie because
of the esteem in which he was held by
the Kirk and the country in general,
in the Earl's opposition to the royal
wishes in the Convention [= Parlia-
ment], and in the jealousy of the
courtiers".

28. Pitcairn, II, 231.

29. *Ibid.*, II, 231.

30. *Ibid.*, II, 231. *Cf.* 22-24 *supra.*

31. Pitcairn, II, 232.

32. Pitcairn, II, 223-31, prints only the
*Ad Lectorem pro intemerata Narrationis
huius fide. Praescriptio.* The title page
carries the following text (which is
not from the Vulgate): "*Ecce improbi
tendunt arcum, aptant sagittas suas nervo
ad jaculandum in caligine contra rectos
corde. Atqui istis propositis destruentur:
Iustus enim quid operatus est? Psal.* 11,
vers. 2 et 3".

33. Pitcairn, II, 223, note 1.

34. *Cf.* 63-69 *supra.*

35. Pitcairn, II, 293-99.

36. *Cf.* 81 *supra.*

37. *Cf.* 87-88 *supra.*

38. Pitcairn, II, 232.

39. *Ibid.*, II, 244. Two Bailies were sent
to tell the Privy Council "the tounis
mynd; and to inquyre quhen the said
bellis sall ryng, and quhow lang"
(*ibid.*, II, 244).

40. *Ibid.*, II, 245.

41. *Ibid.*, II, 246.

42. *Ibid.*, II, 245. There were cannonades
from the Castle on both 6th and 11th
August (*ibid.*, II, 238).

43. *Ibid.*, II, 245.

44. *Cf.* 88 *supra.*

45. Pitcairn, II, 247, from Fleming's MS.
Chronicle under 29th September.

46. *Ibid.*, II, 247 from Fleming.

47. *Cf.* 85-86, note 8 *supra.*

48. Pitcairn, II, 233-34.
49. *Ibid.*, II, 301 from Calderwood. According to Birrel (30th September), the King commanded 5th August to be kept as a solemn day (*ibid.*, II, 246). Fleming's MS. Chronicle (29th September) says that, in recognition of the King's escape, "preiching [was] appointit ewerie Tuisday in euerie burch" (*ibid.*, II, 247). For the reference to a Tuesday in *Macbeth, cf.* 112-13 *infra.*
50. Pitcairn, II, 237.
51. *Ibid.*, II, 223, note 1.
52. *Cf.* 91 *supra.*
53. Pitcairn, II, 235-36.
54. Pitcairn, II, 247 from Fleming's MS. Chronicle.
55. *Aeneid*, VI, 853.
56. Pitcairn, II, 243.
57. *Cf.* 127, 132-60 *infra.*
58. As early as 6th August 1600, George Nicolson informed Sir Robert Cecil that John Ramsay and Dr. Herries had been knighted the evening before and that "the [Gowrie] lands are to be given to these new knights and others". (Pitcairn, II, 314).
59. *Cf.* 118-19 *infra.*
60. But his deposition on the Gowrie affair, made in November 1600, describes him as "of the age of threttie-sex zeiris". (Pitcairn, II, 181).
61. Robert Birrel says that Erskine was made Lord of Dirleton on 15th November 1600 (Pitcairn, II, 246). So does an anonymous Scottish chronicler (*ibid.*, II, 298). But the lordship did not in itself confer a title.
62. Pitcairn, II, 246. Wilson was a servant, not of Sir Thomas Erskine, but of his brother James (*cf.* 80 *supra*).
63. The date given by the knowledgeable Birrel for the knighting of both Ramsay and Hugh Herries (Pitcairn, II, 246), and also by an anonymous Scottish chronicler (*ibid.*, II, 298). *Cf.* 105, note 58 *supra.*
64. Fleming's MS. Chronicle says "West Barnes" (*ibid.*, II, 247).

65. Alexander Nisbet, *An Essay on . . . Armories,* 1718, 142-43.
66. Sir Henry Savile, quoted in *The Complete Peerage*, VI, 534, note d.
67. Resigned in 1615 in favour of his kinsman Sir George Ramsay of Dalhousie.
68. *Cf.* 95 *supra.*
69. *Cf.* Alexander Nisbet, *op. cit.*, 142-43 and Plate IV. The Lord High Treasurer's Accounts for November 1600 record a payment of twenty pounds "to the painteris for Schir Johnne Ramsayis pinsell" [= pennon] (Pitcairn, II, 241).
70. *Cf.* 102 *infra.* Murray's wife was Dorothea, daughter of Lady Mary Ruthven, Countess of Atholl.
71. *Cf.* 101 *infra.*
72. To say nothing of their resumption in 1608, with the trial and execution of George Sprot, notary in Eyemouth in Berwickshire, for not disclosing at once the existence of letters of a treasonable character exchanged between Gowrie and Robert Logan of Restalrig, near Edinburgh; and with the forfeiture of Robert Logan's eldest son, also called Robert, who had succeeded him.
73. *Cf.* 45-46 *supra.*
74. *The Scots Peerage.*
75. Calderwood, VI, 46. *Cf.* 100-1, 107, note 119 *infra.*
76 Pitcairn, II, 156.
77. *Ibid.*, II, 148-51.
78. *Ibid.*, II, 233.
79. The Lord High Treasurer's Accounts show that in August 1600 forty shillings were paid to John Bennet, messenger (-at-arms), who accompanied by a trumpeter carried letters to the Market Crosses of Falkland and near-by Cupar to warn men and women surnamed Ruthven not to come within ten miles of the King (Pitcairn, II, 240). Robert Birrel mentions such a Proclamation on 13th August (*ibid.*, II, 246), and on 18th November 1601 another requiring all of the name of Ruthven to

change their name and not come
within ten miles of the King on pain
of treason (*ibid.*, II, 247).

80. Pitcairn, II, 233.

81. *Ibid.*, II, 233.

82. *Ibid.*, II, 234.

83. The Lord High Treasurer's Accounts
record a payment of ten pounds at an
unspecified date in August to "the
herauldis, trumpetouris and officeris,
passand [= passing] with displayit
coittis [= coats of arms], to divulgat,
at the marcat croce of Edinburgh, the
Treasoun intendit aganis his Maiesteis
persoun at Perth". (*ibid.*, II, 238).

84. Robert Birrel notes that on 15th
November 1600 Gowrie, his brother,
"and his fathers brother" with others
were "all forfaulted" (Pitcairn, II,
246). And an anonymous Scottish
chronicler says that on 15th November
"the Erll of Gowry, his broder and
fader-broder [= uncle] was foirfaltit"
(*ibid.*, II, 298).

85. *Cf.* 84 *supra*.

86. Pitcairn, II, 157-59.

87. According to Calderwood, three other
persons, respectively named Oliphant,
Leslie, and Younger, had been suggested as the man in the turret before
the identification rested on Henderson;
and at one stage James himself had
declared that Henderson was not the
man—"he knew that smaick [= scurvy
fellow] well enough" (Pitcairn, II,
251, note 1). *Cf.* Arbuckle, 12-13.

88. Pitcairn, II, 221-23; *cf. ibid.*, II, 174-79.

89. *Ibid.*, II, 234.

90. *Ibid.*, II, 219-21. *Cf.* 86, note 23
supra.

91. Familiarly known as "Tam o' the
Cowgate", he was a staunch friend of
James. He became Lord President of
the Court of Session and held other
high offices. He received several titles,
including Baron Binning and Byres,
Earl of Melrose, and Earl of Haddington. He procured the imprisonment of
one of James's most powerful opponents among the clergy, Andrew

Melville, in 1607 and in 1608 the
execution of George Sprot (*cf.* 105,
note 72 *supra*) for his links with the
Gowrie Conspiracy.

92. Pitcairn, II, 148.

93. *Ibid.*, II, 148.

94. *Ibid.*, II, 148. For "airt and pairt", *cf.*
50-51 *supra*.

95. Pitcairn, II, 148-54.

96. Cranston is said to have made three
depositions, though only that of 6th
August (Pitcairn, II, 156-57) seems to
have survived. McDuff's deposition
has likewise not apparently come
down; nor has its date been recorded.

97. *Cf.* 45-47 *supra*.

98. The fifteen jurors were all indwellers
in Perth, except presumably "Robert
Broune, Kepar of his Maiesties wyne
sellar; James Liddell, Potifar [= apo-
thecary] to his Maiestie; James Bog,
aid to the Maister Portar" (Pitcairn,
II, 148).

99. *Ibid.*, II, 148.

100. *Ibid.*, II, 155.

101. *Ibid.*, II, 155.

102. An unreliable letter, already quoted
(86, note 23 *supra*), states that
Cranston, Craigengelt, and "sevin
honest men of St Jhonstoun" were
executed (Pitcairn, II, 319).

103. Pitcairn, II, 160.

104. *Ibid.*, II, 160. The Lord High
Treasurer's Accounts for October
1600 note the payment of twenty-one
shillings and fourpence to Andrew
Home, messenger (-at-arms), for
"passand [= passing] to the marcat
croce of Edinburgh, and thair, eftir
sound of trumpet, inhibit[ing] the
ressait or intercomoning" with Moncreiffe, Eviot, and Harry and Alexander Ruthven (Pitcairn, II, 241).

105. In August 1600 the Lord High
Treasurer paid out five pounds for
eighteen copies of the two
summonses, and five pounds, six
shillings, and eightpence for the
translation of them from Latin "in
Inglis" (Pitcairn, II, 240).

106. The Lord High Treasurer's Accounts from August to November record many disbursements to Blinschell and his auxiliaries for their expenses in their comings and goings in consequence of the Gowrie affair and for their attendance at the November meetings of the Scots Parliament (*ibid.*, II, 238-42). They also note a payment for the carrying of "a clois [= sealed] Lettre and sum vther directiones to young Tullibardin [*cf.* 95 *supra*], for transporting the corpis of Gowrie and his brother" (Pitcairn, II, 241).

107. William Ruthven had been "at the schools" in Edinburgh. (*The Scots Peerage*, IV, 264), which could mean "at the University".

108. Pitcairn, II, 167.

109. *Ibid.*, II, 236.

110. Had charges against them proclaimed by a herald accompanied by a trumpeter, at market crosses and elsewhere.

111. *Cf.* 101-2 *infra*. The Letter's issue can be inferred from the King's Advocate's presentation of his case on 15th November.

112. Pitcairn, II, 161.

113. *Ibid.*, II, 241.

114. *Ibid.*, II, 241.

115. *Ibid.*, II, 242.

116. *Ibid.*, II, 159.

117. *Ibid.*, II, 160.

118. *Cf.* 96-97 *supra*.

119. They were protected by Queen Elizabeth. James issued a proclamation against William on 27th April 1603, only a month and three days after Elizabeth's death. But William escaped, this time to the Continent, where after becoming a chemist and philosopher (which probably means an alchemist) he died. According to Bishop Burnet, "it was given out that he had the philosopher's stone" (John Bruce, *Papers relating to William, first Earl of Gowrie, and Patrick Ruthven*, 1867, 57).

Patrick was arrested and lodged in the Tower of London before 24th June 1603. But his imprisonment does not seem to have been very rigorous, although it lasted for nineteen years. He studied medicine and became a distinguished physician with the degree of M.D. and also an alchemist. He practised medicine so as "to administer health to others, but not for any gain to himself" (*The Scots Peerage*, IV, 265). In 1616 he obtained a grant of £200 a year "for apparel, books, physic, and such other necessities" (*ibid.*, IV, 264). On 4th August 1622, the day before the twenty-second anniversary of the Gowrie Conspiracy, he was allowed to go to Cambridge; and on 11th September of the same year "our well-beloved Patrick Ruthven, Esquire", received an annuity of £500 (*ibid.*, IV, 264). His bounds were enlarged on 4th February 1624; but he was still forbidden to approach the Court. On 12th November 1641 he was rehabilitated against the forfeiture of his brother, the last Earl; and he seems to have taken this as implying a restoration of the peerage as well. On 25th March 1645 he appealed to the House of Lords about the estate of his son-in-law, Sir Anthony Van Dyck (who in 1640 had been forced to marry Mary Ruthven). He was styled Earl of Gowrie, Lord Ruthven in 1648, but signed only by the latter title. He died within the King's Bench and was buried at St. George's, Southwark on 24th May 1652.

120. *Cf.* 99 *supra*.

121. Pitcairn, II, 160.

122. *Ibid.*, II, 162-63.

123. *Ibid.*, II, 161.

124. *Cf.* 100 *supra*.

125. Pitcairn, II, 162. *Cf.* Arbuckle, 22.

126. Pitcairn, II, 163.

127. *The History of Scotland*, 1787, I, 84.

128. *Cf.* 100-1 *supra*.

129. Pitcairn, II, 163. *Cf. ibid.*, II, 191-92 for the questions put to the witnesses.
130. The two Abbots were laymen and "Commendators" of what had been Church lands before the Reformation.
131. Henderson's deposition, as read by the Advocate, was substantially the same as the one by him published in the official account. But there are minor differences, as Arbuckle notes (23-24).
132. *Cf.* 97-98 *supra.*
133. Pitcairn, II, 192-208. Blinschell, according to the Lord High Treasurer's Accounts, was paid for summoning John Moncreiffe, Alexander Blair younger of Bathiock (= Baldernock in south-west Stirlingshire), and others to compear and bear witness (*ibid.*, II, 241). But it is not clear whether in fact they ever testified. The Accounts also note a payment "to the witnesses" without naming them (*ibid.*, II, 240).
134. *Cf.* 98-99 *supra.*

135. Pitcairn, II, 163.
136. *Ibid.*, II, 167.
137. The Lord High Treasurer records the payment of sixteen pounds for "the armes of the persones that wes foirfaltit" (Pitcairn, II, 241). As a sign of degradation the painted arms of a traitor were torn in pieces and trampled on, when the sentence was carried out.
138. Pitcairn, II, 167-68.
139. *Ibid.*, II, 168. The Lord High Treasurer's Accounts record a payment "for carying the quarteris of the lait Erle of Gowrie and his brother, to be affixit on the maist eminent places of Striuiling [= Stirling], Perth and Dundee"; and for a creill [= basket], hay, and salt; and for the delivery of the King's warrant to the Magistrates of the towns (*ibid.*, II, 241).
140. Arbuckle, 24.
141. *Cf.* 107, note 119 *supra.*
142. Pitcairn, II, 171.

7

'Macbeth' and the Gowrie Conspiracy

Stones have been known to move and trees to speak;
Augurs and understood relations have
By magot-pies and choughs and rooks brought forth
The secret'st man of blood.

Macbeth, III, iv, 123-26.

Shakespeare could not fail, as I have said earlier,[1] to have known of threats to the life of King James, when he was engaged on a Scottish theme on "The deep damnation of [the] taking-off" (I, vii, 20) of an earlier Scottish king. He could not have avoided what I might call contemporary overtones in the circumstances; and he would, I submit, have meant his audience to "understand relations" (= divine connexions or similarities) between the historical and the contemporary.

But the circumstances of the Gowrie affair are far closer to those of Duncan's murder by Macbeth than are the entirely different ones of the Gunpowder Plot; and I believe that it was the former, not the latter, which was echoing in Shakespeare's mind when he was writing his play, for the simple reason that the latter had not yet occurred. It is true that the Porter in *Macbeth* (II, iii, 1-46) is given drunken maunderings to mutter, in which Shakespeare's Jacobean audience was meant to catch cryptic allusions to Henry Garnett, the Provincial of the English Jesuits, who was one of those tried and executed for complicity in "Gunpowder Treason and Plot". But they are the only certain allusions that Shakespeare makes to it, and they amount to very little. They could be cut out without any dramatic or sensible loss whatever; and there is indeed some evidence for regarding them as a mere extraneous interpolation in an already-existing play.[2] On the other hand, the Macbeth story, both in Holinshed and in Shakespeare, has a general or over-all parallelism to the Gowrie Conspiracy; and there are some particular parallels between it and the play which do not derive from Holinshed but are reiterations, as it were, by Shakespeare of details in the official version of the Gowrie affair.

The over-all parallel is that of the actual murder under trust of Duncan and of the attempted murder under trust of King James—the parallel between an accomplished and a frustrated *homicidium sub praetextu amicitiae* of a Scottish king.[3] Both were cases of high treason in a supreme degree. So, no doubt, was the Gunpowder Plot; but it was to have resulted in a spectacular and public massacre before all the world, not in a single assassination *in camera*. The murder of Duncan was effected by his host in that host's own house, even as the intended murder of James was to have been in Gowrie House. And James was lured there by invitation. As I pointed out in Chapter 3,[4] Shakespeare underlines the "invitation" to Macbeth's castle; and Sir George Mackenzie, in discussing murder under trust, regarded the "invitation" as constituting "one branch of this trust".[5] Shakespeare is as insistent on the invitation to Banquo, though in that case Macbeth proceeds with more cunning.[6] Nothing could have been more pressing and out of the ordinary than the inviting of King James to Gowrie House. Alexander Ruthven set out from Perth in darkness and arrived at Falkland Palace almost at first light, in order to reach the King before he set out to hunt about six in the morning. Alexander was able to get to the King's side, to take him out of earshot, to tell him a story to pique his curiosity, and to urge him to come without delay to Perth in order to investigate the mystery. Though James's interest was to some degree aroused, he declined to forgo his hunting for all that Alexander could urge. The latter, however, was not to be put off. He hung about the area of the chase and at any pause in it renewed his invitation and pleas. It was only when the chase was over, about eleven o'clock or somewhat later, that James yielded to Alexander's insistent solicitation and agreed to ride to Perth. Nor was that all which might be regarded as being of an inviting character. For, as the party neared Perth, Alexander rode ahead to advise the Earl of the King's approach; and the Earl, with a large number of friends and retainers, came out to receive the royal party and conduct them as guests to his house.[7]

Another factor common to *Macbeth* and the Gowrie Conspiracy, but totally absent from the Gunpowder Plot, is the magical and supernatural. No doubt such a feature comes into Holinshed. But it has quite a different quality and flavour there. Thus the oracular trio whom his Macbeth and Banquo encounter are "three women in strange and wild apparell, resembling creatures of an elder world".[8] After delivering their prophecies "the . . . women vanished immediatelie out of their sight. This was reputed at the first but some vaine fantasticall illusion by *Makbeth* and *Banquho*. . . . But afterwards the common opinion was, that these women were either the weird sisters, that is, (as ye would say) the goddesses of destinie, or else some nymphs or feiries, indowed with knowledge of prophesie by their necromanticall science".[9] Shakespeare's witches likewise prophesy what comes to pass and can vanish out of sight. But they are very far from being either goddesses of destiny or nymphs or fairies. Hags, old, ugly, and malignant, they in fact derive from the general notions of witches in popular superstition and in the charges and evidence at contemporary witch-trials.[10] But, while that is so, Shakespeare has made his witches far more impressive and mysterious—inexplicable and anomalous beings

> That look not like the inhabitants o' the earth,
> And yet are on't.   (I, iii, 41-42).

> The earth hath bubbles, as the water has,
> And these are of them.   (I, iii, 79-80).

To return, however, to Holinshed's sybils: their triple prophecy is referred to once later in his story of Macbeth; but they themselves make no second appearance and Holinshed's Macbeth does not seek them out in their cavern or receive further presages from apparitions conjured up by them, as does Shakespeare's Macbeth in IV, i. Instead, Holinshed's Macbeth "learned of certaine wizzards, in whose words he put great confidence (for that the prophesie had happened so right, which the three faries or weird sisters had declared unto him) how that he ought to take heed of *Makduffe*, who in time to come should seek to destroie him. And surelie hereupon had he put *Makduffe* to death, but that a certaine witch, whom he had in great trust, had told him that he should never be slain with man borne of anie woman, nor vanquished until the wood of *Bernane* came to the castell of *Dunsinane*".[11]

Undoubtedly in reconceiving much of the supernatural in his play, Shakespeare was influenced in the direction of contemporary witch-lore by the fact that King James was the author of a notable book on *Daemonologie* published in 1597, that the King believed himself to have been a special target of witches, and that he regarded himself as possessed of a nose for smelling out practitioners of sorcery and exposing their machinations.

And that is why James was so interested in the cabbalistic characters found in Gowrie's pockets;[12] why the depositions of James Wemyss of Bogie and William Rynd which testify about Gowrie in relation to magic, prognostications, and amulets were published along with the official account of the events of 5th August;[13] why the official account itself declared that for many generations the Ruthvens were known through the whole land as dabblers in the occult;[14] and why Patrick Galloway in his sermon on 11th August at the Market Cross in Edinburgh expatiated before the King on Gowrie's magical books and conjurations.[15]

That is to say, Macbeth and Gowrie were both traitors and both intermeddlers with the diabolical.

Again, unlike the pedestrian Holinshed, Shakespeare invests his whole story with supernaturalisms, manifest or latent. The world of *Macbeth* is full of things strange. The order of nature is perturbed and anguished by the moral disorder in the affairs of men; and over these affairs brood prophecy and fateful inevitability, signs and omens. Apart from the witches themselves, the most categorical supernaturalism in the play is the apparition of Banquo, of which there is no anticipation in Holinshed. Supernatural, too, though in a lesser degree, is the visionary dagger with on its "blade and dudgeon gouts of blood" (II, i, 46) which Macbeth sees before the murder of Duncan; the voice which cried after the murder:

> Still it cried 'Sleep no more!' to all the house:
> 'Glamis hath murder'd sleep, and therefore Cawdor
> Shall sleep no more; Macbeth shall sleep no more'.
>   (II, ii, 41-43);

the "terrible dreams That shake [Macbeth] nightly" (III, ii, 18-19); and even Lady Macbeth's sleep-walking (V, i). Like Banquo's ghost, all of these are purely Shakespearian inventions, or with only suggestions in Holinshed. So, too, is Macbeth's inability to speak an Amen:

One cried 'God bless us!' and 'Amen' the other;
As they had seen me with these hangman's hands.
Listening their fear, I could not say 'Amen',
When they did say 'God bless us!' . . .
But wherefore could not I pronounce 'Amen'?
I had most need of blessing, and 'Amen'
Stuck in my throat.   (II, ii, 27-33).

This passage may be a recall of the fact that Gowrie, when run through the heart by Ramsay died "without once crying vpon God".[16]

There are two passages in particular in which Shakespeare refers to disorders and strange phenomena in nature near the time of Duncan's murder. One of them I shall refer to later[17] when discussing the role of Lennox in the play. The other is in II, iv when Ross and an Old Man speak of the signs and wonders on the day following the murder. Some of them come from Holinshed's account of mysterious sequels to the murder, not of Duncan, but of the earlier King Duff. One item in it is: "There was a sparhawke also strangled by an owle".[18] In *Macbeth* this becomes:

On Tuesday last,
A falcon, towering in her pride of place,
Was by a mousing owl hawk'd at and kill'd.
(II, iv, 11-13).

It is curious, in the first place, that the Old Man refers the event to a Tuesday; for the day on which the Gowrie Conspiracy came to its abortive end was a Tuesday, as is expressly and unmistakably stated on the title pages of all the editions of the official account, as well as in the texts within; and James on 24th August 1600 ordered that, since his delivery occurred on a Tuesday, every Tuesday was to be a day of regular preaching as an act of celebration and thanksgiving in every burgh within the Edinburgh Synods and perhaps beyond.[19] It is not less curious, in the second place, that a hawk figured rather prominently at Gowrie House, or, more correctly, a falcon (the words "hawk" and "falcon" being interchangeable in common parlance). The hawk had been with the King's hunting party, carried on the wrist of one of the gentlemen, John Murray of Arknay, known familiarly as "Meikle John Murray".[20] He took the hawk with him from Falkland to Perth; and there, as John Ramsay said in his deposition, after Ramsay himself had dined, he "tuk his Maiesteis halk fra Johne Murray, to the effect the said Johne micht haue dynit".[21] When Ramsay rushed up the turnpike stair on hearing the King's cry for help, he burst into the room at the top, "the deponer haveing in the mentyme his halk on his hand. . . . And his Maiestie, seing the deponer, said, 'Fy! Strik him laich [= low], becaus he hes ane pyne dowlit [= secret doublet or shirt of chain mail] vpoun him!' Quhairvpoun [= whereupon] the deponer kaist [= cast] the halk fra him, and drew his quhinger [= whinger, knife to cut food or serve as a weapon], quharwith [= wherewith] he strak the said Maister Alexander: And immediatlie . . ., his Maiestie schoitt him doun the stair. . . . Thaireftir this deponar addressis him to ane window, and . . . cryit, 'Schir Thomas [Erskine], cum vp this turnepyke, ewin to the heid'. In this mentyme, his Maiestie pat his fute vpoun the halk leische, and held hir ane lang tyme, quhill [= until] the deponar come and tuk hir vp agane".[22] No doubt, until the King stepped on the hawk's jesses, it fluttered wildly about the room. This particular detail is not on record; but it was easily inferrable from the rest of the story and somehow it struck the popular fancy, for it got into the iconography of the Gowrie Conspiracy. Among the attempts to illustrate the dramatic scene is one by Jan Luyken (1649-1712), which, to judge from the costumes, is a copy, perhaps at several removes, of an engraving or cut made soon after the event; and in it, fluttering very prominently and much out of scale above the figures, is a hawk volant, hooded, and vervelled (= with a jess ending in a ring or vervel), as a heraldic blazon would describe it.

According to Pitcairn, the hawk had been presented to the King on 5th August by John Murray.[23] But the Lord High Treasurer's Accounts for July 1600 record the payment by the King's special command of five pounds six shillings and eightpence "to George [possibly a scribal mistake for "John"] Murray, to be gevin to ane boy in drinksiluer, at the presenting of ane halk to his Matie".[24]

When reading Macbeth's story in Holinshed, Shakespeare had come on the name Gowrie (with which the news of the Conspiracy had already familiarized him), not as the territorial title of a nobleman, but as designating a district in Perthshire. The relevant passage in Holinshed is as follows: "Further, to the end [Macbeth] might the more cruellie oppress his subjects with all tyrannicall wrongs, he builded a strong castell on the top of an high hill, called *Dunsinane*, situate in *Gowrie*, ten miles from *Perth*, on such a proud height, that standing there aloft, a man might behold well neare all the countries of *Angus*, *Fife*, *Stermond* [= Stormont], and *Ernedale* [= Strathearn], as it were lying underneath him".[25] So the story of the traitor Macbeth, linked as it is to Dunsinane, Birnam, and Scone, must have recalled by an inescapable association the story of the traitor Gowrie in whose country they all lie.

In including Lennox among the Scottish nobles in *Macbeth* Shakespeare departs from his source, Holinshed; and he gives to his Lennox some specially significant things to do and say. Lennox is the only noble at Duncan's side when news is brought to the King of the victories of Macbeth and Banquo over Macdonwald, Sweno, and Cawdor (I, ii). Lennox is again the only noble in attendance when Macbeth and Banquo arrive with Ross and Angus to receive the king's thanks (I, iv). That is to say, Lennox is from the very beginning closely associated with his king. All that he actually says is two lines in the first of the two scenes so far mentioned; but they may be more significant than at first sight appears, by their playing on the idea of strangeness which is to pervade the whole action:

> What a haste looks through his [*i.e.* Ross's] eyes! So should he look
> That seems to speak things strange. (I, ii, 46-47).

Lennox is again mentioned in the stage directions as in Duncan's suite on their arrival at Inverness Castle, though he is given nothing to say (I, vi). But far more important is his next appearance, at the very height of the tension, for it is Lennox and Macduff who startle Macbeth and Lady Macbeth (and every spectator of the play) by the greatest *coup-de-théâtre* in dramatic literature, as De Quincey so eloquently recognizes—the knocking at the Castle gate (II, iii, S.D.)[26]

Incidentally, is it possible that Shakespeare had taken a hint for this wonderful effect from what he had heard of the Scottish process of serving a summons of treason at the door of a traitor, as described by John Blinschell, Islay Herald: "at euerie ane of the saidis duelling housses rex^ue [= respectively], with my displayit coitt [= coat] of armes and sound of trumpett, eftir I had knokit sex seuerall knokis at euerie ane of the saidis duelling housses", etc.?[27]

To return to Lennox and Macduff: They have come "to call timely on" the king (II, iii, 51). Lennox greets the agitated Macbeth with a "Good morrow, noble sir" (II, iii, 49), and a few lines later asks "Goes the king hence to-day?" (II, iii, 58), which calls forth Macbeth's equivocal reply, "He does: he did appoint so" (II, iii, 58). But Lennox, rather unexpectedly, switches to the wild and ominous night just over:

> The night has been unruly: where we lay,
> Our chimneys were blown down; and, as they say,
> Lamentings heard i' the air; strange screams of death,
> And prophesying with accents terrible
> Of dire combustion and confused events
> New hatch'd to the woeful time: the obscure bird
> Clamour'd the livelong night: some say, the earth
> Was feverous and did shake . . .
> My young remembrance cannot parallel
> A fellow to it.   (II, iii, 59-68).

So, by this very atmospheric speech assigned to Lennox, Shakespeare has worked in such phenomena as the age believed to herald or mark the falls of princes, before Duncan's death has been actually discovered.

It is Macduff, not Lennox, who goes to waken the King. When Macduff rushes back in horror from Duncan's bedside, Lennox blurts out, at the same time as Macbeth, "What's the matter?" (II, iii, 70) and then "Mean you his majesty?" (II, iii, 75). When Macduff bids them see the worst for themselves, Lennox and Macbeth go to view the body. Thus Lennox witnesses, so to speak, the off-stage killing of the two grooms by Macbeth, by no means an unimportant occasion. And when the newly-arrived Malcolm asks who had killed his father, it is Lennox who replies:

> Those of his chamber, as it seem'd, had done't:
> Their hands and faces were all badged with blood;
> So were their daggers, which unwiped we found
> Upon their pillows:
> They stared, and were distracted; no man's life
> Was to be trusted with them.   (II, iii, 106-11).

Lennox, who is but a young man, had accepted what Macbeth wanted him (and everybody else) to accept. But that phrase "as it seem'd" in line 106 just hints at an uncertainty in Lennox which is later to turn into a certainty and receive its first utterance from him.

As yet in the play, however, no one breathes a suspicion of Macbeth. Not even Banquo, who has his own special reasons for suspicion and who has already, before Duncan's murder, indicated to Macbeth that he has not forgotten the weird sisters and their prophecies and, at the same time, that he, Banquo, was not the man to win "honour" by dishonourable means (II, i, 20-29). In the scene of the discovery of the murder, Banquo on entering is staggered by Macduff's bald declaration. He says very little, only his cutting rebuke to Lady Macbeth:

Lady Macbeth.   Woe, alas!
   What, in our house?
Banquo.   Too cruel any where.
   Dear Duff, I prithee, contradict thyself,
   And say it is not so.   (II, iii, 92-95).

He does not speak again till more than thirty lines later:

                Look to the lady:
   And when we have our naked frailties hid,
   That suffer in exposure, let us meet,
   And question this most bloody piece of work,
   To know it further. Fears and scruples shake us:
   In the great hand of God I stand; and thence
   Against the undivulged pretence I fight
   Of treasonous malice.   (II, iii, 131-38).

That is to say, the cautious Banquo asserts his horror and his own loyalty, but he does not point his finger at Macbeth as the perpetrator of the "treasonous malice". Suspicion is certainly rife; but it has no focus or direction, the idea of the guilt of Duncan's grooms having been for the moment tacitly dropped. Even Malcolm and Donalbain, who are left to finish the scene in whispers, express only a general fear of danger to themselves as Duncan's sons and so the most likely to be the next for assassination.

In II, iv there is still no expression of a suspicion of Macbeth's guilt. In fact the suspicion is given a quite different direction. When Ross asks:

   Is't known who did this more than bloody deed? (II, iv, 22),

Macduff replies:

   Those that Macbeth hath slain . . .
              They were suborn'd:
   Malcolm and Donalbain, the king's two sons,
   Are stol'n away and fled; which puts upon them
   Suspicion of the deed.   (II, iv, 23-27).

It is true that Macduff states that he will not go to Scone for Macbeth's coronation, thereby incurring Macbeth's suspicion, as we learn in III, vi; but Macduff in II, iv gives no reason for his abstention from the coronation.

At the beginning of III, i Banquo does at last give explicit expression to suspicion of Macbeth's guilt, but only in soliloquy and only as a probability, not as a certainty:

   Thou hast it now: king, Cawdor, Glamis, all,
   As the weird women promised, and, I fear,
   Thou play'dst most foully for't.   (III, i, 1-3).

His soliloquy in fact shows him as more interested in the possible fulfilment of the witches' prophecies in relation to himself and his descendants. When Macbeth and Lady Macbeth come on the stage after the soliloquy, it is their first appearance as king and queen; and "Lennox, Ross, Lords, Ladies, *and* Attendants" accompany them. Banquo behaves with a respectful dignity to the newly-anointed and crowned king, who invites and presses him to attend the "great feast", the "solemn supper" (III, i, 12, 14). As if to highlight the invitation before the murder under trust, nobody speaks but Macbeth, Lady Macbeth, and Banquo, until the stage empties except for Macbeth and an Attendant who is simply ordered to bring in two men, the two Murderers.

In the banquet scene, III, iv, the stage direction is: "*Enter* Macbeth, Lady Macbeth, Ross, Lennox, Lords, *and* Attendants". So Lennox, as usual, is at the king's side, be that king Duncan or Macbeth. Lennox says nothing until, at another of the climactic moments of the play, he asks the seeming-simple question: "May't please your highness sit" (III, iv, 39), just after the awesome ghost of Banquo has entered and sat down in the vacant place. Lennox's question is the means by which Shakespeare makes his audience realize that the ghost they see is invisible to all on the stage; invisible for the moment even to Macbeth, for he is looking in a different direction and enacting a calculated hypocrisy:

> Here had we now our country's honour roof'd,
> Were the graced person of our Banquo present;
> Who may I rather challenge for unkindness
> Than pity for mischance!   (III, iv, 40-43).

It is only when Macbeth turns at Ross's invitation "To grace us with your royal company" (III, iv, 45) that he sees the ghost. I think that he recognizes the apparition immediately, and plays for a little time to recover from the shock, until his nerve snaps. It is Lennox who, so to speak, twists the knife in Macbeth's wound:

Macbeth. The table's full.

Lennox.   Here is a place reserved, sir.

Macbeth. Where?

Lennox. Here, my good lord. What is't that moves your highness?

Macbeth. Which of you have done this?

Lords.   What, my good lord?

Macbeth. Thou canst not say I did it: never shake
   Thy gory locks at me.   (III, iv, 46-51).

Lennox says no more till he speaks for the dismissed guests:

> Good night; and better health
> Attend his majesty! (III, iv, 120-21).

In III, vi, which occurs at an indeterminate but considerable interval after the banquet scene, Lennox is assigned the specially important function of being the first person explicitly to denounce Macbeth as a murderer and tyrant. This he does in scathing irony to an unnamed Lord, taking up again with him the theme of a previous conversation off-stage:

> My former speeches have but hit your thoughts,
> Which can interpret further: only, I say,

Things have been strangely borne. The gracious Duncan
Was pitied of Macbeth: marry, he was dead:
And the right-valiant Banquo walk'd too late;
Whom, you may say, if't please you, Fleance kill'd,
For Fleance fled: men must not walk too late.
Who cannot want the thought how monstrous
It was for Malcolm and for Donalbain
To kill their gracious father? damned fact!
How it did grieve Macbeth! did he not straight
In pious rage the two delinquents tear,
That were the slaves of drink and thralls of sleep?
Was not that nobly done? Ay, and wisely too;
For 'twould have anger'd any heart alive
To hear the men deny't. So that, I say,
He has borne all things well: and I do think
That had he Duncan's sons under his key—
As, an't please heaven, he shall not—they should find
What 'twere to kill a father; so should Fleance.
But, peace! for from broad words and 'cause he fail'd
His presence at the tyrant's feast, I hear
Macduff lives in disgrace: sir, can you tell
Where he bestows himself? (III, vi, 1-24).

This scene is in fact the turning point in Macbeth's fortunes. He has had a kind of bloody success in all his schemes till now: from now on he encounters a series of bloody failures. And the critical speech is put in the mouth of Lennox. The rest of the conversation of Lennox and the unnamed Lord, running to some twenty-six lines, is about Malcolm's reception by Edward the Confessor, Macduff's escape to England in order to sue for help to overthrow the usurper, and the nation's yearning for peace and happiness under its legitimate king.

In IV, i, after Macbeth's consultation with the witches and his enthralled gaze at the apparitions evoked, Lennox enters the cave, having been heard outside and summoned in. He is conventionally respectful to King Macbeth, with "your grace's will" (IV, i, 135), "my lord" (IV, i, 136, 137), and "Ay, my good lord" (IV, i, 143); and he explains that the galloping horses Macbeth had heard belonged to:

two or three, my lord, that bring you word
Macduff is fled to England.   (IV, i, 141-42).

Lennox is off-stage till V, ii, when he appears with Menteith, Caithness, and Angus at the head of an army to oppose Macbeth—the "many worthy fellows that were out", as reported by Ross to Malcolm and Macduff in England (IV, iii, 183). It is Lennox who knows that Donalbain is not with his brother Malcolm, and who has "a file Of all the gentry" (V, ii, 8-9) in the force from England led by Malcolm, Macduff, and Siward, which includes:

Siward's son,
And many unrough youths that even now
Protest their first of manhood. (V, ii, 9-11).

I

And he finishes the scene with a flourish:

Or so much [*i.e.* of blood] as it needs,
To dew the sovereign flower and drown the weeds.
Make we our march towards Birnam. (V, ii, 29-31).

The point of all this is, as I have already indicated,[28] that in Holinshed
Lennox is not one of the Scottish nobles in and about the court of either Duncan
or Macbeth. According to Shakespeare and Holinshed respectively, the Scottish
nobles are:

Shakespeare.	*Holinshed.*
Macbeth.	Macbeth.
Banquo.	Banquo.
Macduff.	Macduff.
Lennox.	
Ross.	Ross.
Menteith.	
Angus.	
Caithness.	Caithness.
	Sutherland.
	Stranaverne [= Strathearn].

Into the middle of his account of the reign of Macbeth, Holinshed thrusts
a long digression to give the descent of the House of Stewart from Banquo and
Fleance down to James VI.[29] The earlier generations of the descent are fictions;
they had been devised before Holinshed, who simply accepted them in good
faith from earlier chroniclers, to supply a link by male descent between the
Stewarts and the ancient line of Scottish kings from Fergus Mac Erc (d. A.D. 501)
and others stretching back to the mists of antiquity. In the course of this digression from Macbeth's story, Holinshed mentions a Robert Steward, presumably
flourishing in the second half of the thirteenth century, "from whom descended
the earles of *Levenox* [= Lennox] and *Dernlie*" [= Darnley],[30] in an unspecified
century (but probably the sixteenth). Later, in the same digression, Holinshed
refers to Murdo Steward [= Murdoch Stewart], Duke of Albany (d. 1425),
who, he says, married "the earle of *Lennox* daughter".[31]

It should be added that Holinshed tells how, at the very beginning of his
reign, Malcolm Canmore made the thanes of Fife (= Macduff), Menteith,
Atholl, Levenox (= Lennox), Murrey (= Moray), Caithness, Ross, and Angus
the first bearers of the rank of earl in Scotland.[32] Shakespeare inserts this detail
in the speech of Malcolm which concludes the play:

My thanes and kinsmen,
Henceforth be earls, the first that ever Scotland
In such an honour named.   (V, viii, 62-64).

But I repeat, to underline the fact, that there is no Lennox in Holinshed's
narrative of the reigns of Duncan and Macbeth.

To come to the Lennox of James VI's time and the Gowrie Conspiracy:
he was Ludovick Stuart, second Duke of Lennox from 1583. He was eight
years younger than his half-cousin James VI, having been born in 1574. His
father Esmé Stuart (?1542-1583), Seigneur d'Aubigny and in 1581 created first

Duke of Lennox, was a first cousin of Henry Stewart, Lord Darnley, James VI's father. Duke Esmé's death in France, where he had been forced to retire by order extorted from James by the Ruthven Raiders, was a great grief to the young King, who seems to have regarded his near kinsman as a second father. James held Duke Ludovick in the same high regard and affection. Duke Ludovick's first wife, as has been noticed before, was Gowrie's sister, Lady Sophia Ruthven, who died before 1592.[33] He was much about the King in Scotland, where he held high office, in spite of his youth, as President of the Council during the King's absence in 1589-90 and as Lord High Admiral from 1591. He played a considerable part in the Gowrie affair and like the King's other supporters he received many signs of the royal favour during the rest of his life. The first of these was his appointment in 1601 along with Sir Thomas Erskine as a special Ambassador to Henry IV of France, with the delicate task of setting right the French record on the Gowrie Conspiracy. On James's accession to the English throne in 1603 Lennox was summoned to accompany him to London. In the same year Lennox became an English Privy Councillor and Steward of the Household. He returned for a period to Scotland as High Commissioner to the Scottish Parliament. Many appointments at Court, besides those already mentioned, came his way; and he was awarded several additional peerages: Baron Settrington (in Yorkshire) and Earl of Richmond in 1613 and Earl of Newcastle-upon-Tyne and Duke of Richmond in 1623. His sudden death in 1624 was, says David Calderwood, "dolorous both to English and Scottish. He was weill liked of for his courtesie, meekness, liberalitie to his servants and followers".[35] He was buried in Henry VII's Chapel in Westminster Abbey.

Lennox was the most important of James's companions all through the eventful 5th August 1600. He practically never left the King's side. He was one of the hunting party which set out in the morning from Falkland Palace. It was he whom James made his confidant on the ride to Perth. He was a witness of all that occurred there, except when James was absent with Alexander Ruthven. He was at the head of the party that stormed through the locked doors to the turret study of Gowrie House. And his deposition was the most vital document in the whole dossier, the first in order and, except for Andrew Henderson's, the longest and most circumstantial.

I submit that, for these very reasons, Shakespeare deliberately and in spite of Holinshed's omission of a Lennox from among the thanes of Duncan and Macbeth, gave his Lennox a considerable and dramatically important role, very much the kind of part actually played by the Duke of Lennox in the Gowrie affair.

In the play there are other wide differences from Holinshed in respect of the characterization of Macbeth and Lady Macbeth, Duncan, and Banquo, some of which were, I think, suggested by features of the same affair at Perth.

Shakespeare retains for his "gracious Duncan" (III, i, 66; III, vi, 3, 10) all the softness, gentleness, and clemency which Holinshed refers to.[35] But Shakespeare, besides presenting Duncan as elderly rather than about the same age as Macbeth, plays down the neglect and ineffectiveness attributed to him by

Holinshed.[35] Shakespeare may well have wanted his audience to take Duncan
as a prototype of his descendant James, even as they were to think of James as
the legitimate inheritor of "the king-becoming graces" (IV, iii, 91) of the
saintly Edward the Confessor and of his healing touch (IV, iii, 140-59).

As for Banquo, Shakespeare suppresses his complicity in the murder of
Duncan, which in Holinshed is unequivocally stated: "At length therefore,
communicating his proposed intent with his trustie friends, amongst whom
Banquho was the chiefest, upon confidence of their promised aid, [Macbeth]
slue the king at *Enverness* [= Inverness], or (as some say) at *Botgosvane* [= Pit-
gaveny, near Elgin, or Balgowan, near Methven in Perthshire], in the sixth
yeare of his reigne".[36] The suppression of Banquo's participation was a tactful
modification, in order to clear the Patriarch of the House of Stewart from any
taint of treason.

Probably for the same kind of reason, Shakespeare says nothing of the fact
that Duncan and Macbeth were first cousins, sons of the two daughters,
Beatrice and Doada, of Malcolm II, and likewise nothing of Macbeth's belief
that Duncan had done "what in him lay to defraud him of all manner of title
and claime, which he might, in time to come, pretend unto the crowne".[36]

But more important and more to the point are the changes Shakespeare
makes in the characters and motives of Macbeth and Lady Macbeth and in the
relationship between them. Holinshed's Macbeth needs no instigation from any-
body else to kill Duncan, waiting only for a favourable opportunity to carry
out what he had himself planned. This is in no way contradicted by the following passage: "The words of the three weird sisters . . . greatlie incouraged him
hereunto, but speciallie his wife lay sore upon him to attempt the thing, as she
that was verïe ambitious, burning in unquenchable desire to beare the name of a
queen."[36] That is all Shakespeare had to go on for the taut and tense col-
loquies of husband and wife in I, v, 55-74, I, vii, 28-82, and II, ii, 14-74. It is
also the only sentence in Holinshed about Macbeth's wife. In Shakespeare, on
the other hand, Lady Macbeth is actuated, not by her own personal ambition,
but by what could be fairly described as a selfless ardour for her husband's
greatness. Shakespeare takes her out of Holinshed's single sentence and makes
her almost as important as Macbeth himself to the end of III, iv and, up to
that point, by far the stronger character. Though Shakespeare's Macbeth is a
good and brave soldier, capable of a wonderful resolution and courage in the
field, "valour's minion" (I, ii, 19), "Bellona's bridegroom" (I, ii, 54), he is less
than single-minded and resolute otherwise. Indeed he is exactly what his wife
knows him to be (I, v, 17-26) and what she accuses him to his face of being
(I, vii, 35-59), double-minded and irresolute. It is she who plans the murder of
Duncan and thinks of every detail. Though Holinshed's Macbeth takes counsel
with his friends in order to make good his claim to the throne, not in the
planning of the murder itself, Shakespeare with a far more dramatic effect joins
his Macbeth and Lady Macbeth in a close conspiracy of two.

The Gowrie affair was likewise a close conspiracy of two, to all outward
appearance. The design, said Thomas Hamilton, the King's Advocate, in a letter
probably written towards the end of August 1600, "hes bred within these twa

brethris awin [= own] breistis . . . and is liklie to be buriet with thame self".[37] The other persons who paid the penalty for being in some degree involved were mere retainers under orders, not fellow-conspirators. The two Ruthven brothers were very secretive in all their operations. They kept what they were up to, whatever it was, from all their servants and associates, dissembling, prevaricating, misleading, giving orders imprecise or unexplained, or failing to give orders at all, apparently so as to let nobody else into the heart of their secret.[38]

William Rynd, the pedagogue, had something interesting to say in this regard, in the deposition made on 22nd August 1600, two days after his main deposition, both of which were published in the official account.[39] Asked if he had ever heard Gowrie express himself "anent the duetie of a wise man in the execution of an high enterprise" (a question unlikely to have been put unless the authorities already had reason to expect an affirmative answer), Rynd said "that, being out of the countrey, he had diuerse times heard him reason in that matter, and that he was euer of that opinion, that 'he was not a wise man, that hauing intended the execution of a high and dangerous purpose, communicate the same to any but to himselfe; because keeping it to himselfe, it could not be discouered nor disappointed': which the deponer declared before, vnrequired, to the Controller, and Master William Cowper Minister at Perth".[40]

Cowper had already learned something to the same effect, as is related by Archbishop John Spottiswoode. The Archbishop recalls 'that, meeting with Mr William Cowper, then minister at Perth, the third day after [the Gowrie affair] in Falkland, he shewed me that not many daies before that accident, visiting by occasion the Earl at his own house he found him reading a book entituled, De coniurationibus adversus principes, and having asked him what a book it was, he answered, "That it was a collection of the Conspiracies made against Princes, which, he said, was foolishly contrived all of them, and faulty either in one point or another; for he that goeth about such a business should not, said he, put any man on his counsell". And he [i.e. Cowper], not liking such discourses, desired him to lay away such books, and read others of a better subject. I verily think', adds Spottiswoode, 'he was then studying how to go beyond all Conspirators recorded in any history.'[41]

Moreover, there is a temperamental parallel between Macbeth and his wife on the one hand and Gowrie and Alexander Ruthven on the other. Contrary to the usual run of things in personal relationships, the woman in the first pair, to the end of III, iv in the play, and the younger brother in the second are the activists egging on their half-reluctant partners. Like Lady Macbeth, Alexander, not his moody elder brother, was the moving spirit or mainspring in the Conspiracy.

It might be argued that such a dominance by the younger brother is belied by his dying words: "Allace! I had na wyte of it!" As I said earlier, the bare meaning of the words is: "Alas! I am not to blame for it!"[42] But the unspoken context of the remark, so to speak, imputes blame to another, who in the circumstances could only be Gowrie himself. Certainly there is something pathetic about a lad of eighteen stabbed to death. But every youth who dies tragically in a criminal enterprise is not necessarily guiltless; and his last words are not necessarily true. Besides, though Alexander did die shortly after his last words, it is not at all certain that he knew and felt that he was dying. There have been not a few persons, as for example the Empress Elizabeth of Austria, who have been fatally stabbed without realizing for an appreciable interval that they had received more than a mere blow or touch. What I suggest is that the rash and impulsive Alexander, who was something of a gambler with fate, did not realize the imminence of his death and tried to throw the blame on his brother, with some dim hope both of saving himself and of succeeding to the earldom.

The studious Earl, who had attended universities at home and abroad, who had made a deep impression by his thoughtfulness on Beza in Geneva,[43] and who had read Machiavelli,[44] may well have discussed on the academic level with his brother such dangerous subjects as assassination; just as Macbeth also had obviously discussed with his wife the possibility of his removing Duncan from his path to the throne, and had "broken this enterprise" (I, vii, 48) to her, in a scene which must once have existed, but which at some stage in the play's very chequered history was cut out.[45] But the Earl was more a muser than a doer.

The only explanation of the strange behaviour of the two brothers that seems to make sense is that the headstrong younger brother caught fire from the elder's speculative talk about conspiring against the King and removing him either by seizing his person as had been done in the Ruthven Raid of 1582 (in which their father had been a leading actor) or by actually killing him; and that Alexander in his turn talked the Earl into agreeing or half-agreeing to a tentative plan which was to await a favourable opportunity. I think that the Earl was the kind of man who, if left to himself, would never have thought any opportunity favourable. But he was not left to himself. Alexander, I submit, grew tired of delays and procrastination and, by bringing James to Perth on his own initiative, took such action as forced the Earl to back him in a way, if not give the lead. It is not difficult to imagine Alexander using such words as these to his brother when he brought news of the King's early arrival:

> He that's coming
> Must be provided for: and you shall put
> This night's great business into my dispatch;
> Which shall to all our nights and days to come
> Give solely sovereign sway and masterdom. . . .
>   Only look up clear;
> To alter favour ever is to fear:
> Leave all the rest to me.   (I, v, 67-74).

But such an unwilling and half-hearted backing as was given by Gowrie, who dragged his feet to the last, was of course worse than useless, even if Alexander's scheme had not been hastily improvised and clumsy. As was noted earlier,[46] when James arrived at Gowrie House, so far from there being any sign of preparation to entertain a King, the place was at sixes-and-sevens. The King had to wait an hour or more for an indifferent dinner, for no order in advance had been issued to the kitchen.[47] And the master of Gowrie House had all the awkward appearance of a man put out at being landed in a distasteful situation or of a nervous player unsure of his lines and dreading the coming of his cue.

He hung ineffectively about as the King dined, uncertain what to do, going in and out of the room, mumbling over his shoulders to his servants, and being so poor an entertainer that the King had to rally him and teach him the art of hospitality. Macbeth exhibited a similar nervous restlessness when Duncan was at table:

> *Macbeth.* How now! what news?
> *Lady Macbeth.* He has almost supp'd: why have you left the chamber?
> *Macbeth.* Hath he ask'd for me?
> *Lady Macbeth.* Know you not he has?
> (I, vii, 28-30).

And what Lady Macbeth says to her husband earlier might well have been Alexander's attempt to stiffen his limp brother:

> Your face, my thane, is as a book where men
> May read strange matters. To beguile the time,
> Look like the time; bear welcome in your eye,
> Your hand, your tongue: look like the innocent flower,
> But be the serpent under't. (I, v, 63-67).

> Away, and mock the time with fairest show:
> False face must hide what the false heart doth know.[48]
> (I, vii, 81-82).

In the end, Alexander, getting no real support from his brother, determined, not to call the whole thing off, but to go it alone, staking all recklessly on a last throw and stopping up

> the access and passage to remorse,
> That no compunctious visitings of nature
> Shake my fell purpose, nor keep peace between
> The effect and it! (I, v, 45-48).

I think of Alexander as feeling and deciding like Macbeth in a similar dilemma:

> For mine own good,
> All causes shall give way: I am in blood
> Stepp'd in so far that, should I wade no more,
> Returning were as tedious as go o'er:
> Strange things I have in head, that will to hand;
> Which must be acted ere they may be scann'd.
> (III, iv, 135-40).

Pitcairn has an interesting note which supports the view I have put forward of Alexander's desperation: "Henderson infers that [Alexander] did not leave the back of the door [of the turret study, when he went out ostensibly to confer with his brother], either from his [*i.e.* Henderson's] not hearing his retiring footsteps, or from his too precipitate return; which last, alone, would show he had had no conference on so momentous an occasion. The fact seems to be, that [Alexander] Ruthven was completely abashed by the dignified and collected demeanour of the King; and having become quite unnerved by the desperate situation in which he now felt himself placed, he availed himself of the King's proposal to call for Gowry [*sic*], to retire and 'screw his courage to the sticking-place' [I, vii, 60]. Appalled by the awful circumstances of his Treason, and conceiving that it was now too late to retrace his steps, he seems to have stifled every feeling of reason and religion, and desperately to have rushed forward to the conclusion of his conspiracy, with headlong and insane fury."[49]

Notes

1. Cf. 70, 90 supra.
2. Cf. 9-11 supra.
3. Cf. 45-47 supra.
4. Cf. 48-51 supra.
5. Mackenzie, Laws, 129.
6. Cf. 50-51 supra.
7. Cf. 75-76 supra.
8. I, 339.
9. I, 340.
10. The accounts of witch-trials both in England and in Scotland have been well-combed for such suggestions as Shakespeare took from them.
11. I, 347-48.
12. Cf. 81-83 supra.
13. Cf. 89 supra.
14. Cf. 81 supra.
15. Cf. 88 supra.
16. Cf. 80 supra.
17. Cf. 114 infra.
18. I, 299.
19. Cf. 92-93 supra. Cf. also: IV, i, 133-34:
    Let this pernicious hour
    Stand aye accursed in the calendar!
20. Pitcairn, II, 183, note 1.
21. Ibid., II, 183.
22. Ibid., II, 183. Andrew Henderson also, in his deposition (the one read at the trial, not the one published with the official account), said that on entering the room at the top of the turnpike, Ramsay had "ane halk in his hand" (ibid., II, 179).
23. II, 183, note 1.
24. Ibid., II, 237. Both a John Murray and a George Murray are mentioned in the Lord High Treasurer's Accounts for July 1600 as receiving green frieze for hunting garments (ibid., II, 237).

25. I, 347.
26. On the Knocking at the Gate in Macbeth in The Collected Writings of Thomas De Quincey. Edited by David Masson, 1897, X, 389-94.
27. Cf. 46-47, 99 supra.
28. Cf. 113 supra.
29. I, 344-47.
30. Ibid., I, 345.
31. Ibid., I, 346.
32. Ibid., I, 351.
33. Cf. 74, 86 supra. The Duke married for the second time in 1612 and for the third in 1621.
34. Calderwood, VII, 595.
35. I, 335. Cf. 90 supra for what the author of A Short Discourse, etc. says of James's "dangerous . . . excesse" in "clemencie, goodnes and truste".
36. I, 340.
37. Calendar of State Papers, Scotland (Elizabeth), LXVI, no. 51. Andrew Lang did not believe that the King's Advocate was the signatory (James VI and the Gowrie Mystery, 52). But Arbuckle has no doubt of the handwriting (102, note 3).
38. This does not exclude the possibility that Gowrie dropped dark hints, in a way by no means uncommon in criminals before or after a crime, hints which the hearer of them interprets only by hindsight and discloses out of a desire for notoriety. Such a remembrancer of dark hints was Robert Oliphant, one of Gowrie's retainers and a brother of the Laird of Bachiltoun. He was the first person to be named as the man in the turret

study at Gowrie House, before the identification settled on Andrew Henderson. He did not figure in the trials following the Conspiracy. But the Register of the Privy Council minuted on 5th December 1600 (VI, 671) that Oliphant had admitted to having some foreknowledge of the Conspiracy. On the same day, George Nicolson, who kept his ear to the ground and heard all the gossip in the Scottish Capital, reported to Sir Robert Cecil that Oliphant had said that "there was no justice in Scotland, for faulters [= wrongdoers] skaped fre and innocents were punished. Mr Thomas Cranston was execute being innocent, and Henderson saved. That therle [= the Earl] of Gowry had moved that matter to him [i.e. Oliphant] in Paris and here, that he had with good reasons deverted him, that therle thereon left him and delt with Henderson in that matter, that Henderson undertooke it and yet fainted, and Mr Ths Cranston knew nothing of it and yet was executed" (C.S.P., (Elizabeth), LXVI, no. 107). Arbuckle, to whom I am indebted for this quotation (100), adds: "This talk had leaked out and Oliphant fled. No more was heard of him until 1608, when he was seized in London and imprisoned, but later liberated on the orders of James, who said that 'he had tried his innocency'" (R.P.C., VIII, 565). It is clear that James must have been fully satisfied, and probably convinced that the big-mouthed Oliphant had, like others, an ill-will towards Andrew Henderson.

In 1608 "the conjectures which the King and his Ministers formed [in 1600 as to Gowrie and his brother having no fellow-conspirators] were . . . fully disproved, in their own opinion, when Logan of Restalrig and Bour appeared to have been conscious of the purposes of Gowrie" (Pitcairn, II, 221, note 1 after Lord Hailes). But

Robert Logan and James Bour were dead by 1608; and it is not clear what Gowrie's purposes were or how far he had let Logan and Bour into his secret. George Sprot, notary of Eyemouth, was found guilty of being privy to exchanges, by letter or in conference, between the other parties and was executed.

39. Cf. 83 supra.

40. Pitcairn, II, 221. The Comptroller of the Treasury was Sir David Murray of Gospertie (cf. 95-96 supra).

41. III, 88-89. Lord Hailes (cf. Pitcairn, II, 221, note 1) was inclined to think that Gowrie's book may have been the Latin translation of Machiavelli's Discorsi sopra la prima deca di Tito Livio (out of which grew the much more famous Il Principe). It includes a chapter (iii, 6) describing and commenting on actual conspiracies of the past. In the 1591 edition (Nicolai Machiavelli Florentini Disputationum De Republica quas Discursus nuncupavit Libri III, 438-75) the chapter in question is entitled De coniurationibus and there is a marginal title Coniuratio adversus principem. In this chapter Machiavelli emphasises "the danger of discovery that attends any conspiracy involving confederates; the importance, with a view to avoiding this hazard, of not communicating a plot to any accomplice until just before it is to be put into execution; and the risk of attempting to revise carefully laid plans in order to meet unforeseen circumstances, adherence to the original plans being likely to prove the safer course" (Arbuckle, 103).

Gowrie seems to have used, in association with the family arms for which the motto was Facta probant, a device of a man in armour pointing with a sword to an imperial crown along with the further motto Tibi soli. Did he perhaps take Tibi soli as expressing a principle of action for himself?

42. *Cf.* 80, 86 note 16 *supra*.
43. *Cf.* Arbuckle, 106, 110.
44. *Cf.* 125, note 41 *supra*.
45. *Cf.* 8-9 *supra*.
46. *Cf.* 76 *supra*.
47. *Cf.* II, i, 17-19:

> Being unprepared,
> Our will became the servant to
>   defect;

Which else should free have wrought.
48. *Cf.* III, iii, 8-9:

> How now, my lord! why do you
>   keep alone,
> Of sorriest fancies your companions
>   making?

(III, ii, 8-9).

49. II, 178, note 1.

8

King James, the Players, and the Clergy

Two truths are told,
As happy prologues to the swelling act
Of the imperial theme.
Macbeth, I, iii, 127-29.

James VI and I showed himself to be his mother's son in loving what may be comprehensively called "shows"; and his love of them was, if anything, confirmed from 1589-90 by his marriage to Anne of Denmark, whose taste for the drama and masquing amounted to a passion. If John Knox fulminated against the levities of Mary and her Court, James was to find an adversary and censor scarcely less redoubtable in Robert Bruce, the Knox of his generation.

James's brushes with his clergy over players do not figure prominently in the histories of his reign. But they have a symbolical significance for James's strategy and tactics in his campaigns about authority in the Scottish Church; and they illustrate his "kingcraft", to use his own word, which was perhaps shrewder than it is always given credit for and which was certainly dogged. That is to say, his backing of players was as much for political ends as for the amusement of his leisure hours, since it was or became, by reason of the clergy's attitude, an assertion of his royal authority over Presbyterian opposition, even more than an encouragement of the drama for its own sake. And perhaps, since kingcraft was a subtle game, James may have wanted to demonstrate his friendliness to visitors from the England over which he hoped soon to rule and reign, in line with Hamlet's injunction to Polonius: "Good my lord, will you see the players well bestowed? Do you hear, let them be well used; for they are the abstract and brief chronicles of the time: after your death you were better have a bad epitaph than their ill report while you live."[1]

It might be said that, from an early age, James had resolved to do nothing to prejudice his chance of succeeding Elizabeth on the English throne. In the year 1587 his tact, if such it can be charitably called, was put to its severest test by the execution of his unfortunate mother. But it took the strain, and he adroitly, if ignobly, adjusted himself even in that awkward situation, as he had done and was still to do in other minor crises. His longing gaze was always towards the glittering prize of St. Edward's Crown, and his hopes always for the time when he would be a King indeed in a rich country where the monarchy was all-powerful, instead of being, until well into the fifteen-nineties, a King in little more than name, in a country with but a meagre revenue and resources.

127

His domestic problems, from the time when he began to escape from pupilage and minority and to rule in some fashion as well as to reign, were threefold: [1] How to exercise and strengthen the royal authority in a country in which his writ and his officers were often flouted by Highland chiefs and Lowland nobles with their ready resort to private war, and by a consequently low regard for law and order among the people generally; [2] how to control the Presbyterian clergy who refused to recognize him as Head of the Church as well as Head of the State, and to prevent their interfering in matters far beyond what he considered to be their sphere; and [3] how to make ends meet financially and have something over to render life worth living. James must have watched with admiration Elizabeth's effective exercise of her royal command, and with envy the much less complicated situation in Church and State in England compared with the perplexities and frustrations in which he was so often involved. But he was, as I have said, both wily and persistent; and he gradually, before he went south, brought more and more of his turbulent nation to tractability. The first of James's problems, the enforcement of law and order, is outside the orbit of this Chapter. The other two, or aspects of them, are not: they are interrelated and the hub, as it were, of their imbroglio was the royal patronage of players.

Unlike England, Scotland did not develop a vigorous dramatic tradition in the middle ages or in the sixteenth century. The main reason was probably that the country was too poor and the population too small and scattered. The State authorities before the Reformation were pretty easy-going as regards the supervision of things dramatic. As for the pre-Reformation Church in Scotland, it was not different in attitude from the Catholic Church elsewhere in Western Europe with regard to *spectacula*, which term may be taken to cover anything in which persons dress up and gesticulate, from processions, pageants, and acrobatics to the enactment of plays with real plots. Like the rest of the Catholic Church, it showed, occasionally and sporadically, a certain hostility to such *ludi* as were in the nature of seasonal folk-plays of pagan origin; and some churchmen expressed disapproval from time to time of clerical participation in lay revels, of wanton singing in churches and Sabbath indecorum, and of the attendance of priests and persons in orders at entertainments given by strolling minstrels or *histriones*, who, though tolerated everywhere, were in low repute generally. But the Church is not known to have discouraged in any way miracle and mystery plays put on by trade guilds or the observance of the great Festivals or of saints' days by dramas or pageants; nor did it interfere with the laity's other amusements of a more or less dramatic kind. So there is undoubtedly evidence, though of a fragmentary sort, of plays and playing in Scotland in the middle ages and in the earlier sixteenth century, at least south of the Highland Line. That evidence has been most carefully assembled and presented by Dr. Anna Jean Mill in *Mediaeval Plays in Scotland*. But the significant fact remains that practically no dramatic texts have come down—only two to be exact;[2] which can be explained by there never having been many and by such as there were not having an inherent survival value. It would certainly seem from this that the early Scottish genius did not take kindly to the dramatic form.

In Reformed Scotland, as in unreformed Scotland, the secular authorities did not trouble themselves, except occasionally and quite locally, about plays and similar amusements, unlike the secular authorities in England where there developed much more in the way of regulation and surveillance. The Reformed Church of Scotland, however, did take a great interest in the laity's amusements. It adopted, with somewhat greater consistency and rigour, the Catholic attitude before the Reformation to seasonal folk-plays and shows by professional minstrels, as well as to indecorum in general. Such plays of the type of miracle and mystery plays or plays for saints' days as survived (they had never been many or important), were fairly soon suppressed. But the early Reformers in Scotland, like their brethren in England and on the Continent, had no objection to a dramatic vehicle for what they regarded as acceptable matter, though with some reserves about the exchange of garments between the sexes and about women acting. They were quite prepared to use the drama, especially in a form like the morality plays in England, as a means for propagating Protestantism and denigrating Catholicism. John Knox, though so stern a critic of secular shows at Mary's Court,[3] actually himself attended a propagandist play at St. Andrews, written by the ardent Protestant John Davidson[4], whose like-minded brethren were later to be the clerical thorns in King James's side.[5]

Protestant propaganda was also countenanced in pageants or the like, on such occasions as a royal entry into the Capital, as when Mary arrived from France in 1561[6] or when the young James in 1579 was received with special solemnity and expense to open a Parliament on his return from virtual imprisonment at Stirling under the Regent Morton.[7] The speeches made in the course of such entertainments were, to judge from English examples, far removed from the dramatic: they consisted of compliments, exhortations, and admonitions spoken by type characters, mythological figures, or personified abstractions.

Again, plays to be performed by schoolboys were tolerated and indeed encouraged in Reformed Scotland. Some were probably not so much partisan as moralistic, in the line of "Christian Terence". But also both sides in the religious conflict, until the Catholics were outmanœuvred, were ready on occasion to use school plays for polemical purposes. King James certainly witnessed one or more tragedies performed by the boys of the High School in 1579, which may have been their contribution to the afore-mentioned pageantry of that year. School plays of an improving and tendencious kind continued to be staged during the rest of James's reign in Scotland, the Church apparently taking no action to forbid or discourage them.

It can be said, then, that the Reformed Church of Scotland did not denounce and ban everything dramatic, though its approval was decidedly qualified. But as the years of the later sixteenth century elapsed, the Church in its General Assemblies, Synods, and Presbyteries, by country-wide or by local decisions, gradually imposed "irksome and almost impossible conditions",[8] which would have virtually extinguished the last embers of the drama in Scotland.

But by no means everybody saw eye to eye with the extremists in the Church. There developed a division of opinion over theatrical and other diversions, with the Court and its adherents in their favour and a larger body of clerical critics and censors, the bulk of the population being on the whole uncommitted in a varying and inconsistent way. The Court in Scotland, how-ever much it wanted to be entertained, was too impoverished, until late in the period under review, to provide a regular or frequent patronage; it was seldom long in one place and it was not, under Mary and for most of James's reign, the focus of the nation's gaze. Nor, be it said, were any of the nobility, unlike Elizabeth's courtiers, inclined to back companies of players with money or pro-tection. The clerical censors, on the other hand, were more positive and vocal and more able to exert their influence and authority than were the theatro-phobes in England. The latter were not representative of the English people as a whole or of their clergy. But the Reformation in Scotland had been a much more root-and-branch affair than in England; and the ministers of its Reformed Church in general inclined to austerity and, if not to the total banning of organized entertainment in the shape of plays, masques, shows, pageants, and even professional acrobatic displays, certainly to the discouragement of the pursuit of happiness by such means. They carried along with them many of the graver laity, who readily accepted clerical dictation in morals and manners, as well as in faith and doctrine, as part of the Reformed way of life. But this is not to say that civic or burghal authorities were, any more than many individuals, always or uniformly in agreement with ministerial opinion; or that the general population did not contain in the later sixteenth century, as at other times, a large number ever ready to gape at shows and disinclined by the strong presence of the natural man in them to a too strict observance of austerity.

Though James VI was carefully educated to be a Reformed monarch in a Reformed country, he was not prevented from enjoying such modest enter-tainment of a theatrical kind as might be available. His paramount pedagogue, George Buchanan, was an uncompromising Reformer in ecclesiastical matters and a strict disciplinarian in all that pertained to education. But he was also a humanist who sacrificed to the Muses. He had won a European reputation as a Latin poet, not least by his two tragedies written in the fifteen-forties, *Jephthes, sive Votum* and *Baptistes, sive Calumnia*, which were first published in 1554 and 1578 respectively; and he issued "interpretations" of Euripides's *Medea* in 1544 and of his *Alcestis* in 1556. Besides, Buchanan provided various *pompae*, presumably of a semi-dramatic or masque-like kind, under Mary;[9] and, according to Sir James Melville of Hallhill, he was given to rehearsing "at all occasions moralities short and instructive, whereof he had abundance, in-venting where he wanted".[10] Like other humanists, then, he was more than willing that his royal pupil should benefit from such instruction as the didactic drama could supply.

Buchanan was himself something of an actor or mimic, to judge from an anecdote of how he corrected his pupil's careless transaction of business, as for example in signing documents without reading them. One paper presented by Buchanan for signing was in fact a formal transfer to himself of the royal authority for fifteen days. On the strength of it, Buchanan assumed the char-acter of a sovereign "and with that humour for which he was distinguished . . .

the demeanour of royalty", much to the astonishment of the Court and not least of James himself who at first thought his tutor to be deranged. In due course Buchanan resumed his true character and rubbed into the King the obvious lesson.[11]

When Sir Henry Killigrew, who was Elizabeth's Ambassador in Scotland at the time, visited the young King at Stirling, the royal tutors wanted to make a good impression by showing their pupil off to advantage. James was accordingly invited to make "pretty speeches"[12] which Buchanan had probably composed, to translate a chapter of the Bible from Latin to French and from French to English, and to dance, which he did "with a very good grace",[12] having been carefully taught[13] an accomplishment not held in high esteem by radical Reformers.

James Melville the Reformer, not the Sir James already quoted, was even more impressed by a similar display of James's accomplishments, also at Stirling, when he went with his uncle Andrew to consult Buchanan on university matters. "It was the sweetest sight in Europe that day," says Melville, "for strange and extraordinary gifts of ingine [= invention], judgement, memory, and language. I heard him discourse, walking up and down in the auld Lady Mar's land, of knowledge and ignorance."[14] The speeches "of knowledge and ignorance" sound like a part of a *débat*, written perhaps by Buchanan in his moralistic vein.

Buchanan's endeavour, as a tutor who interpreted his function as extending far beyond the merely pedagogic, was to make the young James regard himself as a King circumscribed by and subordinate to the law. His *Baptistes* embodied his ideas of a limited monarchy and of the rights of the people; and he dedicated it on its publication in 1578 to the twelve-year-old King in complete confidence in its suitability and its high didactic value for one called to a throne. It "seems with greater reason", than other works addressed by Buchanan to the King, "more confidently to claim the patronage of your name; for . . . it calls young men from the vulgar strains of dramatic poetry to the imitation of antiquity, and endeavours . . . to excite in their minds a regard for piety. . . . But this work seems peculiarly to have a reference to you, because it clearly sets forth the torments and miseries of tyrants, even when they seem to be most flourishing; and this I deem not only beneficial for you to know now, but even indispensable, in order that you may early begin to hate what you should always avoid".[15]

The year after publishing his didactic tragedy for the admonition of kings in general and one in particular, Buchanan decided to issue another work of a similar tendency, which he had written ten or a dozen years before and which had lain almost forgotten among his papers. This was a Latin dialogue between himself and Thomas Maitland, younger brother of William Maitland of Lethington, on civil government, *De Jure Regni apud Scotos*, which caused a commotion in Scotland and far beyond for a century or more. In the dedication to the young King, Buchanan explains that, whereas publication had been inexpedient at the time of its composition since the affairs of the nation were then in too turbulent a state, he now in 1578 thought publication expedient in the hope that the dialogue might contain many precepts necessary to James's tender age and that it might both testify to the tutor's zeal in the pupil's service and instruct the pupil in his duty to the community. In the course of the dialogue Buchanan developed and expounded in a way meant to be Socratic his "doctrine that the source of political power is the people, that the king is bound by those conditions under which the supreme power was first committed to his hands, and that it is lawful to resist, even to punish, tyrants".[16]

Buchanan went incidentally over the same ideas again in another work dedicated to James and meant to teach him many lessons by historical examples. This was his *Rerum Scoticarum Historia*, which was finished in 1580 but not published till 1582, the year of its author's death. About 1580 Buchanan expressed once more his views on sovereignty in a Latin poem, addressed to Thomas Randolph who was one of Elizabeth's agents in Scotland, and giving the author's ideal of a prince.

Such a doctrine of the royal office as Buchanan forced down James's young throat was probably unpalatable to him as soon as he was old enough to understand it and to compare his Scottish monarchy with the absolutisms of England and the Continent. At any rate the *De Jure Regni* and the *Historia* were condemned by Act of Parliament and all copies in circulation were confiscated in 1584,[17] only two years after Buchanan's death and in the very year in which James became eighteen, the recognized age of regal majority.

A new idea was striking root in the young King's mind. He probably derived the germ of it from a Scottish Catholic, Adam Blackwood, whose studies had been generously financed by Mary when she was in France and who in gratitude frequently visited her during her imprisonment in England and was untiring in his efforts to serve her.[18] He dedicated to her in 1575 the two books[19] of his work on the relation between religion and government, *De Vinculo; seu Conjunctione Religionis et Imperii*. It demonstrated the duty laid on rulers to extirpate heresy and condemn heretics as rebels against constituted authority.[20] Blackwood also set himself to the heavy task of grappling with Buchanan, whose views on sovereignty he denounced with great bitterness and severity in his *Apologia pro Regibus, adversus Georgii Buchanani Dialogum de Jure Regni apud Scotos*, published in 1581.

It was easy for James, in revolt from Buchanan's concept of a king under the law and answerable to it and to the people from whom his power derived, to develop out of Blackwood a theory of divine right and unchallengeable kingly authority, which, as he grew older, he seldom lost an opportunity to expound and maintain and which it was the main object of his kingcraft to exercise.[21] But it has been not unfairly said by Hume Brown that "these tendencies . . . received their strongest propulsion from his very subjects who were most opposed to them. The absolutism of James was forced upon him in large degree by the excessive claims of the Presbyterian clergy",[22] including, I would add, the right and duty to censure the pleasures of their flocks and of even the King himself.

James had never set foot outside his own kingdom until late in 1589 when at the age of twenty-three he went to fetch his Danish bride; and until that year he had seen little of a dramatic or even semi-dramatic kind except humdrum and improving interludes and *débats* with perhaps equally moralistic imitations in sixteenth-century Latin of Terence and Seneca, all of which must have been, in the words of Mad Margaret about penny-readings, "not remarkably entertaining".[23] But he was of an enquiring turn of mind; and he no doubt had the curiosity, as he certainly had the opportunity, to enquire from Elizabeth's ambassadors and other Englishmen visiting his Court, as well as from subjects of his own who had been in London, about conditions in the country which was the goal of all his hopes. He would want to know about the splendours of the English Court and the royal palaces and, sooner rather than later, about the lavish entertainments, especially at Christmas and Shrovetide, and also about the many companies of professional actors and their performances in and around London and on provincial tours as well as before the Court. He would be cognisant of the fact that Elizabeth herself and not a few of her courtiers gave their patronage to companies of players, which was from time to time of value to them in their bouts with the Lord Mayor and the City Council of London and in the difficulties occasionally encountered on provincial tours. Besides such information, James could not but know that his Sister of England had an important functionary in her Master of the Revels, whose duty was to arrange for her amusement by plays, masques, and the like, and whose authority had extended far beyond his immediate scope into the sphere of censorship and play-licensing. That players and playing were strictly regulated would not surprise James, if he knew about it; nor would the fact that dramatists and actors occasionally offended and were punished in consequence. Such episodes merely illustrated the enviable functioning of an effective authoritarian system. Whether James had read any of the printed plays is a moot point; but at least one Scot, William Drummond of Hawthornden, began his collection of English play quartos from early in the seventeenth century. Lastly, if James heard that there were theatrophobes in England, he would be pleased to know that they were a minority faction and by no means so troublesome to the authorities south of the Border as were their counterparts in Scotland.

In 1589 James took the first step towards a contact with "show business" in England, in order to make the festivities in celebration of his forthcoming marriage the more enjoyable. He appears to have appealed to Elizabeth for her help, probably in July or August. She responded in September by dispatching a masque for six masquers and six torch-bearers,[24] who were all probably members of her company of players. About the same time, Roger Ashton,[25] one of James's Gentlemen of the Bedchamber, wrote on James's instructions to Lord Scrope, Governor of Carlisle and Lord Warden of the English West Marches, "signifying . . . that yt was the kinges earnest desire for to have her Majesties players for to repayer into Scotland to his grace".[26] So wrote Lord Scrope in a letter of 20th September 1589 to William Ashby, Elizabeth's Ambassador at the Scottish Court. Lord Scrope's letter continues thus: "I dyd furthwith dispatche a servant of my owen vnto them wheir they were in the furthest parte of Langkeshire, whervpon they made their returne heather to Carliell, wher they are, and haue stayed for the space of ten dayes, wherof I thought good to gyve yow notice in respect of the great desyre that the kyng

K

had to have the same to come vnto his grace; And withall to praye yow to gyve knowledg therof to his Majestie."[27]

So James must have known somehow[28] that Elizabeth's players were in the North of England. Otherwise he would not have applied to such a frontier official as Lord Scrope, but to Ashby the Ambassador for the transmission of his request to London. Knowing the nearness of the company to his border, James seems to have wanted to get word to them by a speedier method than an ordinary dispatch to London and a consequential message carried by a horseman with a roving commission and but a hazy idea of where he might find his billet. That is to say, James was taking no chances of the company's return to the inaccessible South; and his surprising awareness of their presence in the North of England and his eager short-circuiting of formal diplomacy are further indications of his interest in English players.

Queen Elizabeth's company had been got together by Edmund Tilney, Master of the Revels, in 1583 by recruiting twelve of the best actors from already-existing companies.[29] Thomas Heywood, who was well-informed on theatrical matters, mentions as among the most famous actors of a past generation no less than seven of the Queen's men: [?William] Knell, John Bentley, Tobias Mills, John Laneham, John Singer, and the two most celebrated of all, Robert Wilson and Richard Tarleton.[30] The acting ability of the members and several resounding theatrical successes combined with the prestige deriving from the Queen's patronage to give them the premier place among the companies during the fifteen-eighties.

In addition to a dozen or so of members whose function was mainly acting, the Queen's players probably had a few musicians and singers and several handymen, any of whom could be roped in to play small roles or to provide crowd effects. Minor acting service might also have been got from the tumblers or acrobats and tightrope-walkers[31] who were attached to the Queen's men from 1588-89 or earlier. As Chambers says: "The players have amongst other elements in their ancestry the mediaeval mimes, and they inherit the familiar mimic tradition of multifarious entertainment.... The companies of the 'eighties and even the early 'nineties were composed of men ready at need to eke out their plays by musical performances and even the 'activities' of acrobats."[32]

The heyday of the Queen's men was from 1583 to 1591,[33] if indeed they had not passed their zenith by 1589 through losing their prime favourite, Richard Tarleton, the year before. He seems to have been the life and soul of the company; and besides becoming a legend in his own lifetime, he continued to be remembered long after his death. The only companies to challenge them for first place both at Court and with the public in the fifteen-eighties were the Lord Admiral's men with Edward Alleyn as their star. Nevertheless, though in decline, the Queen's men still enjoyed a considerable esteem; and in the provinces, to say nothing of Scotland, their position among dramatic companies was still high in the early fifteen-nineties.

King James was probably not displeased, if he was aware as he might well have been, by the Queen's men's involvement on the side of the bishops in the furious Martin Marprelate controversy of 1588-89. This rollicking war had begun with a number of anonymous pamphlets in a very lively style, attacking Episcopacy and advocating Presbyterianism in its stead. Various known writers, including John Lyly and Thomas Nashe, came to the bishops' defence in other pamphlets, which were, however, hardly a match in witty scurrility for the Martinists. And the Queen's company and at least one other, the Children of Paul's, pitched in with anti-Martinist business on the stage of a robust and Aristophanic kind. The authorities may have welcomed this theatrical assistance to begin with. But they soon used their influence to suppress it. It probably did not suit Elizabeth's temporising policy to countenance too far retaliation on the bishops' tormentors or the liberty taken by players and playwrights in handling matters concerning Church and State on the public stage.

An obscure remark in a pamphlet printed in October 1589 is to the effect that *Vetus Comoedia* had been "long in the country". This has been interpreted as meaning that the players who had held Martin up to scorn in the manner of the Old Comedy of the Greek theatre as written by Aristophanes had been forced by the authorities to desist, had in consequence gone on tour in the provinces, and had been away from London for an unusually long time. Had they perhaps reached Edinburgh?

One cannot say into how many groups the Queen's players divided for the long touring season begun in 1589. But one group, working the North of England, was at Lathom House, one of the Earl of Derby's mansions in Lancashire, on two days between 12th and 18th July; and at Knowsley Hall, another Derby house in Lancashire, on a day between 6th and 12th September (probably Saturday, 12th September) and on Sunday, 13th September. It was this group of the Queen's men who twice visited Carlisle; the first time between visits to Lathom House and Knowsley Hall; and the second after they had been recalled by Lord Scrope. This second visit could not have begun before 15th or 16th September at the earliest.[34]

The question, then, is: Did the Queen's men strike north from Carlisle to Edinburgh soon after they had received King James's invitation? My surmise is that they, or perhaps only some of them, did. Owing to the division of the Queen's company into at least two groups, it is not easy to trace their provincial tours in England from the scanty records in the archives of the towns visited. Certainly the company, probably in next to full strength, appeared at Court for the Christmas festivities on 26th December 1589 and for Shrovetide on 1st March 1590.[35] But there was ample time between 20th September and Christmas for the company at Carlisle to have visited Edinburgh,[36] to have made a prolonged stay there, and to have been back in London again. No doubt, in recalling them to Carlisle from "the furthest parte of Langkeshire", Lord Scrope told them why he desired their presence in Carlisle; and the company surely did not hurry back well over a hundred miles if they did not intend to carry on to Edinburgh. In fact all the likelihood is that the Queen's men were eager to accept the invitation of a King who might at no distant date reign over them.

I assume, then, that the Queen's men set out from Carlisle as soon as possible after 20th September. With all their gear, it would take them at least till the end of September before arriving, longer if they tried to pay their way by giving performances. Unfortunately there are no Scottish provincial records by which the northern trek, if it was undertaken, can be followed. Nor, it has to be admitted, is there any evidence that the company ever reached Edinburgh —or, for that matter, any that it did not.

If the English comedians did reach Edinburgh, they must have found the King and the Court in a state of tension. On 18th August 1589 a marriage by proxy of James and Princess Anne of Denmark had been transacted; and the marriage proper had been arranged for September, subject to the Princess's arrival. She set out for Scotland early in September, but was driven back by contrary winds. Several weeks thereafter passed in uncertainty and fear, until, as William Ashby wrote on 23rd October with a subacid humour to Lord Burghley, "The King's impatience for his love and lady hath so transported him in mind and body, that he is about to commit himself, Leander-like, to the waves of the ocean", in order to bring his bride back with him.[37] His decision to go himself to Scandinavia, contrary to protocol, was hastily taken; certainly after 10th October when Scots and Danes were in dispute about whether to make another attempt to tranship Anne in the late autumn of 1589 or to wait till the following spring. The King embarked on 24th October[38] in stormy weather and amid general forebodings, out of which may have sprung what Coleridge in *Dejection* calls "The grand old ballad of Sir Patrick Spence".[39] A proclamation was issued thereafter to announce the arrangements for the carrying-on of government during the King's absence.

James reached Norway in safety and his marriage to Anne was formally re-celebrated at Opslo (= Oslo) on 24th November. One of the officiating clergy was David Lindsay, who had accompanied James as his Chaplain and who figures prominently later in this Chapter. After some months of festivity, interspersed with learned discussions with Danish savants, James and his Queen reached Leith on 1st May 1590, not without further storms, which were attributed to the devilments of a great wizard-and-witch assembly held at North Berwick during the King's homeward voyage. Lindsay and Robert Bruce completed the matrimonial ceremonials by crowning Anne at Holyroodhouse on 12th May 1590.

From at least the beginning of September 1589 through all the uncertainty of that month and the next, great preparations had gone on for the reception of Anne in the Scottish Capital, though there is no positive evidence for designs of a theatrical or dramatic kind. But in his restless fidgets James may well have got the English comedians, if they were in Scotland, to help him to pass the time. The facts that there are no known records of any dramatic performances at Holyroodhouse or in and about Edinburgh and that the royal expenses for 1589 throw no light are not in themselves conclusive. In any case, if the English comedians ever were in Edinburgh in 1589, they could not have remained indefinitely. Suppose they arrived from Carlisle at the end of September or the beginning of October, when hopes for the Princess's coming any day were still high; they might conceivably have agreed to wait for anything up to a fort-night or three weeks. But with the recession of any hope for the Princess's early arrival, they would be thinking of their departure; and they would pretty certainly be on their way south, as soon after James's decision to go in person to Scandinavia was known and as soon as they could pack their traps. Whether any of them were invited or chose to stay is a completely open question.

But an entry in the municipal records may lend some slight support to the speculation that the English troupers had indeed visited Edinburgh and perhaps outstayed their welcome in the eyes of the town authorities. For on 22nd October 1589, two days before James's embarkation for Scandinavia, the Town Council in their desire to clear Edinburgh of the entertainers or nondescripts who had congregated for the pickings at the expected marriage celebrations, "statute & ordanet that na vagabunds evill steilleris [= pickpockets and the like] sturdy beggares nor idill persounis havand [= having] na maister nor honest occupatioun and that na nichtwalkeris dyssers or cairteris [= card-sharpers] na singeris of vngodlie sangs pypers fydlers commoun menstralles that hes nocht the privelege of the acts of parliament Remayne within this burght".[40]

It is not until Februry 1594 that we come on any further evidence of English actors about the Scottish Court. In that month the Lord High Treasurer paid "be [= by] co'mand of his ma^ties precept to certane Inglis c'medianis" £333·6·8 which was "the comp'oun [= composition] of the escheit of ye laird of Kilcrewch and his complices".[41] Such a reward must have been for several performances. The designation "certane Inglis c'medianis" may indicate that they were newcomers: otherwise the likelier phrase would have been simply "the English comedians". It is possible that the actors had come or been invited, as in 1589, in view of another great royal occasion, this time the birth of James's first child. Prince Henry was born on 19th February 1594. There was apparently a spectacular interlude at Stirling on 30th August in celebration of the Prince's baptism there, in which the English visitors could have performed. But that is pure surmise. The only item in extant records which seems relevant is an entry in the Lord High Treasurer's accounts for £257·16·3 paid by the King's special command and direction "for transporting of the lyoun" from Holyroodhouse to Stirling and back and for the expenses for the men and horses involved.[42]

As for the personnel of the English troupe, they could well have been members of the disintegrating company of Queen Elizabeth on an extended tour. But the only one of them to whom a name can be assigned, and that only inferentially, is Lawrence Fletcher. His antecedents before his coming to Scotland are unknown. He is not known to have been a Queen's man; but the composition of the company is very uncertain, and he could have been one of their juniors who acted only on provincial tours and who, coming to Scotland in 1589, decided to stay on or to make a return visit in 1594. As he became a favourite of King James, he must figure prominently in any account of the King's interest in the theatre.

The first actual mention of Fletcher is in a letter from Edinburgh, written on 22nd March 1595 by George Nicolson, English Ambassador at the Scottish Court, to Robert Bowes, one of Lord Burghley's secretaries. "The k. hathe hard", wrote Nicolson, "that ffletcher the player that was here is hanged for his cause. And in mirry wordes told Roger [Ashton][43] and me thereof as not belieueing it, sayenge very pleasantlie that if it were so he wold hange vs."[44]

It is obvious from this extract that Fletcher had been in Edinburgh before 1595, probably in 1594 and perhaps before that, and that he had been long enough there and performed frequently enough before the King to have become a prime favourite. The phrase "ffletcher the player that was here" implies that for the time being he was no longer in Edinburgh or even in Scotland. But James's interest extended from Fletcher present to Fletcher absent and returned to his native land. Moreover, the interest was such that someone, perhaps James's Ambassador in London, had thought it worth while to report to him news of the actor. Unfortunately we do not know what was behind the report; how it originated at all; what Fletcher had done or was alleged to have done to have deserved hanging; and how it could possibly have been "for his [i.e. James's] cause". James's informant must have given some indication that the hanging story was untrue. But it is difficult to see why, in such circumstances, he thought it worth reporting at all. If it comes to that, why did James go on to make a false report about a strolling player the subject of a pleasantry to the English Ambassador? And, still more curious, why did Nicolson think it important enough to include it in a dispatch meant for Lord Burghley's eyes, though addressed to his secretary?

There is no further evidence for the presence of English actors in Scotland till 1598. Several items from that year show that they were about; and it is clear from the first item that they had been in the country for some time, conceivably since 1594.

This first item is a letter of 15th April 1598 from George Nicolson for the information of Lord Burghley, in which he says: "It is regrated[45] to me in quiet sorte, that the Commediens of London shoulde in their play scorne the k. and people of this lande, and wished that it may be spedely amended and staied; lest the worst sort gitting vnderstandinge thereof should stir the k. and Contry to anger thereat. A matter which beinge thus honestly and quietly deliured [= delivered] vnto me by mr uddert[46] sometyme Prouost of this Towne and a very substantious honest man, I haue thought mete to commend to your Lordes good consideracioun, for present stay of suche courses."[47]

As Hamlet says, "That would be scann'd".[48] In the first place Nicolson was reporting at second hand; and it looks very much as if Uddert also was passing on a second-hand rumour and had never seen or heard the play in question. By the way, does "their play" mean one particular play or simply their playing or gagging in general? Secondly, why did Uddert think it necessary to speak "in quiet sorte"? What was there about his disclosure that required it to be whispered? Dozens or hundreds of people, including "the worst sorte" (whoever they may have been) and the King (to whom the news was certain to have been carried), must have heard or heard about whatever had been said in the theatre. The cat was well and truly out of the bag. And if Uddert wanted the thing "spedely amended and staied", why did he not go straight to the Scottish authorities, instead of dropping a word behind his hand into the ears of the

English Ambassador? It is true that the English authorities kept a jealous eye on acting companies when they were at home; and the same authorities were doubtless interested in the players' doings abroad, especially if their conduct was likely to cause international trouble. Presumably Uddert hoped that Nicolson would himself reprimand and warn the players. But there is no evidence that he did anything of the kind. If he had done so, he would have told Lord Burghley in his letter what action he had taken to rebuke the players and smooth down the ruffled feelings of the Scots. Instead, he merely commends the matter to Lord Burghley's "consideracioun". Lord Burghley, who was not at all himself an enemy of players and who "even at the end of his long life . . . had not forgotten the services of the stage to his earlier statecraft",[49] probably did nothing, in a business which even to Nicolson on the spot seemed quite trivial. But the most important thing to observe is that no visiting company of players, foreigners in a not wholly friendly land, would have wanted to insult and gone out of their way to insult their royal patron on whose support and protection they were so dependent, or wanted to mock and antagonize a nation which could so easily have retaliated.

It is all but certain that either Uddert or his informants had misconstrued whatever was in fact said at one or more performances. Persons with no sense of humour can take offence by missing a point and jumping to the conclusion that what they do not understand is *ipso facto* an insult. Persons of a literal mind with little experience of the theatre might regard any representation of national characters on the stage as offensive. Besides all this, puritanical antagonists of the drama in any shape or form would be likely to reinforce their moral-religious hostility by detecting imaginary grounds of complaint which might in their opinion have weight with the authorities.

As already noted,[50] English companies of players often included tumblers, acrobats, and the like. It may be that two scraps of 1598 information refer to the activities of such members of an English company in Scotland at the time. One was the Town Council's reward of £2, paid over on 26th May by Lord Provost Henry Nisbet, "to the Inglis man that playit with the horse in the abay yairdis".[51] The other was the exploit on 10th July of "ane man, sume callit him a juglar", who performed "sic sowple [= supple] tricks upone ane tow [= rope], q^lk [= which] wes festinit [= fastened] betwix the tope of St Geills kirk steiple and ane stair beneathe the crosse, callit Josias close heid, the lyk wes nevir sene in this countrie, as he raid doune the tow and playit sa maney pavies [= lively antics] on it".[52] Though the Presbytery of Edinburgh on the following day censured the magistrates "for suffering sic spectacles",[53] £6·13·4 was paid on 12th July from the Burgh Exchequer to the daring funambulist, whose name is given as Robert Stewart, "maister of activitie".[54] With such a surname, Stewart may in fact have been a Scot. But Queen Elizabeth's company certainly had one or more tightrope-walkers.[55]

Another 1598 record is definitely relevant to the presence of English actors in Scotland. The St. Andrews Kirk Session records, under the date of 1st October which was a Sunday, have an entry of an application on that day by "ane Jnglishman" for the "libertie of the session to mak ane publik play in this citie", which permission was refused.[56] This tantalizing glimpse is typical of the sources for a history of the early drama in Scotland. One cannot believe that this anonymous Englishman, Fletcher back again or another altogether, appeared out of the blue, tried nowhere else than in St. Andrews to display his quality, and offered to put on a play single-handed. He and his associates would never have pushed on as far as St. Andrews to make their first appearance in Scotland, even though their wanderings before or after are unrecorded. Again, James and his Queen were unlikely to be unaware of the near presence of English actors or to have let them go without a performance, though the royal accounts are clear of any related entry.

It is not unlikely that English actors were involved in an occasion later in 1598 which shows the Edinburgh clergy as puritanically opposed to yuletide merry-making in general and not least in the royal household. On 26th December, presumably as a result of the high jinks of the day before, the Edinburgh Presbytery was not slow to express its opinion and put it on record thus: "The presbyterie being informit of the greit abuse that hes bene in the kingis maiesties house, in the town of edinburgh and vther partis about the keiping of yule hes ordanit that his maiesteis ministeris speik his maiestie that ordour may be takin with his house And that the ministeris of edinburgh and that the rest of the ministeris about tak ordour with thair flockis be [= by] ressoun godis word, the actis of the kirk & lawis of the realme hes damnit [= condemned] the samin" [= same].[57]

James was not the man to take such clerical advice in good part. But what he did or said by way of a riposte is not on record. As for the actors and acrobats of whom we get earlier glimpses in 1598, they may have lingered on and joined a London company which arrived in Edinburgh in October 1599.[58] Much more can be told of this troupe than of any earlier ones, owing to the flare-up their acting caused between the King and his militant clergy.

The time of their arrival was late in the year for a London company to be on the road so far from its base. The year had been singularly free from deaths from plague in London. The company, therefore, had not been forced to a protracted tour because of any plague inhibitions. Their late arrival probably points to an intention to make a prolonged stay, which is what happened; and it may be conjectured that the company came at James's invitation to become His Majesty's players under the same kind of royal patronage as Queen Elizabeth's men enjoyed, which is also what happened.

The leader of the troupe was the already-mentioned Lawrence Fletcher,[59] with one Martin Slater or Slaughter as his second-in-command. Where Fletcher had been since 1594 does not appear, except that he must have at least visited London. My guess is that for some or most of the time he was in Scotland. Martin Slater, who is often referred to only by his Christian name, is first heard of as one of the Lord Admiral's men from 1594 to 1597; then there is a gap in his history[60] till his appearance in 1599 in Scotland. No other names of members of the troupe are known, except perhaps "Mr cobler".[61] The troupe was evidently not one of the constituted English companies. It was probably made up of fairly young actors, game for an adventure and only loosely attached, if at all, to any known company. But from the Church's alarm, it looks as if it cut quite a pretentious figure.

Having come, as I believe, at James's invitation, they naturally offered their first-fruits in October 1599 to their royal patron by acting "sundry Comedies in presence of the King",[62] perhaps in the tennis-court at Holyrood-house.[63] The performances were evidently acceptable, and, somewhat unusually and therefore significantly, the reward of £43·6·8 was "delyverit to his hienes selff to be gevin to ye Inglis c'medianis" in the same month of October.[63]

After they had acted several times before James, the English comedians obtained from him a warrant to act in public, with a precept to the Bailies of Edinburgh to provide a house for that purpose.[62] The date may have been late in October, but was probably early in November. In November, too, the King directed that £40 be given through Sir George Elphinstone to the players "to by [= buy] tymber for the preparatioun of ane hous to thair pastyme".[64] Apparently the players were intending to make substantial alterations with a view to a long future. And they must have bestirred themselves; for early in November[65] "they gave warning be [= by] trumpets and drums, through the streets of Edinburgh, to all that pleased to come to Blackfriars Wynd to see the acting of their Comedies".[66]

This narrow side-street, running along the line of the present, much wider Blackfriars Street between the High Street and the Cowgate, was the most important of all the ancient wynds of Edinburgh. Moreover, it had long been and long continued to be one of its most aristocratic districts. It contained some of the finest town-mansions, including those of Cardinal James Beaton and the Regent Morton, and the princely palace of the Sinclairs. Several of the buildings contained large rooms, capable of serving as chapels or meeting-houses at a somewhat later date; but there is no telling which of them was Edinburgh's first theatre. It is an odd coincidence that both Edinburgh's first theatre and one of the first three to be established in London were on land once belonging to the Dominicans. The point to notice, however, is that Fletcher and his company were assigned, or were perhaps able to choose, a site not hole-and-corner in a slum.

The establishment of the first regular theatre in Scotland had much the same effect there as had the establishment of the first three permanent theatres[67] in London in 1576. That is to say, puritanical theatrophobes joined in protests. But whereas the protesters in England were a minority with little influence, those in Scotland constituted a formidable clerical opposition. In early November 1599, probably Wednesday, 7th November or even the preceding Monday or Tuesday, "The Ministers of Edinburgh, fearing the profanity that was to ensue, specially the profanation of the Sabbath day, convocated their four Sessions of the Kirk. An act was made be [= by] common consent, that none should resort to these profane Comedies, for eschewing offence of God, and for evil example to others; and an ordinance was made, that every Minister should intimat this act in their own several pulpits. They [i.e. the English comedians] had indeed committed several abuses, specially upon the Sabbath at night before" (that is, Sunday, 4th November).[66]

It is true that the Church could and did, in Kirk Sessions, Presbyteries, Synods, and General Assemblies, decide on moral regulations meant to be binding on clergy and laity alike and to be enforced under the accepted code of Discipline. In such matters the Church legislated as for the whole population without regard to minorities, Catholic or merely indifferent; and the scope of moral regulation was taken to be wide indeed, if also ill-defined.

But in this instance the King himself decided that the Presbytery of Edinburgh had trespassed beyond its moral orbit into the sphere of the civil authority. Or, to put it on a more personal level, the King had been insulted by the Edinburgh ministers through their attack on the English actors whom he had taken under his wing. "The King", therefore ,"taketh the act in ill part, as if made purposely to cross his warrant and caused summon the Ministers and four Sessions *super inquirendis* [= concerning matters requiring investigation] before the Secret Counsell."[66]

To continue the nearly-contemporary narrative: "They [*i.e.* the Edinburgh Presbytery] sent doun some in Commission to the King [on Thursday, 8th November], and desired the matter might be tryed privatly, and offered, if they had offended, to repair the offence at his own sight; and alledged, they had the warrant of the Synod presently sitting in the Town."[66]

This is characteristic of the deferential stubbornness of the clergy, offering in one breath "to repair the offence" to the King's satisfaction, and in the next claiming the authority and support of the Synod.[68] But James probably surmised that the Presbytery was divided into a timid and temporising majority and a strong-minded minority not disinclined for a fight. Such was in fact the case; and the minority was spearheaded by Robert Bruce. The clergy, it will be noticed, wanted, for face-saving reasons no doubt, to reach a private settlement with the King. But, we are told, "The King would have the matter to come in publick",[66] declining to be satisfied with an apology from a delegation of the offenders tendered only in the presence of his Privy Council, after the whole body of the Presbytery had defied him so openly in their specially convened meeting and by their ordinance intimated to all their congregations from their several pulpits.

Accordingly, when the delegation appointed by the Presbytery arrived at Holyroodhouse, none were called into the presence of the King and his Privy Council but Peter Hewat, the undistinguished minister of Greyfriars parish, and Henry Nisbet, an able layman who had held many offices including the Lord Provostship and who because of his skill as a negotiator had been repeatedly employed on trade missions for the City in France and Flanders. "After they were heard, the sentence was given out against all the rest unheard."[69]

It was in the following uncompromising terms: "The Kingis Majestie and Lordis of his Secreit Counsall considering the lait contempt and indignitie done to his Hienes be [= by] the foure Sessionis of the burgh of Edinburgh, in taking upoun thame be [= by] ane publict act to contramand the warrand and libertie grantit be [= by] his Hienes to certane commedianis to play within the said burgh, and in ordaning thair ministeris publictlie to discharge thair flokis to repair [= charge their flocks not to repair] to the saidis commedeis, thay haveing nawayis [= in no wise] acquentit his Majestie of befoir [= before-hand] with ony lawfull caus or ground moving thame thairunto, nor na utherwayis acknawlegeing [= informing] his Hienes, as thay aucht and sould have done afoir [= before] thay had sa avowedlie opponit [= opposed] thameselffis to his Majesteis warrand and directioun foirsaid,—Thairfoir his Majestie and the saidis Lordis ordanis ane officiar of armes to pas to the mercat croce of Edinburgh and thair, be [= by] oppin proclamatioun in his Hienes name and authoritie, to command and charge the haill personis of the saidis foure Sessionis, becaus thay ar ane multitude,[70] to convene thameselffis in thair accustomat place of convening within thrie houris nixt eftir the said charge, and thair be [= by] ane speciall act to cas [= quash], annull, and discharge the uther act forsaid, and with that to gif [= give] ane speciall ordinance and directioun to thair haill ministeris that thay, eftir thair sermonis upoun the nixt Sonday, publischlie admonische thair awne [= own] flockis to reverence and obey his Majestie, and to declair to thame that thay will not restreane nor censure ony of thair flokis that sall repair to the saidis commedeis and playis, considering his Majestie is not of purpois or intentioun to awthorize, allow, or command onything quhilk [= which] is prophane or may cary ony offence or sclander with it; and to charge thame heirto, under the pane of rebellioun and putting of thame to the horne;[71] and to charge the saidis ministeris that thay, eftir thair saidis sermonis, conforme thameselffis to the directioun and ordinance to be sett doun be [= by] the saidis Sessionis heiranent [= in accordance there-with] under the said pane of rebellioun, and, giff [= if] ony of the saidis personis dissobayis, to denounce the saidis dissobeyaris rebellis."[72]

In this declaration and sentence one hears the very voice of King James himself dictating to the Clericus Registri and determined to assert his royal authority more decisively than he had ever done before over his stiff-necked and obstructive clergy, as part of his general policy in the relation of Church and State. He had, with remarkable persistence and success, built up the power of the Crown to such a height as it had never reached in Scotland before; and, as an absolutist whose strength was of but recent growth, he could let no challenge to it pass.

But, desirous as he was of ruling in the strong Tudor fashion and checking his clerical malcontents, he had also a taste for wrangling. Accordingly, when the delegation "craved to be heard", the King suffered himself to be "moved" by the Privy Council, after a show of unwillingness.[73]

John Hall, one of the St. Giles' ministers, was appointed by the delegation to be their mouthpiece, perhaps because he was at the time the Moderator of the Edinburgh Presbytery. But he did not get very far: " 'Wee are summoned, Sir,' said Mr. John, 'and craue to understand, to what end.' 'Its true,' said the King, 'ye ar summoned, and I have decerned [= given judgement] already.' Mr. John made no reply."[73] He was evidently overawed and at a loss for a come-back in such a foreclosed argument.

However, a much more awkward clerical advocate was ready to put on a bolder face before the King and the Privy Council. This was one of John Hall's colleagues at St. Giles', Robert Bruce, who was to be James's most difficult

problem in the aftermath of the Gowrie Conspiracy. Bruce was the most powerful preacher of his day and a man of commanding and impressive appearance,
who exercised an influence "almost without parallel in the history of the Scottish
Church".[74] James had recognized his administrative ability by appointing him
in October 1589 to be an extraordinary Privy Councillor during the royal
absence in Scandinavia in 1589-90, and had warmly thanked Bruce for his
services. The King's admiration was perhaps tinged with a certain apprehension in
consequence of Bruce's stand against James's prelatical tendencies in 1596, which
had led to Bruce being exiled for a time from Edinburgh and his charge there.

    When John Hall kept his peace, it was Bruce who took up the debate.
" 'If it might stand with your pleasure,' he said, 'wee wold know, wherefore
this hard sentence is past against us'."[73] To this disingenuous opening gambit,
the King brusquely replied: " 'For contraveening of my warrant' ";[73] that is to
say, the warrant to the players to act in public and the related precept to the
Bailies to provide appropriate accommodation. " 'We haue fulfilled your warrant,' said Mr. Robert, 'for your warrant craved no more but an house to them,
which they haue gotten'."[73] It is difficult to see how the Presbytery could be
said to have "fulfilled the warrant" since it was not addressed to the Presbytery
and the clergy had done what they could to spoil the whole venture. Nor had
they had anything to do with the provision of "an house". After the preliminary sparring, James went to the heart of the matter by asking more
pointedly: " 'To what end, I pray you, sought I an house . . . but only that
the people might resort to their Comedies?' "[73] Bruce, then, with deliberate
obtuseness, returned to the terms of the warrant. "Your warrant bears not that
end", he said, and added the more provocative remark: "and we have good
reason to stay them from their playes evin be [= by] your own acts of Parliament".[73] The King's retort was the angry: "Ye are not the interpreters of my
lawes"; which was evidently an interjection, for Bruce carried on as if he had
not heard: "And, farther, the warrant was intimat but to one or two".[73]
Presumably by "one or two" he meant the Edinburgh Bailies, though this
does not square with his contention that the Presbytery had "fulfilled the
warrant". Perhaps, too, he was implying that an intimation to "one or two"
was very different from a general proclamation. So Bruce in conclusion "therefore desired the King to retract the sentence".[73] The King, according to one
authority, "wold answer nothing";[73] and, according to another, would "alter"
nothing.[75] " 'At the least then,' said Mr. Robert, 'let the paine strike upon us,
and exeem [= exempt] our people' "[73]—a rather rhetorical plea, for James
could not have punished the laity even if he had wanted to. When James "bade
him make away", Bruce "in departing . . . turned and said, 'Sir, please you,
nixt the regard wee owe to God, wee had a reverent respect to your Majesties
royal person, and person of your Queen; for wee heard, that the Comedians,
in their playes, checked your royal person with secret and indirect taunts and
checks; and there is not a man of honour in England wold give such fellows so
much as their countenance' ".[76] On that note the clerical delegation withdrew.

    Bruce's last speech was an attempt to shift his ground by making out that
the Presbytery had really been actuated by regard for the royal dignity which

the comedians had allegedly disparaged. The allusion to conditions in England was neither well-founded nor tactful. Though such terms as "rogues and vaga-bonds" were sometimes still thrown in England at strolling players and master-less entertainers of various sorts, the regularly-constituted companies of actors there were indeed countenanced by men of honour, the Earl of Leicester, the Earl of Warwick, the Lord Admiral, the Lord Chamberlain, and many others, not to mention Queen Elizabeth. As for the tactlessness of Bruce's last sentence, it might more properly be described as the last word of an angry man who throws up his brief with an exasperated insult by implication—no man of honour in England countenanced players and so a countenancer of such persons in Scotland was no man of honour.

James was certainly a man to be touchy about his royal dignity. But he must have known that there was little substance in Bruce's allegation of dis-paragement by the players; that Bruce was not speaking from anything but second- or third-hand evidence, since he himself would never have darkened the door of a theatre; and that he was simply raking up, eighteen months later, whatever was behind the story told by Nicol Uddert to George Nicolson in April 1598.

In accordance with the royal decree of 8th November 1599, the four Sessions obeyed the summons proclaimed from the Market Cross by the officer-at-arms on 9th November and convened within three hours. The Sessions, which consisted of both ministerial and lay members, referred the matter to the clergy for their advice. This was to the effect that counsel's opinion should be taken; which may indicate that the extremists among the ministers thought that they still had a fighting chance. The two advocates consulted, however, William Ogilvie and John Sharp, recommended the rescinding of the offending resolution of the Sessions, for the rather odd reason that "the King's charge did not allow slanderous and undecent Comedies".[77] When the clergy, who had retired during the hearing of counsel, were called back so that a debate could be held and a vote taken, Bruce was the first to be asked to speak. He did so with a kind of wry illogicality: "His Majestie is not minded to allow any slanderous and offensive Comedies; but so it is, that their Comedies are slanderous and offensive: Therefore the King in effect ratifieth our acts".[77] The fact is, of course, that Bruce would have regarded any of the plays as offensive and used the term "slanderous" as meaning not so much "maliciously defamatory of individuals or institutions" as "presenting the indecorous and unseemly". "The rest of the Ministers", we are told, "voted after the same manner" as Bruce against the rescinding of their pronouncement.[78] The elders or lay members of the Sessions, on the other hand, voted the other way, "partly for fear of their estates", as the clerically-biased *Booke of the Universall Kirk of Scotland* puts it, "partly upon information of the Advocates". This first motion, then, having been carried by the votes of the lay majority, the more important second motion was put to the meeting: "Whether the Ministers should intimat the rescinding of the act?" The majority, probably again composed in the main of laity, voted in the affirmative. But "The Ministers assured them, they would not".[77]

The mere rescinding of the resolution in private, without its public annulment, could scarcely be expected to satisfy James. Accordingly a lay deputation, led by Henry Nisbet, undertook "to purchase [= obtain by negotiation] an exemption to the Ministers"—[77] in short, to get them let down lightly without having to eat their words *coram populo*.

Apparently by this time James's anger was evaporating and he was prepared to let the matter blow over with little more than a token compliance, if even so much as that. The deputation of laymen returned on Friday, 9th November, from Holyroodhouse "with this answer, That his Majestie was content that the matter sould be past over lightly; but he would have some mention made of the annulling of the act",[77] that is to say, from the pulpits of Edinburgh on the following Sunday. But this, as before, the ministers refused to do. Whereupon the lay brethren again waited on the King and "returned with this answer, Let them neither speak good nor evil in that matter, but leave it as dead".[79] It is hard to believe that James did not say a good deal more than this to the deputation. But it was probably in an affable and jocose vein, at the expense of the absent clergy and not without raising the smiles of the present laity.

The clergy, however, were not themselves in so gracious a mood. On Saturday, 10th November, they "conveened apart to consult" on their action, in the absence of the laity; and the unbending Bruce said: "It behoved them either to justify the thing they had done or else they could not goe to a pulpit". He got some support; but others said: "Leave it to God to doe as God sall direct their hearts".[79] Thus inconclusively in respect of joint action the meeting concluded. On Sunday, 11th November, Bruce and his supporters "justified [their action] . . . in some smal measure, and yet were not quarrelled".[80]

But at the meeting of the Privy Council on the preceding Saturday, the King and his Councillors had agreed on an act and its public proclamation at the Market Cross of Edinburgh; "quhairthrow [= in consequence of which let] nane pretend ignorance of the same". Like the act of Council of 8th November, this bears all the marks of royal dictation. It rehearses causes and effects as seen from the palace angle, rather than as fully warranted by the facts: [1] That the King had issued a warrant permitting English players to act in Edinburgh; [2] that "some sinister and wrangous reporte" had been made to the Sessions by "certane malicious and restles bodyis quha [= who], upoun everie licht occasioun, misconstrowes his Majesteis haill doingis and misinterpreitis his Hienes gude intentionis quhatsumevir" (= whatever they be); [3] that the Sessions were moved "verie raschely and unadvisitlie" to countermand the royal warrant, to order the ministers to publish this countermanding, and to threaten the Kirk's censures against the disobedient; [4] that the King was given no previous intimation of "ony lawfull ground or caus" for such a move; [5] that the ministers were now better advised of their "errour and oversicht"; [6] that all the ministers had convened to discuss the matter and were "willing nawise [= in no way] to be contentious with his Majestie, bot in all reverence and humilitie to obay his Hienes as becumis gude and obedient subjectis, in respect of the pruif quhilk [= proof which] thay have evir had of his Majestie, that his Hienes hes not commandit nor allowit ony thing careying with it ony offence or sclander"; [7] that, "eftir the dew acknawlegeing of thair formar errour, [and] rasche and unadvised proceidingis", the Sessions have now quashed and repealed their former act and the conformable admonitions to the congregations; and [8] that therefore the players may freely enjoy the privileges of the royal warrant, and the lieges in Edinburgh or anywhere else may attend performances "without ony pane, skaith, censureing, reproche or sclander" from either ministers or magistrates.[81]

On Monday, 12th November 1599, George Nicolson, the English Ambassador, dispatched a copy of the proclamation to Sir Robert Cecil, and devoted most of his covering letter to the whole episode. He states something difficult to believe, namely that the Sessions in taking their decision of 7th November[82] had not known of the existence of the King's warrant to the players. But we can accept his report of the gist of the ministers' sermons. They exhorted their flocks, he said, "to forbeare and not to come to or haunt prophane games sportes or playes now when they aught rather to make their recourse to god by praier and fasting to prevent the displeasure of God hanging over them and threatening them by the sword now by reason of cruell slaughters among them, by the late plagues here and the great famyne of late and appearance of it in no lesse measure this yeare". And Nicolson adds this interesting passage: "The bellowesbloweres [= spreaders of rumours] will and do say they [i.e. the English comedians] are sent in by vs to suow [= sow] contencion betwene the k. and kirke. Thus this matter standes over, with an increase of dislike betwene the parties k. and kirke."[83]

Another Englishman, Sir John Carey (later Lord Hunsdon), who was Deputy Warden of the English Eastern Marches and Marshal of Berwick, likewise reported the episode briefly to Cecil on 23rd November 1599 and prophesied that "muche trubeles it had like to wraighte" [= work].[84]

The clergy of Bruce's intransigent party may have derived some encouragement and renewed boldness from the comparative mildness of the King. They still dominated the clerical scene; and when the Presbytery of Edinburgh, which was a larger body than the four Sessions, met on Tuesday, 13th November, the day after the proclamation was read, the members "all in ane voce [= voice] findis thir playis made be [= acted by] the inglischmen come in the countrej unlauchtfull and sclanderouss".[85] This was a reassertion, no doubt inspired by Bruce, of charges which James had rebutted in their exchange on 8th November. As, however, the Presbytery's unanimity resulted in no more than a declaratory minute of a private meeting of ministers and representative elders, James chose to be officially unaware of it. At least there is no record in the Register of the Privy Council or elsewhere of his troubling to correct or rebuke the Presbytery.

This inaction and also his forbearance earlier may have been in part his politic preparation for a conference to be held at Holyroodhouse from 17th to 19th November, when he was to meet the leading clergy, summoned by his missives, and discuss with them, in an informal and preliminary way, grave questions of ecclesiastical polity that were to come before a General Assembly of the Church in the near future. The issue was, of course, the grand one of

Prelacy versus Presbytery. It will be sufficient for this Chapter merely to quote this compact summary of the proceedings by David Masson: "The most resolute defender of the strict Presbyterian theory . . . was Andrew Melville; the King himself took a leading part, and managed the debate on the other side. On the whole, though there was a disposition to acquiesce with the King as much as possible, the result was far from satisfactory to him; and, when he dismissed the conference, it was with an expression to that effect, and an intimation that he hoped the coming General Assembly would be more tractable."[86]

More relevant to this Chapter is the fact that the Presbytery of Edinburgh continued to worry and gnaw over their old bone of contention, the theatre, the players, and their comedies. Instead of letting bygones be bygones, as James appeared to want after having secured his point and won his victory, the Presbytery reverted to the "Inglisch playeris" on 27th November 1599 and ordained "thair brether *Maister* patrik galloway Johnn brand and the moderatour To ga to the kingis maiestie and to ressone with his maiestie That the Inglische players may be dischargit" and to report the King's answer on 4th December.[87] What the Presbytery expected to get from further reasoning with the King other than a second No is not very apparent; and a second No is in effect exactly what the deputation got and reported back to the Presbytery on the day specified: His Majesty would cause the comedians' plays to be examined and "gif [= if] ony fault wer in thame his maiestie suld causs reform thame".[87]

In spite of, or because of, the protests and arguments of clerical disputants, James honoured the English comedians by attending performances in November or December 1599, to judge from the handsome reward to the company of £333·6·8 paid by the Lord High Treasurer in December.[88] It may be that James ordered a specially generous sum to be paid in view of the company's losses through the clerical ban.

It is perhaps worth remarking that up to this point the company is always referred to, even in the Lord High Treasurer's accounts as "the English comedians": they are never called "the King's players".

What looks like the last shot in the campaign of 1599 was fired by the Presbytery, when on 18th December it commissioned two of its clergy "to ga to the kingis maiestie and to crawe [= crave] that yoolkeiping may be stayit".[89] The Presbytery had lodged an objection to the royal yule the year before, but on 26th December 1598, the day after the height of the offending.[89] But in 1599 the Presbytery was beforehand with its deprecation; and almost certainly the reason was the fear that the merry-making would be the more "slanderous and offensive" because the English comedians would be called on to contribute. Unfortunately, however, there is no record of their participating.

From the end of 1599 no more is heard of English actors either in Edinburgh or elsewhere in Scotland until the late summer and autumn of 1601. It is possible and even likely that, during the twenty months from which no record of them has survived, Fletcher's men remained in Scotland and helped to support themselves by occasional provincial tours from their base in Blackfriars Wynd. There may, of course, have been some changes in the personnel and some going and coming of members between Scotland and London. But Fletcher himself and Martin Slater do not figure during the period in question as attached to any company operating anywhere in England. As a further slight indication of the continuing existence of Fletcher's men in Scotland, I would note that the references to them in the summer and autumn of 1601 begin to speak of the company as "the kingis or his maiesties servandis" and of Fletcher himself as "comediane serviture to his maiestie".

But before coming to the 1601 references to the players, another of James's campaigns with his clergy must be reviewed; for, though it was not ostensibly about players and playing, nevertheless in it the clergy, who had been worsted by the King in 1599 on the theatrical issue, were to a not inconsiderable degree actuated in the autumn of 1600 by a desire to get their own back by an apparently high-minded resistance to him on quite a different issue.

In Chapter 6 on *The Sequels of the Gowrie Conspiracy* I mentioned, only in passing, one particular consequence which King James had done not a little to provoke, both by his measures immediately after the Conspiracy and by his attitude to the Church practically ever since he had ruled as well as reigned. This sequel was the reaction of a clerical party, led by the redoubtable Robert Bruce, to the King's mandates for sermons and national thanksgivings on the score of his miraculous escape from the machinations of traitors.

As we have already seen, it was by no means the first confrontation of the King and his clerical opponents. There had been many brushes between them as results of various differences of opinion, in addition to the theatrical issue. But behind them all and activating them all was the much larger issue of Erastian Episcopacy on the one hand and Calvinistic Presbyterianism on the other. James was convinced that Monarchy and Episcopacy were inseparable. "No Bishop, no King" was for him the condensed enunciation of a constitutional ideal, if as yet not a constitutional fact: he himself to be fully sovereign, like his Sister of England who was the recognized Head of its Church, must determine the affairs of the Scottish Church with compliant bishops to help him. He had made it abundantly clear where his sympathies lay, and was making slow but persistent progress, not without set-backs, towards the establishment of a bench of Erastian bishops, even though, for a time at least, he had to compound for the lesser title of commissioners.

The Presbyterian leaders, with Edinburgh itself as their anti-prelatical stronghold, made equally clear where they stood, and also where in their opinion the King himself stood in matters ecclesiastical. Their unqualified conviction was completely in line with what Andrew Melville, the most authoritative and influential figure in the Scottish Church, bluntly said to James at Falkland in September 1596. "Telling James that he was 'but God's sillie [= weak, frail] vassal', he seized him by the sleeve and added: 'Sir, as diverse tymes before, so now again I must tell you, there are two Kings and two Kingdomes in Scotland; there is Christ Jesus and His Kingdome the Kirk, whose subject King James the sixth is, and of whose Kingdome not a King, nor a head, nor a Lord, but a member'."[90]

In the wrangles with the clerical opposition especially from the critical

L

year 1596 when, as is noted below, Bruce and others were banished for a time from Edinburgh, the advantage may be said to have lain on the King's side. But it was an advantage that he could not afford to lose or weaken. That is why he stood firm at every juncture; as, for example, in 1599 on the theatrical issue, even though it had no very weighty bearing on the major issue of the government of the Church. I may mention another earlier instance of James's firmness in dealing with a clerical opponent, because it does bear on the major issue. In 1596 David Black, Minister of St. Andrews, used in his sermons "certain unreverent, reproachfull and infamous speeches",[91] to which James, growing every day surer of his power and authority, took strong exception. He determined to bring Black to account and decide by a test-case the question of whether a minister was subject to the civil jurisdiction for what he said in the pulpit. Black was summoned before the King and the Privy Council on 18th November, but, on the advice of a ministerial committee appointed to deal with the situation and others like it, declined to recognize a lay jurisdiction in matters spiritual. Black repeated his refusal on 30th November and on 2nd December was found guilty of making objectionable statements from the pulpit, the penalty therefor being referred to the King's will and pleasure. This was given positive expression in an act of Privy Council on 9th December, which dissolved the standing committee of ministers and ordered the departure of sixteen of their leaders from Edinburgh, including Bruce, and of Black himself, who was held in temporary ward, beyond the Firth of Forth. He was also extruded from his charge at St. Andrews.

It was bad enough for the clergy opposed to the King to be punished on the score of what they themselves might choose to preach. But it was still more humiliating for them to have to preach what the King might be pleased to dictate to them. That, as we shall see, was the issue which emerged from James's immediate course of action after the Gowrie Conspiracy.

As far as one can judge, there was a general and spontaneous joy at the King's delivery. If James had taken the ovations he received on his ride back from Perth to Falkland on 5th August 1600 as an earnest of what the rest of the country would likewise offer him, without any dragooning, it would have been better for his peace of mind and for the amelioration of relations between himself and the Church. The clergy, even those who were the most opposed to his general policy for the Church, would probably have readily enough joined in with their flocks in thanksgivings and services and also, discreetly as would become their grave office, in the more secular rejoicing.

But James was not content to let things happen in this agreeable way. He was of course glad for purely personal reasons that he had escaped with his life, as anyone else who was not a King would have been. But he was a King, an anointed King, with very exalted views of "The Right Divine of Kings to govern wrong".[92] The wish to have his miraculous delivery celebrated in a truly signal way was in accordance with these exalted views of sovereignty. James was quickly off the mark along the three lines mentioned in Chapter 6.[93] In fact he may be said to have initiated each on the very day of his ordeal. It almost looks as if he had anticipated trouble, not from the laity, but from some of the clergy, and wanted to forestall it. However, the measures he took to put across his *ex parte* account to the clergy and to compel them, including the recalcitrant, by decree to disseminate the official version of the affair from their pulpits were hasty, ill-considered, and above all over-anxious.

I have already mentioned the general Proclamation which the Privy Council from Holyroodhouse published on 6th August on instructions received from the King, and also its implementation.[94] But James sent additional instructions which concerned the Edinburgh ministers in particular. They appear in the Register of the Privy Council, meeting under the King himself on 12th August, as a preamble to an "Act, aganis the Ministeris of Edinburgh".[95] The preamble, after flourishes about the horrible treason and the happy delivery, relates how the King, immediately on his return to Falkland late on 5th August, wrote to acquaint the Privy Council at Holyroodhouse "and desyrit thame to command the Ministers of Edinburgh to haue convenit thair seuerall flokis in thair awin [= own] kirkis; and thair, publictlie to haue intimat to the people the said Treasoun, and to haue gevin thankis to God for the said deliuerie of his Maiesteis noble persone". Accordingly on 6th August the Privy Council had summoned before them these four Edinburgh ministers: Robert Bruce, James Balfour, William Watson, and John Hall. The Councillors "at lenth oppynnit [= opened] vp vnto thame the haill forme, maner and circumstanceis of the said Treassoun, quhilk [= which] wes alsua [= also] affermit in thair presence be [= by] a honnest and famous gentilman [probably Sir Thomas Erskine] quha [= who] wes present, and a ey witnes at Perth with his Maiestie". As if this was not enough, the Privy Councillors "for thair farther satisfactioun" produced and displayed to the four ministers the King's "awin [= own] Missiue and write in this matter; and thairfoir, according to his heynes directioun, haueing instantlie delt and travellit [= treated] with the saidis Ministeris, and haueing commandit thame to haue repairit to thair pulpettis and kirkis, and to haue certifiet the people of the said Tressoun, and to haue thankit God for the said happie deliuerie; the saidis Ministeris, maist vndewtifullie untrusting his Maiestie and the vndoubtit treuth of this horrible Treasoun, refuisit to obey his heynes and the saidis Lordis".[96]

This preamble to the act of Council was drawn up on 12th August, when the King himself presided and set the tone. What the Lords of the Privy Council had actually said to the four ministers in attendance on 6th August may well have been less domineering. Nevertheless it was in accordance with the King's instructions. A plain and unemphatic request to the ministers would have been a wiser move. It may be, as I have already hinted, that James actually anticipated the ministers' obstinacy and tried to force their compliance. Or it may be that they had a prearrangement to take advantage of any promising opportunity for retaliating to the humiliations they had suffered at his hands since 1596, especially their defeat over the players and their theatre in 1599. But whatever were the motives on either side, James's over-emphatic declarations inevitably suggested to his clerical opponents that his Majesty "protested too much".[97] And from their "undutiful" distrust of the King and his story arose their declining to obey his behests in the way of thanksgivings and sermons.

But disingenuous as were their protestations of conscientious difficulties in accepting and obeying, there was genuine regret among the clerical leaders at Gowrie's tragic and untimely end. One of their weaknesses in relation to James had been, in addition to divisions in the clerical ranks, the fact that there was not a single nobleman of ability and authority, except the young Earl, to give a lay lead and the seal and recommendation of a great name to the Presbyterian cause. It is true that as a boy of about sixteen he had joined the Catholic lords who were defeated in 1593; but he was pardoned in view of his youth and probably as having been drawn into the rebellion by the influence of others, especially the Earl of Atholl. The King's partiality to Gowrie personally may also have told in his favour. By the time of Gowrie's return to Scotland from his foreign travels and studies in May 1600 at the age of about twenty-three, his aberrations in a Catholic direction were forgotten; and the eyes of sturdy Presbyterians were turned towards him as a young man of promise and high rank and as a lay champion for the future, though still on the young side for the time being. He had a handsome person and a fine presence; his bearing and manners were dignified and stately; and he had a reputation for learning and a predilection for solitude and meditation. He had made a deep impression on no less renowned a Calvinist than Theodore Beza,[98] and on his arrival in London, where he was graciously received by Queen Elizabeth, he was described by one Hudson as "one of the best accomplished of his age of that nation, both for learning, travel, and good qualities".[99] The image of a studious young man of a decorous and reserved type is more borne out than otherwise by the contempt of the notorious Patrick, Master of Grey,[100] who had met Gowrie in Italy and who dismissed him as "rather fashioned like a pedant than a cavalier".[99] As touching a tribute as any came from William Cowper, Minister of Perth, who had known Gowrie for years and who at first was unable to believe that he had been guilty of treason; when ultimately convinced, he declared: "quhat [= what] greif then it wrought in me my owne conscience beareth me record: the lose [= loss] of ane earthlie creatur went never so neir my heart".[99]

There was one minister in the Edinburgh neighbourhood on whom James could rely. He was David Lindsay, Minister of South Leith, a humane and moderate man who had been prominent both in Church and in State affairs and who was altogether acceptable in Court circles. As was said earlier, he acted as James's Chaplain during the 1589-90 excursion to bring Princess Anne to Scotland from Scandinavia. It was Lindsay who had been called by the first proclamation after the Gowrie Conspiracy, that of 6th August 1600, to preach in Edinburgh and to lead the people in thanksgiving. Apparently he had gone to Falkland within a day or two thereafter, no doubt summoned by the King for consultation on the report of his brethren's non-compliance with the royal will. He then returned to Edinburgh to reassure the ministers of the truth of the official version of the Gowrie Conspiracy and to try to persuade them to a dutiful obedience. He failed to move them and went ahead on his own, preaching again on the same lines as on 6th August and preparing for the King's return to Edinburgh on 11th August, when he delivered in his own church in Leith the first of the two sermons James heard that day.[101]

By that time, if not before, James had decided on what strong measures to take to bring his disobedient clergy to book. They were embodied in the "Act, aganis the Ministeris of Edinburgh", the preamble to which has been already discussed. The act proper states that five[102] Edinburgh ministers were summoned before the King and Council, Robert Bruce, James Balfour, William Watson, John Hall, and Walter Balcanquall, of whom the last-named had on account of illness been absent from the Council meeting on 6th August. The King and Council "hard thair pretendit excuisses" and found "thame still constant in thair distrust and doubt, . . . yit to assuir and certifie the people . . . nochtwithstanding the constant and trew reporte and declaratioun quhilk thay haue hard",[103] along with the testimony of noblemen who had been at Perth with the King and the assurances of the Privy Councillors and the royal Chaplain, Patrick Galloway. Accordingly the King and Council "Findis, decernis and declairis" that the five ministers "hes maist vndeutifullie behauit thame selffis . . . and that they ar not worthie to be sufferit to speik or preiche publictlie to his heynes peopill, at ony tyme heirefter . . . in ony pairt of this realme . . . vnder the pane of deid: And forder, Ordanis thame to remove and depairt furth of the burgh of Edinburgh, within fourty-aucht houris eftir the dait heirof; and onnawyse [= in no wise] to resorte or repair, in ony pairt, within the space of ten myllis to the said burgh . . . vndir the said pane of deid. And Ordanis intimatioun to be made heirof, be [= by] oppin Proclamatioun at the mercat croce of Edinburgh; quhairthrow [= in consequence of which let] nane pretend ignorance of the same".[103]

On the following day, 13th August, the King and Council went on to a kind of corollary to the act by issuing a charge to those Edinburgh ministers who had not been removed from office and to all the deacons and elders of the city "that they keip thair ordinar tymes of meiting in thair said Sessions, &c. and gif [= if] thay failyie [= fail to do so], or do in the contrair, that incontinent thairefter the said Herauld, macer or officer denunce them rebellis".[103] On the same day the King and Council agreed on an act for filling the Edinburgh charges.[103]

Having got rid of the disobliging or disobedient clergy, James wanted to recall the rest to the duty of loyal thanksgiving. This was done by an act of Council promulgated on 21st August at Falkland. It called for a solemn thanksgiving for his Majesty's delivery in all the churches of the realm on the last Tuesday of September and the following Sunday.[103] The references to "aduyse" from the Commissioners of the General Assembly were to indicate that the Church as a whole, apart from the few dissidents, accepted the official version of the Gowrie Conspiracy and fell in with the royal wishes about national thanksgivings and celebrations.

On 24th August James followed up the act by a letter from Stirling to be delivered by David Lindsay to the Edinburgh ministers who were still in their charges. It added to the method of celebrating the King's "happy deliverie upon a Twisday" the appointment, as advised by the dutiful General Assembly, "that every Twisday heerafter sall be a day of ordinar preaching", presumably with weekly recalls of the Conspiracy and the delivery from it, "within every burgh within the boundis of the Synods".[104]

The letter contained other matter relevant to James's war with Bruce and his party. The King with the Privy Council's advice had resolved that the displaced ministers of Edinburgh "sall never be restored agane . . . since, in that case, We dread noe lesse than the hazard of our life and perrelling of our state". Other persons were to be nominated to the vacant charges—declared vacant, said the letter, on the advice of the Commissioners of the General Assembly. With still more of their advice, James had appointed a meeting of the Commissioners for 2nd October to deliberate on filling the Edinburgh vacancies and to consult on such other matters "as sall be thocht good to be proponned in name of the Kirk, for the weall of our and their estate" at the Parliament to open on 1st November. Two of the "wisest and best affected" of the Edinburgh ministers were to attend on 2nd October, having been "instructed sufficiently to give ther advice and concurrance with the said Commissioneris in the premisses"[104]—which might be translated into the modern idiom of "sign on the dotted line".

But before the October meeting could take place, James and the Privy Council issued from Glasgow on 31st August a charge against the deposed ministers, because "his Maiestie is credebelie informed, the saidis personis, not onlie still continewis in thair infidelitie and blindnes, maliciouslie and wilfullie refuising to acknawleg the certane treuth of this mater; bot, to his Maiesteis forder contempt, they hant [= haunt] and resorte in all pairtis of this cuntrie, dispersing mony vntrew bruitis [= reports] and rumouris aganis his hienes, practising be [= by] all meanis to foster and interteny [= maintain] his Maiesteis subiectis in the lyk errour and blindnes with thame selffis, and to lay vpoun his Maiestie, the burding of [= responsibility for] that, quhilk [= which] maist traiterouslie was deuysit and intendit aganis his hienes awin [= own] persoun".[105] Wherefore the offending clergy were ordered to appear before the King and Council at Stirling or wherever else the King might be, as follows: Watson on 9th September; Balcanquall and Hall on 10th September; and Bruce and Balfour on 11th September; "to vnderly sic forder punischment, as his Maiestie and lordis of his hienes Counsell sall inioyne vnto them; vnder the pane of rebellioun".[105]

The clerical opposition, however, was crumbling. On 10th September Watson, Balcanquall, and Hall appeared before the King and Council at Stirling. They freely declared that they were now fully persuaded of the truth of the official version of the Gowrie Conspiracy; that, since their removal from Edinburgh, they had not, directly or indirectly, publicly or privately, tried to sow doubt or distrust among the lieges; and "that they wald, in publict, manifest and declair thair said persuasioun and assurance . . . , and move his Maiesteis subiectis to do the lyk, and gif thankis to God for the same".[105]

This declaration was "gratiously received"[105] and the converts were given their marching and preaching orders to "repair and adres [themselves] with all guidlie diligence"[105] thus: Watson to Dunbar and Duns; Balcanquall to Tranent, Dalkeith and Musselburgh; and Hall to Dunfermline, St. Andrews, and Perth. They were to hold forth in the churches of the places named on the ordinary preaching days, when presumably the congregations would be large, and to make public and manifest affirmations of their steady conviction of the truth of the official narrative. They were to crave God's pardon and the King's for their long delay in believing, to move all to thank God for the King's delivery, and "schairplie to rebuik all sic personis quha [= who] continewis doutfull heirin".[105] In order that all this should be done to the letter, the itinerant predicants were to obtain certificates from the ministers and elders of the towns visited to the effect that they had obeyed their instructions. There-after, we are told, the King may take "forder ordour with thame, as salbe thocht expedient".[105]

On the prescribed 11th September at Stirling Balfour and Bruce presented themselves before the King and Council. Balfour made the same sort of avowal as Watson, Balcanquall, and Hall; and, as a token of his amendment and an earnest of his duty for the future, as well as to counteract the mischief he had done, he was sent likewise on a preaching mission to Dundee, Montrose, Arbroath, and Brechin.

But Bruce was indeed "made of sterner stuff".[106] He continued, obstinately but courteously, to be "doubtfull and nocht throuchlie resoluit"[107] of the truth of the matter. Consequently he was condemned to leave Scotland by 8th October and not to return for any reason; nor was he to seek refuge in England without James's licence, under the penalty of death. On the same day as the pronouncement of the sentence, Bruce was to make for the family seat at Airth, about eight miles south-east of Stirling; and there, preparing for his journey, he was to remain until his exile began.

On 18th October the King and Council at Holyroodhouse decided that Hall should be allowed to return freely to Edinburgh and be reinstated in his charge.[107] For some reason which does not appear, Watson, Balcanquall, and Balfour had to wait till 21st May 1601 for their amnesty.[108]

To turn to the indomitable Bruce, "The very head and front"[109] in the offending: He did sail away from Scotland, possibly to France where he had once studied jurisprudence, or to Holland. But he was soon back in Scotland, being perhaps allowed to return through the good offices of friends, both clerical and lay. He was summoned to Craigmillar Castle, near Edinburgh, to meet on 15th January 1602 commissioners appointed by the King. According to the briefing they had received, they "proponned three things to him: [1] That he would approve the book sett out upon Gowrie's Conspiracie: [2] That he would purge [= acquit from blame or suspicion] the King, in such places as the King sould appoint him to preach in: [3] That he would crave the King pardon, for his long mistrust and disobedience".[110] Though the conference was lengthy, Bruce, it is hardly necessary to say, turned the proposals down; and it is likely that he had gone to Craigmillar determined not to bend. Thereafter he had three conferences with the King himself: in April 1602 at Brechin; on 24th June 1602 at Perth; and on 5th April 1603 at Holyroodhouse, the very day on which James set out on his southward journey to ascend the English throne, having received the congratulations of hosts of his loving subjects who, like Bruce himself, had come to tender their duty. Among the most remarkable features of these interviews as recorded are the King's patience and placability

with little or no sign of exasperation and Bruce's courtly behaviour and professions of respect while at the same time maintaining his positions with the
most dextrous and evasive logic-chopping. Probably both parties got some
pleasure from these eristic occasions, especially the disputatious James. But all
attempts at reconciling such diametrically opposed standpoints came to nothing.
James had his triumph in bringing the Church of Scotland to an Erastian obedience; but the triumph was spoiled for him by the *amari aliquid* of one man's
not ignoble resistance. Bruce was never forgiven or restored to his Edinburgh
charge, though he was suffered to minister elsewhere from time to time. He
died in 1631, six years after James himself.

James had his confrontation from the autumn of 1600 on with some of
his clergy largely, in my submission, because they wanted to retaliate for their
defeat in 1598 over the issue of the players and their theatre. It is now possible
to come back to the later evidence for the presence of English actors in Scotland. The date is the summer of 1601. The first item of evidence is only an entry
in the accounts of the Burgh Treasurer of Dundee, the payment on 8th August
of £33·6·8 "To the Inglischmen that playit in the tolbuith".[111] The date of the
payment suggests to me that the performance itself may have been on 5th
August as part of Dundee's celebration of the first anniversary of James's escape
at Gowrie House on 5th August 1600. There can be little doubt that the actors
at Dundee were members of the Blackfriars Wynd company; and it is very
unlikely that they went specially and only to Dundee. It is far more likely that
they were on a summer tour and acted also at the several towns along their
route.

The same tour may have taken them on to Aberdeen. At any rate, on
9th October 1601 the Provost, Bailies, and Town Council of Aberdeen ordered
their Dean of Guild to give thirty-two marks (= £21·6·8) "to the kingis
sservandis presentlie in this burght quha [= who] Playes comedies and staige
playes Be [= by] reasoun thay ar recommendit be his majesties speciall letter".[112]
In providing his company with a patronal document James was following the
regular practice in England where theatrical companies were obliged to have
patrons of standing and letters patent from them as credentials. In addition to
the thirty-two marks given to the players, there were two other relevant expenses in the 1601-2 discharge in the Aberdeen Book of Guildry accounts: £22
"to the stageplayaris inglischemen" and £3 "for the stageplayaris suppouris
[= suppers] that nicht thaye plaid to the towne".[113] Besides the performance
"to the towne", which I take to mean in this context the Town Council, there
were sure to have been other occasions of an unofficial kind.

The actors were either still or once again in Aberdeen on 23rd October
1601. It will be seen from an extremely interesting passage in the Aberdeen
records, to be quoted presently, that the actors were nominally in the suite of a
visiting Frenchman, to whom King James was obviously anxious to show
special honour. But the interval between 9th and 23rd October and the length
of time the company seems to have taken to get from Dundee to Aberdeen
leads me to surmise that they had gone on tour from Edinburgh ahead of the
Frenchman and the rest of his escort and had rejoined them at Aberdeen.

In the Aberdeen records the Frenchman is called "Sr. Francis Hospitall of Haulzie". He was in fact François de l'Hôpital, who later distinguished himself as le Maréchal de l'Hôpital. But he was in 1601 only eighteen years of age. He could hardly have come to Scotland at that time on a sort of Grand Tour to complete his cultural education. His motives were more likely to have been a youthful spirit of adventure and a general curiosity about the Scottish Ultima Thule, sharpened by a more particular curiosity about the Gowrie Conspiracy of the year before, which was an episode of the liveliest interest and speculation for the whole Continent, especially France. I fancy, too, that James was anxious to make a favourable impression on his young visitor, who on returning to his own country might do something to reverse impressions less favourable.

The first part of the reference to the Sieur de l'Hôpital's visit to Aberdeen is as follows:

"The Quhilk [= which] day [23rd October 1601] Sr. Francis Hospitall of Haulzie knycht frencheman being recommendit be [= by] his matie [= majesty] to the prouest Baillies and counsall of this burt [= burgh] to be favourablie Interteneit, with the gentilmen his maties servandis efterspect [= mentioned below], quha [= who] war direct to this burt be his matie to accompanie the said frencheman, being ane noble man of France Cuming onlie to this burt to sie the town and countrie the said frencheman w^t the knightis and gentillmen following wer all reesauit [= received] and admittit Burgesses of gild of this burt quha gave their aythis [= oaths] in commun form. Followis the names off thame that war admittit burgesses:—

Hospitall, Sr. Francis, off Halzie, knycht.
Hamiltoun, Sr. Claud, of Schawfeild, knycht.
Grahame, Sr. Johne, off Orkill, knyt.
Ramsay, Sr. Johne, off ester Bairnie, knyt.
Hay, James, James Auchterlony, Robert Ker, James Schaw,
    Thomas Foster, James Gleghorne, David Drumond, Servitoris to
    his Matie.
Monsieur de Scheyne, Monsieur la Bar servitoris to the said Sr.
    Francis.
Law, James.
Hamilton, James, servitor to the said Sr. Claud.
Sym, Archibald, trumpeter.
Fletcher, Laurence, comediane serviture to his matie.
Wod, Mr Dauid.
Bronderstainis, Johne."[114]

In addition to conferring honorary citizenship the Aberdeen Town Council spent £126·3·6 on their guests' entertainment and the "defraying of thair haill chargis during thair remaining in this burt".[115]

If, as I suggested, de l'Hôpital may have wanted to ask questions about the Gowrie Conspiracy, he would have plenty of opportunity to quiz two members of his party who had been present and active at Gowrie House on 5th August 1600: Sir John Ramsay, who rescued the King in the turret room and ran Alexander Ruthven through the body; and Sir John Graham, who was in close attendance on the King all day and fully confirmed the long depositions of the Duke of Lennox and the Earl of Mar.

The whole party at Aberdeen probably returned fairly soon to Edinburgh, though not necessarily together. Fletcher and his company could not afford to travel without stopping to give performances at any likely towns and to rake in the money. The young de l'Hôpital seems to have been back in Edinburgh by 10th December 1601, for on that day George Nicolson, Elizabeth's Ambassador, reported the King's entertainment of his French guest to Sir Robert Cecil.[116] And at an uncertain date in 1601, but probably after the return of Fletcher and his company to the Capital, a payment of £400 was made to them by a royal precept issued through Roger Aschetoun,[117] the Ashton who twelve years before had communicated to Lord Scrope James's eager desire for Queen Elizabeth's players to come on from Carlisle to Edinburgh. The sum paid, £400, looks like a subvention by the King to the company now under his official patronage, rather than a lump sum for a number of performances, even though the entry in the Lord High Treasurer's accounts refers to them as "certane Inglis Comedianes".[117]

Though there is only scanty evidence for the company's continuance in Scotland, there is none at all for their departure.[118] It is reasonable to suppose that they felt more secure under royal patronage in a country where they had no competitors than they would be if they returned to England. The scanty evidence for their presence in Scotland consists of three items in the Lord High Treasurer's accounts for February 1603: £76 for eight ells of "skarlot claith at nyne pund Xs [= £9·10·0] the ell" to make "coit [= coat] and breikis" [= breeches] for "M^r cobler and vthir thrie commendianis"; £106·13·4 for eight ells of "yellow veluote" to edge the garments at £13·6·8 the ell; and £16 for eight ounces of "cramasie [= crimson] silk" at forty shillings an ounce to stitch the trimming on.[119] Similar payments for actors' livery were often made in England. "M^r cobler" is a name otherwise unknown; but his emergence from anonymity may indicate that he was a fairly important member of the company.

It is most unlikely that any of Fletcher's men remained in Scotland when their royal patron and champion went south in April 1603. They may well have formed part, at the express order of the King, of the great and ever-growing cavalcade which accompanied him from Edinburgh to London. James left Edinburgh on Tuesday, 5th April[120] and, owing to his progress being slowed down by civic receptions and presentations, formalities, festivities, and sports including great hunting parties, he did not get to London till 7th May. He had, of course, a very full official programme to fulfil. But in the midst of all the business of state, he found time to take over the patronage of a theatrical company. The letters patent are dated 19th May; but the Privy Seal giving directions for their issue is dated 17th May, and the preliminaries must have begun almost as soon as James arrived in London. His alacrity in the matter is a proof of his devotion to the theatre; and it could be interpreted, without too much fancifulness, as a demonstration, to himself and to his troublesome clergy in Scotland, of his now-unfettered exercise of his royal authority in a sphere where he had been so often thwarted and gainsaid.

The theatrical company which he adopted was unquestionably the best in London, with the best actors and the best repertoire of plays from the best dramatists. It had been known as the Lord Chamberlain's men, under two Lords Hunsdon, father and son, who held office from 1585 to 1603.[121]

The letters patent, described in the margin as *Commissio specialis pro Laurencio Fletcher & Willelmo Shackespeare et aliis*, deserve partial quotation, not only for the names of the chief actors and the order in which they are given, but for the tone of royal cordiality and approval:

"Iames by the grace of god &c. To all Iustices, Maiors, Sheriffes, Constables, hedborowes [= head-boroughs, petty constables], and other our Officers and louinge Subiectes greetinge. Know yee that Wee of our speciall grace, certeine knowledge, & mere motion haue licenced and aucthorized . . . theise our Servauntes Lawrence Fletcher, William Shakespeare, Richard Burbage, Augustyne Phillippes, Iohn Heninges [= Heminges], Henrie Condell, William Sly, Robert Armyn, Richard Cowly, and the rest of theire Associates freely to vse and exercise the Arte and faculty of playinge Comedies, Tragedies, histories, Enterludes, moralls, pastoralls, Stageplaies, and Suche others like as theie haue already studied or hereafter shall vse or studie, aswell for the recreation of our lovinge Subjectes, as for our Solace and pleasure when wee shall thincke good to see them, during our pleasure."

The actors were authorized to "shewe and exercise publiquely to theire best Commoditie", when deaths from the plague fell below a certain weekly figure, in the Globe Theatre "as alsoe within anie towne halls or Moute halls or other conveniente places within the liberties and freedome of anie other Cittie, vniversitie, towne, or Boroughe whatsoever within our said Realmes and domynions. Willinge and Commaundinge you and everie of you, as you tender our pleasure, not onelie to permitt and suffer them herein without anie your lettes hindrances or molestacions during our said pleasure, but alsoe to be aidinge and assistinge to them, yf anie wronge be to them offered, And to allowe them such former Curtesies as hath bene given to men of theire place and quallitie, and also what further favour you shall shewe to theise our Servauntes for our sake wee shall take kindlie at your handes."[122]

Eight of the nine players named in the document had been the principal members in the former Lord Chamberlain's company. Only the first-named, Lawrence Fletcher, was a newcomer from the King's troupe in Scotland; but the prominence given to his name indicates his importance in the King's regard and consequently in the newly organized company. It is probable that some of the rest of the King's Scottish troupe were also absorbed; but Martin Slater became a member of Queen Anne's company, formerly the Earl of Worcester's men, for which a draft patent in similar terms to those in the patent for the King's own company was drawn up at an uncertain date, but probably in May or June 1603.[123]

Other royal persons followed the lead of the theatre-loving King and

Queen in giving patronage and protection to companies of players. They were:
Prince Henry's men, after the Prince's death adopted by Frederick, the Elector
Palatine; the Duke of Lennox's men; Prince Charles's men; and Princess Eliza-
beth's men.

Such royal support for the theatre went far beyond any given by Queen
Elizabeth, whose own company gave its last court performance on 6th January
1594 and, already in decline, faded out almost completely except for provincial
appearances long before the death of their patroness. Was Shakespeare including, among the blessings of the "most balmy time" of 1603, the high hopes of
himself and his fellows for their profession under a royal House so favourable
and partial, when in *Sonnet* 107 he refers to the gloomy forebodings of troubles
to come after Elizabeth's death and their happy contradiction by the un-
challenged and peaceful succession of James:

> The mortal moon hath her eclipse endured
> And the sad augurs mock their own presage;
> Incertainties now crown themselves assured
> And peace proclaims olives of endless age?

But if James had all the theatrical satisfaction he wanted in his southern
Kingdom, his northern Capital (and with it, the rest of the country) was purged
of things dramatic by his old clerical antagonists, if we may judge by a sarcastic
passage in Sir Anthony Weldon's *Description of Scotland* on James's re-entry into
the city on 20th June 1617: "Ffor his Majestie's entertainment, I must needes
ingenuously confesse he was received into the parish of Edenborough (for a City
I cannot call yt) with great showts of joy, but no shewes of charge; for Pageants,
they holde them idolatrous things, and not fit to be used in so reformed a
place. . . . They holde their noses yf youe talke of beare-bayting; and they stop
their eares yf you talke of a playe."[124]

Nevertheless, James had brought such order out of chaos to Scotland as it
had seldom enjoyed before, and had so mastered both Parliament and General
Assembly that he was able to leave behind an all-powerful Privy Council to
govern for him according to his absolute will. In 1607 he declared with pride
and satisfaction to his English Parliament: "This I must say for Scotland, and
may truly vaunt it: here I sit and govern it with my pen: I write and it is done;
and by a Clerk of the Council I govern Scotland now,—which others could not
do by the sword."[125]

Notes

1. *Hamlet*, II, ii, 545-51.
2. *The Droichis* [= dwarf's] *Part of the Play*, perhaps but not certainly by William Dunbar; and Sir David Lyndsay's *Ane Satyre of the Thrie Estaitis*.

3. Mill, 47, 108. During her brief reign Mary took a lively interest in all manner of diversions. They were apparently but seldom in the nature of true dramas. But the Court was frequently entertained with masques

and disguisings accompanied by singing and dancing and with visits by nondescript tumblers and jongleurs.

4. Mill, 88-89.

5. Cf. 149-56 infra.

6. Mill, 188-91.

7. Ibid., 192-94.

8. Ibid., 91.

9. Ibid., 47-50.

10. The Memoirs of Sir James Melville of Hallhill. Edited by George Scott. 1751. 234.

11. Macmillan, 214-15.

12. Ibid., 215.

13. William Hudson, the royal "balladine" [= dancer of a kind of dance of the same name], was on James's instructions paid in December 1580 £101 "for his extraordiner panis taikin in teitcheing of his grace to dance" (Mill, 334).

14. Macmillan, 216.

15. Buchanan, 111-12.

16. En. Brit., IV, 311. The "criminal" monarch in the forefront of Buchanan's mind as he wrote was James's own mother. In 1571 Buchanan published a scathing and venomous Latin denunciation of Mary as an accomplice in the murder of her husband, Lord Darnley, and as an adulteress with the Earl of Bothwell. It is generally known by its later title, Detectio Mariae Reginae.

17. In 1664 and 1688 the circulation of manuscript translations of De Jure Regni was prohibited by proclamation; and in 1683 the University of Oxford had Buchanan's works publicly burned, along with those of Milton and others.

18. Soon after Mary's execution in 1587, Blackwood published a long account of her maltreatment in prison, interspersed with passionate denunciations of her enemies, especially Elizabeth and Knox.

19. A third was added in 1612.

20. De Vinculo developed ideas first expressed in 1574 in Blackwood's eulogistic elegy on Charles IX of France,

who unwillingly gave the order for the St. Bartholomew Massacre of 1572.

21. In 1606 Blackwood published a poem on James's accession to the English throne, Inauguratio Jacobi Magnae Britanniae Regis.

22. Hume Brown, II, 169.

23. Sir W. S. Gilbert, Original Plays. Third Series (including Ruddigore; or, The Witch's Curse). 1924, 253.

24. Mill, 109, note 4.

25. Knighted, probably later.

26. Mill, 299; and Chambers, Stage, II, 265-66.

27. Mill, 299.

28. Perhaps from Ashby, who in a letter of 12th October to Lord Burghley shows he was in touch with the Borders about procuring provisions in time for James's wedding festivities.

29. Chambers, Stage, II, 104.

30. Thomas Heywood, An Apology for Actors. 1612. 43.

31. Chambers, Stage, II, 111.

32. Ibid., II, 550.

33. In 1586-87 they visited, among other places, Stratford, where, according to Edmond Malone, they may have recruited Shakespeare himself (Chambers, Stage, II, 107).

34. The explanation of Lord Scrope's remark to the effect that the Queen's men had been in Carlisle "for the space of ten dayes" (cf. 133 supra) may be that his summons reached the company when they were covenanted to play at Knowsley Hall on 12th and 13th September; that they sent in advance such troupers as they could spare; that this advance party arrived ten days before 20th September; and that Lord Scrope wrote his letter when the rest of the company arrived.

35. Chambers, Stage, II, 111; and Murray, I, 16.

36. Dibdin, 20-21, thought it "by no means likely" that the English comedians paid by the Lord High Treasurer in February 1594 were the first to visit James VI.

37. *C.S.P.*, II, 568-69.
38. Henderson, 172, gives the date as 22nd October.
39. *Ibid.*, 172.
40. Mill, 297.
41. Dibdin, 20.
42. Mill, 109, 335.
43. *Cf.* 133 *supra*. Nicolson's reference to Ashton by his Christian name indicates that the two were on specially good terms.
44. *C.S.P.*, II, 676; and Mill, 299.
45. Thorpe in *C.S.P.*, II, 749, and Dibdin, 21, take this word to be a spelling of "regretted". But it might mean "creaked", "grumbled", or "whispered".
46. The name "uddert" was misread as "struett" by Dr. Mill (301, note 3). But there never was an Edinburgh Lord Provost so called. Nicol Uddert (spelt also "Udward", "Edward", etc.) and his brother Alexander held various civic offices, Nicol being Lord Provost in 1592-93.
47. *C.S.P.*: II, 749; Dibdin, 21; and Mill, 301, note 3.
48. *Hamlet*, III, iii, 75.
49. Chambers, *Stage*, I, 267.
50. *Cf.* 154 *supra*.
51. Mill, 297.
52. *Ibid.*, 297-98.
53. *Ibid.*, 298.
54. *Ibid.*, 298. After the Gowrie Conspiracy, James arranged for a French tightrope-walker to give a performance at Falkland "to mitigat the Quein and peiple" for the Earl of Gowrie's death (Mill, 111, note 1).
55. Chambers, *Stage*, II, 111, 551; and Murray, II, 293, 304.
56. Mill, 287.
57. *Ibid.*, 109-10, note 5.
58. The play presented at Glasgow on 7th June 1599, which was Corpus Christi Day, is "evidence of the persistent survival of the mediaeval communal play in some form" (Mill, 107, 244), not of the presence of visiting professional actors.

59. *Cf.* 138-39 *supra*.
60. Apart from his name appearing in the Southwark token-books; which, however, is an indication only of domicile, not of continuous residence.
61. *Cf.* 158 *infra*.
62. *B.U.K.*, IV, 1002; and Mill, 300. *Cf.* Calderwood, V, 765-67.
63. Dibdin, 22.
64. *Ibid.*, 22. *Cf.* Mill, 300, note 2. The £40 was probably to re-imburse the players for timber already bought.
65. *B.U.K.*, IV, 1002 says "Uppon Munday the 12 of November". This is a misdating. Dr. Mill, 300, note 3, suggests "? 7th Nov.", inferentially from *R.P.C.* But the more likely date for the warning by trumpet and drums is Friday or Saturday, 2nd or 3rd November.
66. *B.U.K.*, IV, 1002; and Mill, 300.
67. The Theatre, the Curtain, and Blackfriars.
68. A larger body with wider powers.
69. *B.U.K.*, IV, 1002; and Mill, 300-1.
70. And so not convenable with ease and speed.
71. Having a messenger-at-arms, accompanied by a trumpeter, proclaim their names and offences.
72. *R.P.C.*, VI, 39. *Cf. B.U.K.*, IV, 1002; and Mill, 301.
73. *B.U.K.*, IV, 1002; and Mill, 301.
74. *Fasti*, I, 55.
75. Calderwood, V, 766; and Mill, 301, note 2.
76. *B.U.K.*, IV, 1002; and Mill, 301-2.
77. *B.U.K.*, IV, 1002; and Mill, 302-3.
78. *Ibid.* According to George Nicolson's dispatch of 12th November 1599 to Sir Robert Cecil, the ministers utterly refused to countermand anything they had said and were resolved to endure the extremity (*C.S.P.*, II, 777; and Mill, 303-4).
79. *B.U.K.*, IV, 1002; and Mill, 303.
80. *Ibid.* Nicolson put it thus to Cecil in the dispatch of 12th November: The ministers in their sermons on the day before "vsed very gentle exhortacions

(as they do ever with great respect) to forbeare all prophanes, in sorte as the wise might know their constancy, and none nevertheless touche them for the same with reason" (Mill, 304).

81. *R.P.C.*, VI, 41-42. In November 1599 payments were made to the officers-at-arms for ordering the Sessions to annul their act and for notifying the public of the King's approval of the players (Dibdin, 23).

82. *Cf.* 162, note 65 *supra*.

83. Mill, 303-4.

84. Mill, 304, note 1.

85. *Ibid.*, 304.

86. *R.P.C.*, VI, 44, note 1.

87. Mill, 305.

88. Dibdin, 24.

89. Mill, 109, note 5.

90. Hume Brown, II, 224.

91. *Fasti*, V, 420.

92. Alexander Pope, *The Dunciad*, IV, 188.

93. *Cf.* 87 *supra*.

94. *Cf.* 87-88, 91-92 *supra*.

95. Pitcairn, II, 233.

96. *Ibid.*, II, 233-34.

97. *Hamlet*, III, ii, 240.

98. Calderwood, VI, 67. Beza in a letter of 15th April (*Scripta in Scotiam*, according to the writer's own note) recalls his grief at Gowrie's death and their friendship (*olim mihi jucundissima*) and refers to *clandestinas improborum machinationes*. Without mentioning their names, he offers an asylum to Gowrie's two young brothers, William and Patrick Ruthven (Arbuckle, 106, 110).

99. Arbuckle, 106.

100. Lord Grey after his father's death in 1609.

101. *Cf.* 88 *supra*.

102. At least two other Edinburgh ministers were present, Peter Hewat and George Robertson; but as they were regarded as having complied with the King's commands, they were not proceeded against. David Lindsay was summoned in the middle of the Council meeting to add his declara-tion of belief in the King's story. For his many services, Lindsay at the end of 1600 was made a Privy Councillor and Bishop of Ross.

103. Pitcairn, II, 234.

104. *Ibid.*, II, 301. *Cf.* 92-93, 112 *supra*.

105. *Ibid.*, II, 235.

106. *Julius Caesar*, III, ii, 97.

107. Pitcairn, II, 236.

108. *Ibid.*, II, 237.

109. *Othello*, I, iii, 80.

110. Pitcairn, II, 304.

111. Mill, 305.

112. *Aberdeen C.R.*, II, 222; and Mill, 305.

113. *Aberdeen C.R.*, II, xxi (in which "suppouris" is wrongly read as "support"); and Mill, 306.

114. *Aberdeen B.*, 161-62. Dibdin, 24, wrongly says that the freedom of the town was conferred on "Fletcher *and each of his company*".

115. *Aberdeen C.R.*, II, xxi-xxii; and Mill, 306.

116. *C.S.P.*, II, 791.

117. Dibdin, 24. Dibdin suggests that other payments in the Lord High Treasurer's accounts to John Kinloch for the expenses of "certain strangers of his company" and for their bedding, etc. in the Canongate may refer to Fletcher and his men. But that is unlikely.

118. An entry, dated 30th May 1602, of a reward of twenty shillings to "his Majesties Players" in the Ipswich Chamberlain's accounts (Murray, II, 294) is not easily explained, except as being a misdating.

119. Mill, 335.

120. He may have considered Tuesday the fifth of the month to be lucky for him, having escaped from the Gowrie Conspiracy on Tuesday, 5th August 1600. *Cf.* 92-93, 112 *supra*.

121. Except for a brief period in 1596-97 when the Lord Chamberlain was Lord Cobham.

122. Chambers, *Stage*, II, 208-9.

123. For some reason this patent never passed the Great Seal; and it was not

till 15th April 1609 that a later patent, in almost identical terms, was issued to the company, which, however, had acted continuously as Queen Anne's men.

124. John Nichols, *The Progresses, Processions, and Magnificent Festivities of King James the First*, III, 340.

125. Hume Brown, II, 240-41.

9

Some Surmises about the Plays performed by English Actors in Scotland

> a poor player
> That struts and frets his hour upon the stage
> And then is heard no more.
> *Macbeth*, V, v, 24-26.

Nothing is known for certain about the repertoires of travelling companies of actors in the English provinces; and it would appear that not a single play-title is noted in any provincial record of a performance. But some reasonable inferences can be drawn and some plausible surmises offered. For one thing, it is all but certain that no Elizabethan play was ever performed by professional actors in the provinces before it had been put on, not once but again and again, in and about London. "How chances it they travel?" asks Hamlet about the troupe expected in Elsinore; "their residence, both in reputation and profit, was better both ways".[1] But the fact is that companies went on tour less by choice than by the force of plague-regulations which closed the theatres from time to time, especially in the warmer months of the year, or on account of other unfavourable circumstances, such as a temporary exile from the London area ordered by the authorities because of some indiscretion, as hinted at by Rosencrantz: "I think their inhibition comes by the means of the late innovation."[2] Companies would naturally take on the road some at least of the plays they had just been performing in the metropolitan area. But they probably catered when on tour mainly for simpler and less sophisticated tastes, by dropping out, except perhaps in Oxford and Cambridge, such plays as Hamlet reckoned to be "caviare to the general"[3] and offering instead established and rather old-fashioned favourites, like the play-within-the-play with its outmoded rhetoric and its verbose rhyming couplets.[4] Hamlet's very first remark about the expected players shows him as thinking that they would be likely to offer conventional plots involving stock characters: "He that plays the king shall be welcome; his majesty shall have tribute of me; the adventurous knight shall use his foil and target; the lover shall not sigh gratis; the humorous man shall end his part in peace; the clown shall make those laugh whose lungs are tickle o' the sere; and the lady shall say her mind freely, or the blank verse shall halt for't".[5]

On arriving at some town where they intended to stay for a day or two, visiting companies would certainly not depreciate their own talents or the variety of their shows. On the contrary, they would make their entry to a town as pretentious and noisy as possible with drums and trumpets, even as the English actors did in Edinburgh when in November 1599 they paraded through the streets to let the citizens know of the opening performance at the first Scottish theatre.[6] And touring companies seem to have distributed and posted up puffing handbills like the one Polonius read from (for that, I suggest, is what he was doing): "The best actors in the world, either for tragedy, comedy, history, pastoral, pastoral - comical, historical - pastoral, tragical - historical, tragical-comical-historical-pastoral, scene individable, or poem unlimited: Seneca cannot be too heavy, nor Plautus too light. For the law of writ and the liberty, these are the only men".[7]

Like the troupe visiting Elsinore in *Hamlet*, members of a travelling company carried many plays in their memories and could at short notice either recite a speech ("The rugged Pyrrhus, he whose sable arms", etc.[8]), even though the play itself "was never acted; or, if it was, not above once",[9] or else put on a whole play, as was to be done with *The Murder of Gonzago* or, as Hamlet renamed it, *The Mousetrap*.[10] Besides having good memories made all the more retentive by constant practice, Elizabethan actors were both versatile and adaptable. They did not regard the texts of their plays as sacrosanct, but rather as fluid material. At any rate, many plays underwent "revisions", perhaps several times, at the hands of jobbing playwrights, including Shakespeare in his apprenticeship. And it is likely that the players themselves or, more particularly, the book-holders who were entrusted with the "platt" (= plot, scenario) would cut and modify as circumstances seemed to require. Like the leader of the troupe at Elsinore, an actor "could, for a need, study a speech of some dozen or sixteen lines",[11] such as Hamlet wanted to be inserted in *The Murder of Gonzago*. But, such written revisions or additions apart, Elizabethan actors or many of them were adepts at improvising and gagging, with a facility matching the Italian performers of the *commedia dell' arte*. Two of Queen Elizabeth's players were specially celebrated for such a talent: Richard Tarleton, who, however, died in 1588 before any of his company visited Scotland; and Robert Wilson, who was still alive in 1600.

Such gagging was not much to Hamlet's taste; and we can take his strictures on it to be Shakespeare's likewise: "And let those that play your clowns speak no more than is set down for them; for there be of them that will themselves laugh, to set on some quantity of barren spectators to laugh too; though, in the mean time, some necessary question of the play be then to be considered: that's villainous, and shows a most pitiful ambition in the fool that uses it".[12] In deprecating such "ad-libbing" Shakespeare could be said to have expressed primarily how he thought his own plays should be acted in the metropolitan theatres; but at the same time he was recognizing that on provincial tours the clowns did in fact take an ampler licence in their patter to please all those who, like Polonius in Hamlet's jibe, were "for a jig or a tale of bawdry".[13]

Every Elizabethan company had likewise members who were competent musicians, able to diversify performances with songs and with jigs, which were lively song-and-dance interludes like "the singing farce of the Merryman and his Maid" in *The Yeomen of the Guard*.[14] Still further variety was often provided by tumblers and acrobats, more in the provinces, I fancy, than in London theatres of a superior type.

It was with the best acting of his time in mind that Shakespeare introduced into *Hamlet* the episode of the "passionate speech" which the First Player is invited to recite: " 'twas Aeneas' tale to Dido; and thereabout of it especially, where he speaks of Priam's slaughter".[15] The speech was from a play which had appealed to high-brow patrons of the drama savouring every allusion and recherché phrase and which in consequence had not been a popular success. Incidentally, it would not have been very suitable for provincial audiences. But the First Player's giving himself so completely to the passion of it as to change colour and weep affords us some idea of a histrionic effectiveness able to move even hearers who did not fully understand the words. Hamlet himself, who did understand both the passion and the words, contrasts in the following soliloquy his own apparent resignation under a real wrong with the First Player's excitement as worked up out of a merely imaginary one:

O, what a rogue and peasant slave am I!
Is it not monstrous that this player here,
But in a fiction, in a dream of passion,
Could force his soul so to his own conceit
That from her working all his visage wann'd,
Tears in his eyes, distraction in's aspect,
A broken voice, and his whole function suiting
With forms to his conceit? and all for nothing!
For Hecuba!
What's Hecuba to him, or he to Hecuba,
That he should weep for her? What would he do,
Had he the motive and the cue for passion
That I have? He would drown the stage with tears
And cleave the general ear with horrid speech,
Make mad the guilty and appal the free,
Confound the ignorant, and amaze indeed
The very faculties of eyes and ears.[16]

The point I would make is that the First Player's rendering of Aeneas's speech and Hamlet's comment thereon are among the contemporary evidence for the acting ability of Elizabethan players. Their manner of acting and their elocution were no doubt of a more bravura type than is customary in the theatre nowadays, largely because the Elizabethans in their everyday living were more demonstrative and less inhibited than we are. But, when good, their action and elocution were very good indeed.

On the other hand, Shakespeare, through Hamlet's advice to the players, expresses both his ideal of acting and his strong disapproval of overacting. As overacting was likely to have been a common failing of touring companies because in them the younger and less experienced members were probably allowed to sustain more important roles than would come their way in London and the suburbs, I venture to quote at length the well-known passage:

"Speak the speech, I pray you, as I pronounced it to you, trippingly on the tongue: but if you mouth it, as many of your players do, I had as lief the town-crier spoke my lines. Nor do not saw the air too much with your hand, thus, but use all gently; for in the very torrent, tempest, and, as I may say, the whirl-wind of passion, you must acquire and beget a temperance that may give it smoothness. O, it offends me to the soul to hear a robustious periwig-pated fellow tear a passion to tatters, to very rags, to split the ears of the groundlings, who for the most part are capable of nothing but inexplicable dumb-shows and noise: I would have such a fellow whipped for o'erdoing Termagant; it out-herods Herod: pray you, avoid it. . . . Be not too tame neither, but let your own discretion be your tutor: suit the action to the word, the word to the action; with this special observance, that you o'erstep not the modesty of nature: for any thing so overdone is from the purpose of playing, whose end, both at the first and now, was and is, to hold, as 'twere, the mirror up to nature; to show virtue her own feature, scorn her own image, and the very age and body of the time his form and pressure. Now this overdone, or come tardy off, though it make the unskilful laugh, cannot but make the judicious grieve; the censure of the which one must in your allowance o'erweigh a whole theatre of others. O, there be players that I have seen play, and heard others praise, and that highly, not to speak it profanely, that, neither having the accent of Christians nor the gait of Christian, pagan, nor man, have so strutted and bellowed that I have thought some of nature's journeymen had made men and not made them well, they imitated humanity so abominably. . . . O, reform it altogether."[17]

The play-within-the-play in *Hamlet* contains a feature which has puzzled the commentators. The difficulty lies in the peculiarity of the opening dumb-show. In other plays of the period, dumb-shows are of one of three kinds: [1] Intermezzi between the acts with no reference to the action in the play proper and with no function but that of relief or variety; [2] allegorical or symbolical anticipations of or sequels to acts, in the nature of choruses without words; and [3] pieces of the action of the play performed in miming so as to cover the ground in a kind of theatrical shorthand. But the dumb-show in *Hamlet* duplicates, exactly and beforehand, the action to follow with words. "Belike", as Ophelia says, "this show imports the argument of the play".[18] I submit, as an explanation of this anomaly, that Shakespeare knew that English theatrical companies touring on the Continent[19] were faced by the difficulty of establishing rapport with audiences having little English or, in most cases, none at all, at any rate in the earlier phase of continental touring. Such a brief miming anticipation of the action as precedes the dialogue in *The Murder of Gonzago* would make the play proper as comprehensible to a foreign audience as, let us say, the acts of an opera in a foreign tongue are made by the introducer of a televised performance. As time went on, English actors on the Continent, some of whom spent many years there, came to learn the languages, translated their English plays into them, and acted other plays originally written in them by continental dramatists. But they may well at first have employed just such miming as in the play-within-the-play in *Hamlet* as a regular aid to rapport. Hamlet's calling out to the trouper playing Lucianus "Begin, murderer; pox, leave thy damnable faces, and begin"[20] may be due to his impatience to get to the critical point in his probation of the King; but it may also indicate that the manner of acting by the visitors to Elsinore was of a "ham" type running to exaggerated gesture and grimace.

Companies of English actors coming to Scotland in the sixteenth century were as much aware of being in a foreign land as if it had been Denmark or Germany. They would be faced at first with the fundamental problem of holding the interest of audiences unfamiliar with dramatic conventions and accustomed to an English almost as different from that of London as Platt-Deutsch. At least the difference between spoken Scots and written but non-literary Scots on the one hand and written Scots with some literary pretension on the other, in the sixteenth and early seventeenth century, was very consider-able; the former having retained its traditional idiosyncrasies of vocabulary, idiom, and pronunciation with little change from the fifteenth century; the latter having approximated to the English of such writers as Ascham, Sir Thomas North, and Holinshed, without, however, becoming identical. I think, therefore, that the first English actors in Scotland would instinctively adopt a declamatory elocution and a breadth of gesticulation; and it might well be that they also improvised dumb-shows as regular preparations before the acts. More-over, they would find, as did English companies on the Continent, that plays on broad lines and familiar plots, depending largely on action and spectacle, with perhaps music and acrobatics, would be more acceptable than those turn-ing on dialogue and an elaboration of motive and intrigue. There is a strong probability, too, that, in the last few years of the sixteenth century and the first three of the seventeenth, they acquired new plays which had never been played south of the Border.

If Queen Elizabeth's players did come to Scotland in 1589 at King James's invitation, as it is reasonable to believe they did,[21] they came without any special preparation and with no more in the way of equipment than would be usual for a tour in the English provinces. The fortunes of the Queen's men had already begun to wane with the death of Richard Tarleton in September 1588. It looks as if none of their known plays was written later than 1591, which may have been due to their inability to buy new ones. In the same year, *The Troublesome Reign of John, King of England* was printed, the first of their plays to reach the press, probably released by the company to raise the wind. In 1594-1595 no less than nine of their plays were printed, a still clearer sign of their financial straits. They gave their last Court performance on 6th January 1594. As Chambers says, "there can be no doubt that the Queen's men, whether because they had ceased to be modish, or because their finances had proved unable to stand the strain of the plague years, were now at the end of their London career. On 8th May 1594 the significant entry occurs in Henslowe's Diary of a loan of £15 to his nephew Francis Henslowe 'to lay downe for his share to the Quenes players when they broke & went into the contrey to playe'.[22] This by itself would not perhaps be conclusive, as there were other years in which the company began its provincial wanderings as early as May. But from the present journey there is nothing to show that they ever returned",[23] though their name continues to be noted in provincial records right down to the end of Elizabeth's reign.

The groups of visiting actors from England in 1594 and later probably came with more deliberation and preparation than did their predecessors in 1589. The evidence for their derivation from known companies is sketchy or non-existent. But it is not unlikely that some or all of them were truants from the Queen's company in its decline who had decided to look for a different royal patron in Scotland.

The two following lists give the names and some particulars of plays known to have belonged or, in some cases which are noted, conjectured to have belonged to Queen Elizabeth's company.

The first list gives the names of lost plays:

1. *Phillyda and Corin.* Presented at Court on 26th December 1584.
2. *Felix and Philiomena.* Presented at Court on 3rd January 1585.
3 and 4. *Five Plays in One.* Presented at Court on 6th January 1585. And *Three Plays in One.* Prepared for presentation at Court on 21st February 1585, but not in fact called for. The *Five Plays* and the *Three* together probably constituted Richard Tarleton's *The Seven Deadly Sins,* one of the eight playlets serving as an Induction. The "platt" of the second part of Tarleton's play survives in a Dulwich manuscript.
5. *The May-game of Martinism.* If this was indeed a play, it was the Queen's men's contribution to the Martin Marprelate controversy in 1589.
6. *Valentine and Orson.* Entered in S.R. on 23rd May 1595 and 31st March 1600. But no quartos have survived. It is not known whether the play was the same as a lost play of the same name by Richard Hathway and Anthony Munday entered in Henslowe's Diary in July 1598.
7 and 8. *The Fair Maid of Italy* and *The Ranger's Comedy.* Neither play was certainly the property of the Queen's men.

The second list is made up of the names of extant plays:

1. *The Famous Victories of Henry the Fifth.* Written by 1588 and entered in S.R. on 14th May 1594. The extant quartos are dated 1598 and 1617. Authorship of the play has been ascribed to Richard Tarleton or Samuel Rowley. Shakespeare took a few suggestions from the older play for *Henry IV,* parts 1 and 2, and for *Henry V.*
2. *The True Tragedy of Richard the Third.* Entered in S.R. on 19th June 1594, but probably written six or seven years earlier. The only surviving quarto is dated 1594. The play may be a continuation of *The First Part of the Contention betwixt the two*

famous Houses of York and Lancaster, 1594. The play has been attributed to Thomas Lodge and George Peele working on a base by Thomas Kyd or, but quite without evidence, to the anonymous author of *Locrine*, 1595. Shakespeare made little or no use of the play in his *Richard III*.

3. *The Troublesome Reign of John, King of England*. Written between 1587 and 1591: not entered in S.R.; and published as in two parts in 1591 (with no author's name), 1611 (as "Written by W. Sh."), and 1622 (as "Written by W. Shakespeare"). Subsequent criticism has variously ascribed the play to: Shakespeare and William Rowley; Christopher Marlowe; George Peele; Peele, Robert Greene, and Thomas Lodge working on a Marlowe base; and the anonymous author of *King Leir*. In *King John* Shakespeare follows the plot of the earlier play fairly closely; but he completely re-writes the dialogue, freely omitting, condensing, and expanding.

4. *The True Chronicle History of King Leir and his three Daughters*. Written perhaps three years before the entry in S.R. on 14th May 1594. The only known quarto is that of 1605, following a second S.R. entry on 8th May of that year. The ownership of the play by the Queen's men is a strong presumption rather than a certainty. The following have been put forward as authors: Thomas Lodge and George Peele; Lodge and Robert Greene; Lodge and Thomas Kyd; Greene along with one or more unnamed collaborators; Peele; and William Rankins. Shakespeare took the play as a basis for his *King Lear*, but made it much more than a revision. The old play ends happily and lacks the Gloucester plot.

5. *The First Part of the Tragical Reign of Selimus*. Probably written in 1591. It was not entered in S.R. The extant quartos are dated 1594 and 1638. The second title page bears the words "Written T.G.", to suggest as the author Thomas Goffe, who wrote two plays on Turkish history but who was born only in 1591. There is good reason for ascribing the play or much of it to Robert Greene. But it has also been attributed to Greene and Thomas Lodge in collaboration or to Marlowe. A good many lines are plagiarized from the anonymous *Locrine*, which was written several years before its publication in 1595.

6. *Sir Clyomon and [Sir] Clamydes*. Written as early as 1570 or even earlier. It was not entered in S.R. and has come down only in the quarto of 1599. The following have been suggested as possible authors: Thomas Preston, author of *Cambyses*, *c.* 1569-70; Robert Wilson, author or part-author of many plays, most of which are lost; Richard Bower, who may have written the early *Apius and Virginia*, 1575, and who died in 1561; and George Peele, who, however, could have written the play only

as a parody of an older manner. The phrase on the title-page
"As it hath been sundry times Acted by her Maiesties Players"
may be a reference to an earlier company of Queen's men than
the one recruited in 1583. If not, the play as put on by the later
company would undoubtedly have undergone revision.

7. *A Looking Glass for London and England.* This joint-work of
   Lodge and Greene, on the story of Jonah and the fall of Nineveh
   as a tract for the times, was entered in S.R. on 5th March 1594.
   The extant quartos are dated 1594, 1598, 1602, and 1617. The
   probable date of composition is 1590.

8. *The Scottish History of James the Fourth, slain at Flodden.* Entered
   in *S.R.* on 14th May 1594, the play has come down only in a
   1598 quarto. Its author, Robert Greene, probably wrote it in
   1590-91. The title of it is misleading. The play is not a Scottish
   chronicle-history at all and there is no death of the King in it at
   Flodden or anywhere else. It is in fact a dramatization of a
   novella by Giraldi Cinthio with new names and a new setting,
   "Entermixed with a pleasant Comedie, presented by Oboram,
   King of Fayeries" (or more correctly "presented to Oboram").

9. *The History of Orlando Furioso, One of the twelve Peers of France.*
   Entered in S.R. on 7th December 1593 and 28th May 1594.
   The extant quartos are dated 1594 and 1599. Robert Greene
   may have written the play in 1591, soon after the appearance in
   that year of Sir John Harington's translation of Ariosto; but a
   case has also been made for a composition in 1588-89.

10. *The Honourable History of Friar Bacon and Friar Bungay.* Greene
    wrote the play about 1589. It was entered in S.R. on 14th May
    1594; and the surviving quartos are dated 1594, 1630, and 1655.
    The 1594 quarto purports to give the play as "plaid by her
    Maiesties seruants". But that was only when the Queen's men
    and the Earl of Sussex's men combined in 1594. The play itself
    seems to have been the property of Henslowe.

11. *The Old Wive's Tale.* Entered in S.R. on 16th April 1595.
    The only known quarto is dated the same year. George Peele
    took some hints for his play from Greene's *Orlando Furioso*; and a
    1591 date is likely for its composition.

The players visiting Scotland in 1589 and those who came later and may
have been more or less permanently there from 1594 to 1603 almost certainly
put on plays in the two lists above. But the lists do not necessarily include every
play which belonged to the Queen's men; and the later group or groups at
least, being beyond the reach of the Master of the Revels and prosecution for
breaches of copyright, might have performed any English plays they could get
a hold of, printed or manuscript, which would look like a representative selec-
tion of London successes and would at the same time be suited to the latitude of
Edinburgh and Holyroodhouse.

In addition English actors in Scotland may well have looked round for plays by native Scots, just as English companies, which spent years in certain continental cities, acquired and acted plays in the languages spoken there. It has to be admitted that the drama in Scotland was not a flourishing kind and budding dramatists were rare phenomena.

One play which has to be considered as a possibility is the anonymous *Philotus*,[24] a comedy, ribald and bawdy as is not uncommon in the Scots literary tradition, on "the greit inconveniences that fallis out in the Mariage betwene Age and Youth", according to the title-page. It was published in 1603 by Robert Charteris and in 1612 by Andro Hart, both quartos being printed in Edinburgh.

Everything about this dramatic nonsuch is mysterious—authorship, date, source, vehicle, style, affiliations, and performance, if indeed it ever was performed.[25] It has been suggested that *Philotus* was the play by Robert Sempill (?1530–95) acted in Edinburgh on 17th June 1568 before the Regent Moray and several other Scottish nobles. The attribution is absurd. Sempill was an ardent Reformer, as his fiery ballads prove; and his lost play, one can be sure, was not straight drama at all, but a piece of Protestant propaganda, performed in the critical months between the Battle of Carberry Hill which sent Mary to imprisonment in Lochleven Castle and the Battle of Langside which drove Mary to seek a refuge in England and dashed for ever the hopes of the Catholics. In fact, *Philotus* is non-political and non-sectarian, and it was not written during Mary's reign or during James's minority, as is obvious from these lines in it:

> Last, Sirs, now let us pray with one accord
> For to preserve the person of our King,
> Accounting ay this gift as of the Lord
> Ane prudent prince above us for to ring [= reign].

Nor was it written under an earlier King, James V. The King in question was undoubtedly James VI, and that after he had come of age, after he was in effective control of affairs, and probably after he had survived the Gowrie Conspiracy. The language and style of *Philotus* agree with this surmise and point to a date of composition nearly the same as that of its first publication.

Another suggestion is that the author of *Philotus* was Alexander Montgomerie (?1556–?1610), who is best known for *The Cherrie and the Slae*, 1597. He was at least alive and writing at the appropriate time and had all the metrical skill for the *Philotus* dialogue in stanzas. Besides, he was attached to the Scottish Court and regarded as its laureate; and he had a relish for the gross and indecent, as his *Flyting betwixt Montgomerie and Polwart*, 1621, shows. The attribution to Montgomerie is, all things considered, more likely than another to King James himself, even allowing for the fact that Robert Charteris printed *Philotus* "Cum privilegio Regali".

An odd fact about this odd play is that at the end of both quartos is printed a madrigal in two stanzas, "What if a day or a month or a yeare", three years before its appearance in England in Richard Allison's *An Howres Recreation in Musicke, apt for Instrumentes and Voyces*, 1606.[26] Whether the madrigal is by Thomas Campion or not (and all the evidence is for his authorship[27]), it can be dated as certainly belonging to the last Elizabethan decade. It has been described, with some exaggeration, as "the most extraordinary combination of English verse that is, perhaps, any where to be found".[28] The verses certainly are subtly antithetic in elaborating the poetic commonplace of the brevity and precarious-ness of human life, exquisitely flowing and modulated in rhythm, and skilfully complicated in rhyming. It was probably the last feature which appealed most to the Scottish dramatist, and not any the less if Montgomerie was the man.

But how did the author of *Philotus*, who was undoubtedly a Scot, know this unpublished English madrigal? Perhaps he learned it from Fletcher's company who had carried the words and music in their memories from London. And if *Philotus* was in fact staged by Fletcher's men in Scotland, they may well have wanted to add to the musical opportunities. That the play was meant for acting is clear, in spite of its being cast in a variety of rhymed stanzas. Such a mnemonic aid could have been, by accident or design, a help to Englishmen in memorizing a Scots play. But in fact the language used approximates more to Elizabethan English about 1600 than do, for example, contemporary Scots proclamations and acts of Parliament or the Register of the Privy Council. The Scots of everyday speech was still more different.

The author of *Philotus*, whoever he was, must have had some acquaintance with dramatic traditions other than that with which his own country could provide him. But the play bears little resemblance to contemporary English drama, especially by reason of its using rhymed stanzas as its vehicle. Such slight likenesses in quality or spirit as can be detected to English comedies, in the thirty-five years or so from Gascoigne's *Supposes* to Shakespeare's *Taming of the Shrew* and *Twelfth Night* in the Italianate-Plautine vein, are not remarkable. But some influence from sixteenth-century continental comedy, French or Italian, is evident. The influence of the Italian novella, too, is clear in the plot,[29] though no original has been discovered for it. An English analogue is *Of Phylotus and Emilia*, one of the nine prose tales by Barnaby Rich in *Riche his Farewell to Militarie Profession*, 1581. Rich seems to claim the tale as his original work; but his phrase might mean no more than that he was the first to tell it in English. On the score of dating, it has been held that the play borrowed from the tale;[30] and this seems a reasonable conclusion. But Moore Smith believed play and novella to have been separately derived from a common source.[31]

No one, I think, has ever entered among the claimants for *Philotus*, for very obvious reasons, the only Scotsman of the time known to have been a dramatist, William Alexander of Menstrie, who was knighted in 1609 and raised to the peerage as Viscount Canada and Lord Alexander of Menstrie in 1630 and promoted as Earl of Stirling in 1633. As tutor to Prince Henry till 1603 and the holder of many other offices later, he was a member of the royal entourage and well-placed if he had wanted to have his dramas performed by a company so dependent on Court patronage and protection as Fletcher's was. King James is said to have been delighted with Alexander's works and to have "honoured their author with his conversation, calling him his philosophical poet".[32] Alexander assisted the King in a metrical version of the Psalms, which was published in 1631 and which was largely, if not entirely, the work of the assistant.

His four "Monarchicke Tragedies", which make up about half of his output in verse, are the work of a man more familiar with the Senecan closet-drama of the sixteenth century than with the normal requirements for plays to be performed in a public theatre, then or at any other time. It is true that, unlike most of his brother-Senecans, he did not feel bound to observe the constricting unities of time, place, and action, which neo-classic theorists regarded as obligatory in drama, however indifferent to them playwrights for the public theatres were. But, like other Senecans, he has a chorus in each of his tragedies; and, like so many of them, he chooses his plots from ancient history, casting the speeches of all the characters, not into blank verse, but into heroic quatrains interspersed with heroic couplets. The result is anything but dramatic by ordinary standards. The reader's attention is not engaged by plot, incident, or situation. There is far too little movement of any kind, and far too much disquisition; and there is no resemblance to the manners, feelings, or utterance of actual life. The plays really exist for the moral and political reflections in which all but the quite minor characters indulge, sometimes to an incredible length. *The Alexandrean Tragedy*, for example, opens with a speech of five folio pages by the ghost of Alexander the Great; and *Julius Caesar* with a speech of similar length by Juno. But it should be added for Alexander's credit that his plays and also his poems have a distinctly metaphysical quality; and the hunter after literary curios will find much to interest him in their packed and recondite allusions.

It would be a mistake to assume that the serious-minded persons of the sixteenth and seventeenth centuries, who produced edifying and rhetorical pseudo-dramas of a monumental dullness, wrote them with absolutely no hope or design of getting them performed. In fact the most unlikely plays were performed, at any rate before special audiences in courts and inns of court, in universities and schools. So Alexander may have tried, at least, to get his tragedies acted. He may or may not have succeeded; but he certainly thought well enough of his dramas to print them, with many corrections in the second and subsequent editions, one five times, another four times, and the other two thrice each, which is oftener than the appearances of any other closet-dramas of the period.

Darius was published in 1603 in Edinburgh, and then along with *Croesus* in 1604 in London; and both of these plays with *The Alexandrean Tragedy* and *Julius Caesar* in 1607, 1616, and 1637, all in London. The first edition of *Darius* was one of the last books printed by Robert Waldegrave before leaving Scotland and resettling in London; and the dedicatory verses to James VI point to its having been in the press before James's accession to the English throne. The author describes it in the prose address to the reader as "the first essay of my rude and unskilfull Muse in a Tragicall Poeme". He was born about 1567; and, though he began to publish work only in 1603 when he was already in his later thirties, he had probably written much of it before committing it to the press. Among Alexander's miscellaneous poems are *Some Verses Written to his Majestie by the Authour at the time of his Maiesties first entrie into England*, in which he speaks in unmistakably plural terms of "dead Monarkes", "olde Heroes", and "the Potentates of former times", whose fates his "tragick muse" had celebrated:

> But this age great with glorie hath brought forth
> A matchlesse Monarke whom peace highly raises,
> Who as th'vntainted Ocean of all worth
> As due to him hath swallow'd all your praises.
> > Whose cleere excellencies long knowne for such,
> > All men must praise, and none can praise too much.

> For that which others hardly could acquire,
> > With losse of thousands liues and endlesse paine,
> Is heapt on him euen by their owne desire,
> > That thrist [= thirst] t'enjoy the fruites of his blest raigne:
> > And neuer conquerour gain'd so great a thing,
> > As those wise subiects gaining such a King.

So at least two and, not improbably, all four of Alexander's tragedies had been written while James was still resident in Scotland, and, I would add, while his actors under Fletcher were still based in Edinburgh.

The four tragedies are in an English not so very different from that of, say, Samuel Daniel or Fulke Greville. Like William Drummond of Hawthornden (1585-1649), his friend younger by nearly twenty years, Alexander belonged from the outset and by choice much more to the English than to the Scottish literary tradition. He was well aware of his linguistic singularity and quite consciously tried to reduce it, in a manner not unlike that of the men of the Scottish Enlightenment in the eighteenth century whose aim was to write with the elegance of Addison and Berkeley, Swift and Chesterfield. Alexander says in the address to the reader of *Darius*, his first publication: "The language of this poeme is, as thou seest, mixt of the English and Scottish dialects; which perhaps may be vnpleasant and irksome to some readers of both nations. But I hope the gentle and judicious English reader will beare with me, if I retaine some badge of mine owne countrie, by vsing sometimes words that are peculiar therevnto, especiallie when I find them proper and significant. And as for my owne countrymen, they may not justly finde fault with me, if for the more part I vse the English phrase, as worthie to be preferred before our owne for the elegancie and perfection thereof." Accordingly, though there are Scotticisms in it, the play would have presented no serious problems to English actors; and it is, in language and the easily memorized dialogue in rhymed verse, just what might have been expected from an erudite Scotsman writing for English actors to play before a Scottish audience and a learned Scottish King who hoped to be called in the near future to the English throne. Between the editions of 1603 and 1604, the first issued in Edinburgh and the second in London, *Darius* was made to appeal more to the English public by the elimination of as much Scots wording as Alexander detected. The 1607 edition of *Darius* and *Croesus* is merely a re-issue of the 1604 text of these plays, along with the first editions of *The Alexandrean Tragedy* and *Julius Caesar*. The 1616 edition extensively revises all four plays to bring them nearer to the southern idiom in the light of Alexander's longer familiarity with it. He gave a final stylistic overhaul to his four plays in 1637. As *Croesus*, *The Alexandrean Tragedy*, and *Julius Caesar* were published for the first time in England, after James's accession and Alexander's migration southwards, they were more anglicized in language from the start and underwent less, though some, revision in subsequent editions. It does not follow, however, that the original composition of some or all of them was not just as "mixt of the English and Scottish dialects" as was *Darius*. Nor does it follow that the promise in the address to the reader of the first edition of *Darius* "to bring foorth hereafter frute of the same kind" refers to literary plans not yet begun. If I am doubtful whether all of *The Monarchicke Tragedies* were written before the Union of the Crowns, I am pretty certain that *Darius* and *Croesus* were.

One play, not extant but known to have been acted by the King's men late in 1604, must be mentioned here as a possible item in Fletcher's repertoire in Scotland. This was a drama on the Gowrie Conspiracy. According to a letter of 18th December 1604 to Sir Ralph Winwood from John Chamberlain, a disseminator of news and gossip to his correspondents: "The Tragedy of *Gowry*, with all the Action and Actors, hath been twice represented by the King's Players, with exceeding Concourse of all sorts of People. But whether the matter or manner be not well handled, or that it be thought unfit that Princes should be played on the Stage in their Life-time, I hear that some great Councellors are much displeased with it, and so 'tis thought shall be forbidden."[33] Whether in fact the performances were stopped is not known.

Chamberlain writes as if "The Tragedy of *Gowry*" was a new play; and the title he gives it seems to imply that it presented Gowrie's fate with at least some compassion. But both inferences may be wrong. Though new on a London stage, it may well have been a propagandist and pro-James play put on first in Scotland at the King's command in 1600-1, at the time when he was actively taking other measures as well to convince or silence those who were reluctant to accept the royal version of the Gowrie Conspiracy. It was the "great Councellors", according to Chamberlain, who were displeased by the play. James himself does not seem to have been offended by his own company's performance of it. At least, he had them play no less than eleven times at Court between 1st November 1604 and 12th February 1605.[34]

A final question, which I have delayed till now, is: Where, if anywhere, does *Macbeth* come in the context of this Chapter? Anything like an adequate answer involves so many considerations that an attempt at an answer must be reserved for another Chapter.

Notes

1. II, ii, 343-45.
2. II, ii, 346-47.
3. II, ii, 457.

4. III, ii, 165-271.
5. II, ii, 332-39.
6. *Cf.* 141 *supra*.

7. II, ii, 415-21.
8. II, ii, 474-86, 490-519, 524, 528-41.
9. II, ii, 455-56.
10. III, ii, 247-51.
11. II, ii, 565-67.
12. III, ii, 42-50.
13. II, ii, 522.
14. Sir W. S. Gilbert, *Original Plays*. Third Series. 1924. 272-73.
15. II, ii, 467-69.
16. II, ii, 576-92.
17. III, ii, 1-16, 18-39, 42.
18. III, ii, 149-50.
19. Elsinore was one of the many centres, from Madrid to Warsaw, to which they penetrated.
20. III, ii, 262-64.
21. *Cf.* 134-36 *supra*.
22. *Henslowe's Diary*. Edited by Sir W. W. Greg. 1904-8. I, 4.
23. Chambers, *Stage*, II, 114.
24. Not to be confused with Philotas, one of the generals of Alexander the Great. Samuel Daniel wrote *The Tragedy of Philotas* and published it in 1605, 1607, and 1611. Daniel's friend, Richard Lateware, had previously used the same plot in a lost play.
25. *I.e.* till it was given by the Edinburgh University Dramatic Society during a recent Edinburgh International Festival.
26. The madrigal has only two stanzas in *Philotus* and in Allison's anthology. Three other stanzas are found in Richard Johnson's *The Golden Garland of Princely Pleasures and Delicate Delights*, 1620 (3rd ed.); but they are not regarded as by the same author.
27. *Cf.* Campion's *Songs and Masques, with Observations in the Art of English Poesy*. Edited by A. H. Bullen, 1903, 270.
28. William Crowe, *A Treatise on English Versification*, 1827, 105.
29. Ben Jonson's *Silent Woman* has a not unsimilar plot, however different otherwise.
30. J. P. Collier, however, in his edition of Rich for the Shakespeare Society, 1846, argues unconvincingly for the priority of the play.
31. *Rich's Story Of Phylotus and Emilia* in *The Modern Language Review*, 1910.
32. Alexander Chalmers, *The Works of the English Poets*, 1810, V, 290.
33. *Memorials of Affairs of State in the Reigns of Queen Elizabeth and King James I*. Collected (chiefly) from the Original Papers of . . . Sir Ralph Winwood. By Edmund Sawyer. 3 vols. 1725, II, 41.
34. Chambers, *Stage*, II, 211; IV, 119.

10

Facts, Deductions, Inferences, and Speculations

> My former speeches have but hit your thoughts,
> Which can interpret further: only, I say,
> Things have been strangely borne.
> *Macbeth*, III, vi, 1-3.

[The numbers in brackets refer to previous pages; and the capital letters in brackets to notes at the end of this Chapter.]

At the end of Chapter 9 on the kinds of plays which might conceivably have been presented by English actors in the Scotland of James VI, I finished with the question: Where, if anywhere, does *Macbeth* come in such a context?

In order to reach my answer, if such I may call it, I feel that I must gather together from previous Chapters such facts as are specially relevant and such probabilities as may be reasonably deduced from them.

CHAPTER 1. In this introductory Chapter, I argued for the presence of a considerable amount of topical material in Shakespeare's plays, against Sir Edmund Chambers's view that there is but little. I suggested that in *Macbeth* in particular there is much of the topical, both such as Shakespeare meant to be recognized and such as he drew from the Scotland of James VI to complete his picture of an earlier period without caring whether it would be picked up or not. In so doing he "treated his Scottish story in a Scottish setting as something of a special case requiring special treatment" (6).

CHAPTER 2. I described *Macbeth* as "the play with the greatest topical content in the Shakespearian canon" (7), by reason of the amount of matter in it reflecting contemporary interests in one way or another. I put 1601 forward as the date of the main composition of the play as distinct from later revisions or insertions (11-13). By so doing, I was flying in the face of practically all previous daters of the play. The date of composition is nearly always given as 1606. A fairly recent exception is Dover Wilson who argued for 1601 or early 1602, on stylistic grounds (12); an opinion anticipated on the same grounds by Saintsbury and Sir Herbert Grierson (39, note 25). But I think that I have been able to adduce harder evidence than is afforded by judgements on style alone.

There is, for one thing, the incontestable fact that in early 1602 Charles Massey wrote for the Lord Admiral's company the lost *Malcolm, King of Scots*. I submitted that the obvious reason for the rivals to the Lord Chamberlain's company wanting a play on so unlikely a period of Scottish history was to catch such share of acclaim as they could by offering a sequel or "second part" to *Macbeth* of the year before (12-13).

But my main reason for dating *Macbeth* in 1601 is the extraordinary parallelism between the play and the Gowrie Conspiracy of 1600 (11, 12, 22, 29; see also below under Chapter 7). As I remarked (11), the daters of *Macbeth* in 1606 have nearly all been Englishmen, with what I reluctantly describe as the typically English lack of interest in or knowledge of Scottish history; and they jumped to the conclusion that the play must have been sparked off, so to speak, by the English sensation of the Gunpowder Plot of 1605, though that Plot bears no resemblance at all to the action of *Macbeth*. But, whatever has been the attitude of later Englishmen to Scottish affairs, the Englishmen of Shakespeare's own day, like everybody in Western Europe at the time, had the liveliest curiosity about the Gowrie Conspiracy, even though the Gunpowder Plot when it *did* occur upstaged the Conspiracy in their minds. After all, the older and more infirm Elizabeth became, the more interested did her English subjects become in the person most likely to succeed her and in all that they heard about him; not least his figuring as a principal in the Gowrie Conspiracy, which had so nearly ended in a disaster as serious for England as for Scotland.

But I would emphasize here that Shakespeare attempted nothing so obvious and straightforward as the unknown author of the lost "Tragedy of Gowry" in 1604. It apparently dramatized the very events of 5th August 1600, with characters bearing the names of the actual participants (13, 177). Shakespeare proceeded much more subtly, allusively, and artistically to present, not a mere piece of ephemeral stage-journalism with an up-to-the-minute plot, but a tragic masterpiece to defy time, on a centuries-old action from Scottish history which nevertheless by a miraculous adaptation and development reflected the recent by means of the past, without any sacrifice whatever of its power as an autonomous drama. If Shakespeare had in fact restricted himself to the story as it is told in Holinshed, his play would have had much less resemblance to the Gowrie affair than it undoubtedly has. But his tragedy from the past only suggests the more recent: it does not represent it. The play is in the nature more of an echo, symbol, or hieroglyph than of a mirror-image. And *Macbeth* still impresses us, who no longer have the Gowrie Conspiracy in the forefront of our curiosity, as much as the temples at Karnak and Luxor impress modern sightseers who cannot read the inscriptions.

While I believe that *Macbeth* originated in 1601, not 1606, I recognized in Chapter 2 that it underwent, between its first composition and its first appearance in print which was in the 1623 Folio, a variety of treatments in the way of cutting, adding, and revising, only some small amount of which was done by Shakespeare himself, the rest being the sacrilegious work of others or, to use a Scots-Law term, their vicious intromission (7-11). Had *Macbeth* been printed in quarto fairly soon after its composition, it would have been saved from the losses and contamination which have left it in such a sorry state.

In discussing Shakespeare's sources for *Macbeth*, I presented evidence (14-18) for his use of William Stewart's *Buik of the Croniclis of Scotland*, as was first done by Charlotte Carmichael Stopes. I agreed with Mrs. Stopes that from the *Buik* he derived important elements in the characterization of Macbeth and Lady Macbeth and in the relationship between them in the first two acts, for which there is no parallel in Holinshed. I reserve for submission a little later my speculation on how and where Shakespeare came to consult Stewart's *Buik*.

CHAPTER 3. In this Chapter I drew attention to certain details in *Macbeth* which show Shakespeare to have had some familiarity, hitherto unrecognized and altogether surprising, with Scots Law and procedure. The details in question do not signal their presence. They are in fact unobtrusively woven into the fabric of the play, largely by metaphors and images, as are the many other legalisms from English Law in Shakespeare's other plays.

The plot of *Macbeth* has, at its hub, treason and two murders of guests by their host: these crimes are the very heart of the tragedy and it hardly needs saying that Shakespeare concentrated on them all his powers and skill. It is quite obvious that he had become aware of certain peculiarities of Scots Law and process in this field and had worked them appropriately into a play set in Scotland. The most notable passage in this respect is Macbeth's soliloquy in I, vii, 1-28, which I quoted in full (43-44). Embedded in it are legal concepts from three Scottish enactments of quite recent date: a 1587 Act of Parliament defining such an aggravated murder as that of a guest by his host as murder under trust and constituting it a statutory treason liable to the same prosecution and punishment as any other level of treason; a 1592 Act elaborating the solemn ritual to be observed in the laying of charges of treason; and a 1591 Act of Sederunt of the Court of Session which admitted as receivable witnesses in treason trials persons unacceptable in other cases, including women, minors of any age, and *famosi* (*i.e.* disreputable characters, known criminals, and accessaries), and which pronounced a single witness as adequate without other confirmation. I analysed out the legalisms in Macbeth's soliloquy (47-48), which, I must recall, bristles with imagery from courts and judgements. The anachronism of throwing the Jacobean enactments back in time to the period of Duncan and Macbeth is of no consequence. Probably Shakespeare only knew of their being items in the Law of Scotland, without concerning himself with when they came into operation.

In presenting two murders under trust, Shakespeare shows himself fully aware of the importance in such crimes of the insidious invitation of a guest by a host with a murderous intention, such "invitation" being, in Sir George Mackenzie's words "one branch of this trust" (48). In fact, by elaborating as he does the inviting of both Duncan and Banquo (48-51), Shakespeare seems to have wanted to make absolutely clear to his audience the criminal category of murder under trust or *homicidium sub praetextu amicitiae*.

Moreover, he knew the full implications in a legal charge of being "art and part" in a crime, which was a long-standing description in Scots Law taken

N

from Roman Law. The evidence is the emphasis Shakespeare lays on Macbeth's scheme to have Banquo killed by hirelings in Macbeth's own absence, and on his recoil in the banquet scene when in spite of all his precautions Banquo's ghost appears in silent accusation (50-51).

I noted in Chapter 3 (51-52) Shakespeare's use in *Macbeth* as a ἅπαξ λεγόμενον of "interdiction", which might be the adaptation of another Scots legalism.

In the same Chapter (51), but more fully in Chapter 4 (58-59), I discussed the possibility or indeed the likelihood of Shakespeare's alluding twice in *Macbeth* to the term given to a scheme laid down in a 1587 Act for a system of sureties and pledges for all persons to be held responsible for the good behaviour of their vassals. The Act was an attempt to bring a measure of order into the more unruly parts of the kingdom; and its provisions came to be known as the General Bond or Band.

CHAPTER 4. In this Chapter I told the story of the long-continuing feud between Clandonald of Islay and Kintyre and Clanlean of Duart which ran on through most of James VI's reign in Scotland and well into the seventeenth century (55-69). My reason for narrating the feud was that a peculiarly perfidious massacre under trust in 1586 by Macdonald of his Maclean guests was the immediate cause of the legislation and enactments of 1587, 1591 and 1592 which put murder under trust into the category of treason and provided for its appropriate publicising, trial, and punishment; and the origin also of other Acts of 1587 designed for the pacification of the more turbulent parts of Scotland, especially Act 92 which established the just-mentioned General Bond or Band (58-59; see also above under Chapter 3).

I had a second reason for giving the story of the feud. In Chapter 2 (30) I quoted Sir Herbert Grierson's view that in Holinshed's *Scottish Chronicle* Shakespeare encountered an ethnic type new to him, together with accounts of the bloody and treacherous acts to which it was sometimes prompted and the moods of conscience and superstitious fear which could follow them. But I suggested that Shakespeare may perhaps have had as well more recent manifestations of the Celtic temperament to go on (30). Certainly, if he had heard of the feud, which he may well have done in following out his interest in murder under trust, he would have been as deeply interested in the contemporary life of the clans for the ethnic background of his *Macbeth*, which, it should be realised, is all about Scottish Highlanders, not about Scottish Lowlanders (A). I quoted a number of passages in the play which at least resemble items in the feud (63-68).

CHAPTER 5. I summarised in this Chapter (71-85) the officially-inspired version of the Gowrie Conspiracy. Whatever else bearing on the Conspiracy Shakespeare may have read (71; see also below under Chapter 6, 87-91), he could not possibly have missed the official version. I have not tried to correct that version in any way, but simply to retell it succinctly and without dropping anything in the least degree significant.

CHAPTER 6. This Chapter is concerned with three results of the Gowrie Conspiracy: [1] The output of printed and unprinted matter, official and otherwise, friendly or critical, both such pamphlets as Shakespeare is unlikely to have missed and such others as were less likely to have been read by him (87-91); [2] the holidays and thanksgivings for the King's escape, with some comparison of James's generosity to his rescuers and that of Duncan and Malcolm to their deserving subjects in the play (91-96); and [3] the legal processes of all kinds, which continued for months and which followed precisely the provisions of the already-mentioned parliamentary Acts of 1587 and 1592 and the Court of Session Act of Sederunt of 1591 for the fitting denunciation, trial, and punishment of treason and murder under trust (96-103).

CHAPTER 7. The purpose of this Chapter is to confirm, at greater length and in detail, the statement in Chapter 2 (11) to the effect that the Gowrie Conspiracy of 1600, not the Gunpowder Plot of 1605, was the threat to James's life which Shakespeare reflected in *Macbeth*. The circumstances of the Gowrie Conspiracy with its attempted *homicidium sub praetextu amicitiae* closely parallel those of Duncan's actual murder by Macbeth as Shakespeare presents it. But the circumstances of the Gunpowder Plot have no resemblance whatsoever to the tragedy (109-13, 120-24).

When Shakespeare read up the Macbeth story in Holinshed, he encountered the name Gowrie, not as the title of a nobleman, but as the name of the district in which stood the Castle of Dunsinane and in which lay also Birnam and Scone. The name Gowrie was on everybody's lips in England and Scotland in 1600-1; and Shakespeare could not have helped associating the traitor Gowrie and his Conspiracy with the district where the catastrophe of his own tragedy was to be set (113).

In dramatizing from Holinshed Shakespeare modified his source in the general direction of the Gowrie Conspiracy and of particulars in the official version of it (109). For instance, he makes far more of Macbeth's invitations to his intended victims, Duncan first and Banquo later, than Holinshed does, and indeed stresses them. So it was also in the Gowrie Conspiracy, for nothing could have been more pressing and urgent than the invitation to James to visit Gowrie House (110). I add, rather unnecessarily, that there was no invitation in the prearrangement of the Gunpowder Plot.

Again in the Gunpowder Plot there was no supernatural factor; whereas in the Gowrie Conspiracy, with a traitor who dabbled in the occult, there was such a factor, and it was strongly emphasised in all the legal proceedings at the instance of the King (110).

Admittedly, Holinshed's story has a certain element of the supernatural; but all told, it amounts to very little. On the other hand, Shakespeare introduces far more, investing his whole play with supernaturalisms and including such inventions of his own as the visionary dagger, the voices in the night, the terrifying dreams, the ghost of Banquo, the apparitions in the witches' cavern, and and in some sense even the sleep-walking (111). Macbeth's inability to say "Amen" (II, ii, 23-33), besides having the suggestion of a supernatural cause, may derive from Gowrie's dying without calling on God, which failure was given a sinister significance (80, 112).

To the same supernatural category belong the signs and wonders of which Shakespeare makes so much, drawing some of them from other passages in Holinshed than the Macbeth story and adding some of his own (112-114). One is particularly interesting, the passage II, iv, 11-13, in which Tuesday and a falcon are associated; because of James's insistence that every Tuesday thereafter be observed as a day of preaching and thanksgiving since that was the day of the week on which he had escaped from death at Gowrie House; and because of the notorious fluttering of a hawk about the turret room on that occasion (112-13).

One of the most important and noteworthy changes Shakespeare made on Holinshed's narrative in order to reflect the events of the Gowrie Conspiracy was to give Lennox, who does not figure at all among the Scottish nobles in Holinshed, a prominent role as one in constant attendance on his sovereign. That was precisely the part which the Duke of Lennox played through the whole day of the Conspiracy. And his account of the events, communicated in the precognition, as the Scots-Law term is for a preliminary examination with reference to a prosecution, was the first and, except Andrew Henderson's, the longest and the most detailed to be read at the great treason trial before the King and the Scots Parliament which began on 4th November 1600 (101, 113-19).

But still more striking is Shakespeare's departure from Holinshed in the characterization and motivation of Macbeth and Lady Macbeth and in their relation, partly in line with William Stewart's Buik of the Croniclis of Scotland, (14-18), but also with an eye on the Gowrie family. Holinshed's Macbeth needs no instigation whatever. Though he has a wife who is said to be very ambitious to be queen, she is dismissed as such in half a sentence, with no further part to play in her husband's career and no influence on it or on him. But Shakespeare makes his Lady Macbeth as prominent as her husband and much the stronger character in the first half of the play, ambitious only for Macbeth, not for herself. His Macbeth in the same half of the play is double-minded and irresolute and has to be forced by his single-minded and resolute wife to take decisive action (120).

This situation in which a supposedly weaker partner, according to con-ventional notions, is in fact the stronger is paralleled in the Gowrie Conspiracy; since in it the younger brother was the energetic and forceful one, not the elder and brooding head of the family. And as in Macbeth, the two conspirators operated in the utmost secrecy with no confidants and only such helpers as were kept completely unaware of what was afoot; whereas Holinshed's Macbeth consulted his friends on his claim to the throne, though not in the actual planning of Duncan's murder (120-24).

There is also the minor but interesting parallel between the agitation of Shakespeare's Macbeth and his distrait absenting himself when Duncan is being entertained to supper and the Earl of Gowrie's moonish behaviour and wandering about from room to room when James was dining in the house. There is nothing corresponding in Holinshed's narrative (122-23).

CHAPTER 8. This Chapter offered a brief history of the stage in Scotland under James VI up to 1603, with an account of the different attitudes to the drama of King and Court, clergy and laity. I described the education James was given to make him a Reformed monarch (130-32), his rebellion, and his adoption of a very different idea of kingship (132). But what I chiefly wanted to note was the King's love of shows and entertainments of all sorts (127-28), his interest in and his knowledge of English actors visiting his country from 1589-90 on, for the most part and perhaps always at his invitation (133-41, etc.), and the favour he extended to them (133-60).

That royal favour was remarkable in view of James's chronic impecuniosity. Proportionately it far surpassed any such countenance as the English actors enjoyed in their own country. James eagerly constituted himself, not only the generous patron, but the champion of players and playing, and waged vigorous campaigns on their behalf against his clergy. I shall have to refer to this topic again more fully a little later.

CHAPTER 9. I described in this Chapter Shakespeare's obvious familiarity with theatrical touring (165-69); and I speculated on what plays English actors visiting Scotland might have brought with them or might have acquired after they had arrived (169-77), concluding with the question with which I opened the present Chapter: Where, if anywhere, does *Macbeth* come in such a context?

Something like that question could be put more explicitly thus: Was *Macbeth* written originally for Lawrence Fletcher and his fellows to perform first in Scotland in 1601 for the satisfaction and complimenting of its King— a King who claimed to be descended both from Duncan and from Banquo; who had very exalted ideas of the kingly office; who took *Beati pacifici* as his motto and made peace at home and abroad his political aim; who had an intense interest in and an absolute conviction of the malign activities of witches; and, not least, who was still marvelling at his providential escape from a traitor and still ordering his people to celebrate it with him?

Other related or consequential questions which suggest themselves are: Did Shakespeare have some special reason for writing *Macbeth*, a reason additional to the normal one of a professional dramatist making his living by a series of plays? And did Shakespeare have a more intimate knowledge of Scotland than could be obtained at a distance and from secondary sources? In short, did he ever visit Scotland? If so, when and in what circumstances?

Macbeth could fairly be described as unique among Shakespeare's plays in several respects. But there are two which are particularly relevant to the questions I have been posing.

The first of these uniquenesses is that *Macbeth* has so much in it to compliment, flatter, and interest King James that it must have been designedly written for his special gratification; so much indeed as to suggest that it was a commissioned work (B). If there was such a commission, the likeliest time for it was in 1601, when James was prolonging his celebrations for his escape from treason at Gowrie House and was gloating over his humiliation of the clerical theatrophobes who had objected to his patronage of players.

The second uniqueness which I single out is Shakespeare's very sensitive handling of his *mise-en-scène* in *Macbeth*. There is a pervasive difference in it from his procedure in all his other plays. Normally he, like other dramatists for the public theatres, treated plots set in foreign parts all pretty much in the same way; that is to say, without really acclimatising them or conceiving of the incidents, the characters, their feelings, sentiments, and reactions, and the world of their being as differing much, except in superficial ways, from that of their contemporary London and England. Ben Jonson, it is true, took a different line in his *Catiline* and *Sejanus*, with their heavily-loaded classical antiquarianism; but he succeeds only in giving such a sense of the life of the past as one gets in an archaeological museum. His *Every Man in his Humour* was at first set in Florence; but in a revised version Jonson was able to transfer it with a minimum of change to the London where it had always belonged. In his other plays set abroad, like *Volpone* in Venice and *The Case is Altered* in Milan, he followed the normal practice of his contemporaries.

Their practice could be compared to that of the Renaissance painters who transferred Biblical or classical situations to Florentine or Venetian palaces, dressed most of their figures in fifteenth- or sixteenth-century costumes, and surrounded them with accessories of the same period, making only token approximations to historical and local considerations. The Elizabethan and Jacobean dramatists were not really historically-minded and not really interested, except to a quite minor degree, in conditions different from their own. For them, it was the story as story, the plot as plot which counted. And in dramatizing a story, they envisaged it in terms of their own experience, or, to put it figuratively, cooked it for the stage according to the standard recipes, which was all that their equally unhistorically-minded and untravelled audience expected.

It might be objected that Shakespeare in his plays based on classical history, *Coriolanus*, *Julius Caesar*, and *Antony and Cleopatra*, tried to create a classical world like Ben Jonson. But in fact he did no such thing. Such classical hints and suggestions as there are, however telling, do not come from a scholarly and wide-ranging familiarity with classical history and literature. They come from no other quarter than Shakespeare's source, Plutarch's *Parallel Lives*, or rather from Sir Thomas North's English translation of Jacques Amyot's French translation which was probably made from a Latin version of Plutarch's Greek.

I know, too, that some people have supposed that Shakespeare must have visited Italy, on the score of an allegedly Italianate flavour in *Romeo and Juliet* and *The Merchant of Venice*. But their flavour is only that of the romantic-poetic drama of the age, except that Shakespeare's has more bouquet.

Shakespeare, however, did something quite different in *Macbeth* from his procedure in any other play set in a country not his own. For his Scottish story was not regarded like any other plot *ab extra*: it was by him carefully and deliberately embedded in Scotland, a Scotland recognized as being notably different from England. The characters, their circumstances and way of life, their social organization and law, their moods, passions, and racial idiosyncrasies are presented precisely for their differences from people and life in London and England. So is their very language, not by its being an attempted imitation of the Scots vernacular, but by being an utterance perfectly keyed to the ethos (33-38). And the action takes place against an unmistakably Highland background with great empty moors and uplands and a paucity of towns, buildings, and inhabitants, and in a climate and atmosphere with more harshness than geniality and more darkness and half-light than sun, except for the striking exception of the passage on Inverness Castle (I, vi, 1-10); a landscape, climate, and atmosphere both appropriate to the deeds done within their ambience and also designed to contrast with conditions in England (29-33).

I cannot believe that the Scottishness of *Macbeth* all came to Shakespeare from his imagination working on secondary sources, and that he was never at closer quarters with Scots and Scotland than Stratford and London; just as I find it impossible to believe, as some have maintained with regard to the *Sonnets*, that Shakespeare wrote them out of mind-stuff alone and had no closer experience of the situation he exploits than he got from reading the outpourings of other sonneteers. It has the *feel* of Scotland, as authentic and convincing as the *feel* of India in Kipling and E. M. Forster; in spite of the fact that a dramatist by the very nature of his medium has to achieve his atmospheric and other effects by mere hints and brief suggestions through a word or phrase dropped by the characters alone; not as the unrestricted novelist can do, who is able to take as much time and print as he needs to create his illusion, more by his own running commentary than by what his characters say.

I said earlier (181) that I would return to the question of how and where Shakespeare consulted William Stewart's *Buik of the Croniclis of Scotland*. It could not have been anywhere in England or, it would appear, any place but one in Scotland. For Stewart's *Buik* existed in a single manuscript which had certainly once been in the royal ownership of James V and which can reasonably be identified with "the Scottis Chronicle wrettin with hand" known to have been at Holyroodhouse in the reign of James VI (14). If one accepts, as I do, the case for Shakespeare's having read Stewart's *Buik*, one is forced, as I am, to the conclusion that he did so in Scotland and that there he had such access to the royal library as would not normally be accorded to a strolling player, but which might have been granted to a special player for a special purpose by none other than the King himself (C).

The idea is not so wild as it might at first appear. In fact, it would not have been at all out of character for James to do such a favour, however unlikely it would have been for Queen Elizabeth to have done it. James was always doing and saying off-beat things. And he was likely to be, not less, but more unconventional in extending his friendship to anyone who catered for his favourite amusement of the theatre. As I have already said (185), James was no enemy to English players visiting his country, but on the contrary their generous friend, patron, and protector. He seems to have kept himself informed of theatrical affairs in England (132-38). In 1589 he began to invite English actors to Scotland (133-37); and, if later groups were not specially invited but came at a venture, they knew that they would be welcome to the King at least

(137-41). Besides favouring players in general, James could take a remarkable interest in individuals among them, as in the case of Lawrence Fletcher (137-38). He would himself give express commands for the payment of the players (137, 148, 158); and on at least one occasion it was he who handed over the money (141). In 1599, when the English actors established themselves as more than summer visitors, James gave the company a warrant to act in public, ordered the Edinburgh Bailies to provide a building for conversion into the first Scottish theatre, and directed that money should be given to the players for material to adapt it (141). The consequence was a war in two campaigns with his puritanical clergy, which James waged with zest in 1599 and 1600-1 (141-48, 149-56). At some time in the course of the war James took the visiting English players into his own service as "his maiesties servandis", probably in the summer or autumn of 1601 (149). In the October of the same year James sent his players with a "speciall letter" of commendation to the civic authorities of Aberdeen. They formed part of the entourage of a French visitor whom James wanted to honour in a signal way. Obviously he would not have sent his players on a journey of this kind if he had regarded them as no better than rogues and vagabonds. And the Aberdeen authorities showed their regard for the bearers of the King's commission by including Lawrence Fletcher among the eighteen "knightis and gentellmen", who, along with the French nobleman and others, were made burgesses on 23rd October (156-58). After this tour the company on its return to Edinburgh received a particularly handsome payment by a royal precept (158). Fletcher and his fellows would have little inducement to remain in Scotland after their royal patron had gone south in April 1603. Almost certainly they went south with the King or at no long interval after him. For cordial letters patent were issued by James on 19th May, following a Privy Seal direction of 17th May (only ten days after the King's arrival in his new Capital), to Lawrence Fletcher and William Shakespeare as the principals of the King's new company, made up of some or all of his Scottish players and the former Lord Chamberlain's men (158-59).

The "speciall letter" of commendation to the Aberdeen authorities prompts me to refer to a tradition, which I see no reason to doubt, linking King James and Shakespeare in a personal relationship. It was first put in print in the Advertisement to an edition of Shakespeare's *Poems*, published in 1709-10 by Bernard Lintot: "That most learned prince and great patron of learning, King James the First, was pleased with his own hand to write an amicable [sic] letter to Mr. Shakespeare; which letter, though now lost, remained long in the hands of Sir William D'Avenant, as a credible person now living can testify" (D). D'Avenant is said to have been Shakespeare's godson; and it would not have been unnatural for the godfather to have made a present to his godson of the "amicable letter" from King James (E).

If the letter ever existed, I venture to say that James did not write it "with his own hand" merely in order to pass the time of day, but with some more positive intention. Nor do I think that the letter was in the nature of a royal command, but rather in the way of a friendly suggestion or invitation. And, since a letter is normally sent to a recipient at some distance away, I offer as a reasonable possibility that the King's "amicable letter" was written in Scotland and contained a friendly invitation to a dramatist of some repute to come north from London for a Scottish welcome.

Be all that as it may, I think I have said enough of James's eccentricities to warrant my adding that he was the very man, if he had heard that one of the London playwrights was in his country for whatever reason, to urge him to write a new play—any play at all to amuse the Scottish King and help him, by its very existence and presentation at the new theatre in Blackfriars Wynd and Holyroodhouse, to flout his troublesome clergy who had taken so badly his patronage of the theatre and also his royal version of the Gowrie Conspiracy; but especially a play on treason with a Scottish subject which involved the history of his own dynasty.

A sojourn by Shakespeare in Scotland, and nothing else, would also explain his knowledge and use in *Macbeth* of certain particularities of Scots Law and procedure, as described in Chapter 3. Most of the enactments involved were of quite recent date. But, though they were recorded officially in volumes of parliamentary and judicial proceedings, they were not to be found by Shakespeare in any book at all likely to have reached him in England, or for that matter in Scotland either. That is to say, I do not think that he got his facts from a book at all. Nor do I believe that he got his information at second hand from someone like Lawrence Fletcher who had been in Scotland and then related it to Shakespeare in London. The legal and procedural items in question are not the kind of thing that a casual visitor to Scotland would be interested in or would pass on as possibly interesting to friends and neighbours in England. But they were just the kind of thing that a dramatist like Shakespeare with a legalistic turn and an eye for apt detail might seize on for use in a play set with such care and deliberation in Scotland as *Macbeth* is. This is as much as to say that Shakespeare picked up his Scottish legalisms in conversation and by observation on the spot, including observation of the differences from English usages in cases of treason, with which he was already familiar.

In 1601 the very hottest news and the liveliest gossip and discussion in Scotland were about the Gowrie Conspiracy and its ramifying sequels, along with the outward and visible operation of the machinery of the law. In fact, the country was buzzing at the time with talk of traitors and treason, murders under trust and trials. The very nature of the processes and operations was such as to strike the imaginations of all and sundry, gentle and simple—the impressive ceremony of proclamation of guilt and outlawry by heralds and trumpeters, the solemn arraignment and trial of the accused, and the grim conclusion of barbarous sentence and execution.

It is worth recalling that two of the participants in the rescue of the King at Gowrie House were in the party sent to accompany James's young French guest to Aberdeen in the autumn of 1601, Sir John Ramsay and Sir John Graham (157). It is clear, as I have already indicated (157-58), that James wanted de l'Hôpital to take back a good impression to France where the royal involvement in the Gowrie affair was looked on with suspicious eyes. Ramsay and Graham may have been meant to expand on the Conspiracy to de l'Hôpital, if, as might have been expected, he asked questions about it. Such a conversation would be in French rather than in Scots or English; and it would not be a private confabulation. Anyone within earshot who knew French would have been able to understand it. And such was Shakespeare (if for the moment we allow the possibility of his having been there), as he shows in *Henry V* in III, iv, and V, ii.

Another of the new-made burgesses at Aberdeen in October 1601 was Archibald Sym, "trumpeter" (157). He was not at all, as his designation might now suggest, of the standing of a town bellman. He was a dignified official of the Lord Lyon's Court; and he must have been frequently engaged on missions for proclamations and other announcements in terms of the 1592 Act and otherwise.

There were two other subjects for native Scots to extend themselves on to visitors from the South, especially perhaps in Aberdeen. One was the clan feud of which I gave an account in Chapter 4. The feud and the atrocities perpetrated in it were just the kind of news about the barbarous North and West of Scotland that the more settled Lowlanders would delight to retail as a justification of their hostility to their more warlike neighbours. Besides oral reports of the feud, a contemporary narrative of it was included in the manuscript *Historie and Life of King James the Sext* (63-69). It is extremely unlikely that any one of the half-dozen manuscript copies in existence was available in England. I do not suggest that therefore Shakespeare read one of them in Scotland; but only that if he had heard about the feud or had a chance to read a coherent account of it, he would have been deeply interested in the manner of life it revealed (55-56).

The other stock subject was that of witchcraft. There was an abundant literature of it in existence; and Shakespeare could have read it anywhere (24-25). And he no doubt was familiar with much more about alleged witches and charms, which merely passed from mouth to mouth. There was of course plenty of such talk in Scotland, not least in Aberdeen where there had been a particularly sensational witch-hunt or series of them in 1596-97. Though no report of the trials was printed till 1841, they would still be talked over and over in 1601. And it has been argued, with some plausibility, that certain odd details not found elsewhere are worked into the witch-scenes of *Macbeth*.

I suggested the possibility that King James's "amicable letter" to Shakespeare contained an invitation to come to Scotland. But in 1601 Shakespeare may have had another powerful motive for taking the air at a distance from London.

The theatrical company to which he belonged and for which he was the principal dramatist, the Lord Chamberlain's men, had been imprudently drawn into the periphery of a wild and stupid plot against the Queen's government. The ringleader, who was perhaps as much led himself as he led others, was the rather showy Robert Devereux, Earl of Essex. He was, despite his many indiscretions and liberties, the most indulged and smiled-on of Elizabeth's favourites after the death in 1588 of his stepfather, Robert Dudley, Earl of Leicester. He kept himself much in the public eye and was very popular, not only with the crowds, but with aspirants to literary fame, being one himself and an open-handed patron of others. His leadership of what might be called the party of the young men inevitably aroused the hostility of Elizabeth's staider counsellors, as well as that of rivals among her courtiers like Sir Walter Raleigh. Essex had successes and reverses by land and sea; and on the score of his successes he had gained a somewhat ill-founded reputation as a man of action and enterprise. In 1599 Elizabeth appointed Essex to the unenviable but highly important office of Lieutenant and Governor-General of Ireland, at a time when the situation in that country was more than usually serious. It would appear that Sir Robert Cecil engineered the appointment and tricked Essex into accepting the Siege Perilous. There was immense popular approval and relief at the news; and Essex set out on 27th March 1599 from London amid the deafening applause of the crowds (3-4).

But he lost his nerve in the face of mountainous difficulties and was a complete failure. He slunk back in disgrace to England, where on 28th September he burst into the Queen's presence at Nonsuch Palace in Surrey and threw himself on her mercy. Elizabeth did not forgive him this time, but was slow to act, probably out of a lingering fondness. Her elderly advisers, however, no doubt fanned the flames of her resentment; and at last on 5th June 1600 Essex was accused before a specially-constituted court of having made a dishonourable and disadvantageous arrangement with Hugh O'Neill, the rebellious Earl of Tyrone, of deserting his command, and of returning to England against the Queen's orders, with his mission unaccomplished and her rule in Ireland imperilled. He was stripped of all his offices and restricted to the confines of Essex House, his mansion in London, till August 1600.

Once again at liberty but ordered not to appear at Court, he smarted under his disgrace. He was not willing to remain in a private station, and attracted about him a band of sympathisers and malcontents. His chief ally was Henry Wriothesley, Earl of Southampton, who had been his Master of Horse in Ireland and who was now groaning under the same royal displeasure. Apparently their aim was to secure the removal from the Queen's side of her elderly and most trusted counsellors and of other enemies and rivals about the Court like Sir Walter Raleigh, by taking forcible possession of the person of Elizabeth and the Palace of Whitehall. But out of that rash scheme evolved, it would seem, a conspiracy with the more sinister aim of putting Elizabeth herself to death.

In his impulsive way Essex along with Southampton led a band of about three hundred supporters into the City on Sunday, 8th February 1601, hoping to rouse the citizens and their train-bands. But they got a poor response and were easily overpowered. Essex and Southampton were put on trial at Westminster Hall on 19th February and condemned to death as traitors. Essex was executed on 25th February. But Southampton was spared and imprisoned in the Tower as for life. He was in fact set free by one of James's earliest acts of clemency after his accession and given many honours.

The already-mentioned involvement of the Lord Chamberlain's men in the Essex affair was due to some of Essex's faction conceiving the idea of pre-disposing the Londoners to their cause by a dramatic representation of the dangers of evil counsellors about the monarch and the drastic remedy of a deposition, as had happened in the case of Richard II. Accordingly a group of half-a-dozen of the conspirators approached some members of the Lord Chamberlain's company, including Augustine Phillips, on either Thursday 5th or Friday 6th February to persuade them "to have the play of the deposyng and kyllyng of Kyng Rychard the second to be played the Saterday next [the day before the intended rising] promysyng to gete them xls. more then their ordynary to play yt" (F). Phillips, in his subsequent examination, declared that the company "were determyned to have played some other play, holdyng that play of Kyng Richard to be so old & so long out of vse as that they shold have small or no Company at yt" (F). But in the upshot they took the money and played the play, no doubt with many of the conspirators, even perhaps Essex and Southampton, watching its effect on the audience.

For reasons which are obscure, Elizabeth had been likened to Richard II. It could not have been because of a similarity in their characters. But it could have been that Elizabeth was thought by her critics to be too much under the influence of the wrong advisers and not unlikely to end with a forced abdication and a death in prison. At any rate, Elizabeth herself was aware of the growls. In consequence of her touchiness on the matter, her censors of the drama saw to it that the most objectionable feature of Shakespeare's play, the abdication or deposition scene in Westminster Hall (IV, i, 162–318), was not printed in any of the three quartos, one in 1597 and two in 1598, published during the Queen's life. The scene was restored in the 1608 and 1615 quartos, as well as in the 1623 Folio. It is to be presumed that, though the scene was not printed till 1608, it was included when the play was being acted; and it is certain that it was presented, as part of the bargain, on 7th February 1601.

The antiquary William Lambarde on 4th August 1601 made a note of a conversation with Queen Elizabeth, in which "her Majestie fell upon the reign of King Richard II, saying, 'I am Richard II. know ye not that?'" Lambarde replied with an indirect allusion to the performance of Shakespeare's play before Essex's rising: "Such a wicked imagination was determined and attempted by a most unkind Gent. the most adorned creature that your Majestie made". The Queen's comment was: "He that will forget God, will also forget his benefactors; this tragedy was played 40^{tie} times in open streets and houses" (G).

It is a remarkable fact and one indicative of Elizabeth's implacability and impassivity that on 24th February 1601, the night before Essex's execution, she saw at Whitehall a performance by the Lord Chamberlain's men. Apparently their having acted *Richard II* the day before Essex's desperate attempt was regarded by Elizabeth as no more than an indiscretion. She may have been inclined towards leniency by the fact that the patron of the company was her near kinsman George Carey, Lord Hunsdon, who was the grandson of Anne Boleyn's sister.

There is no evidence in provincial records that the Lord Chamberlain's men travelled as a touring company during 1601. They were certainly in the London neighbourhood at Christmas of that year, for they performed at

Whitehall on 26th and 27th December; and on 29th December they gave a performance at the Blackfriars Theatre which the Queen attended after having dined with Lord Hunsdon. But the lack of evidence from provincial records by no means proves that the Lord Chamberlain's company never left the vicinity of London.

In any case, whatever the company as such may have done, Shakespeare as an individual may have felt that he was a marked man and thought it prudent to absent himself for a while from his usual haunts and the too-close neighbourhood of officers of the Government. After all, he was the author of the offending *Richard II*. Moreover, in 1599 he had expressed the liveliest hopes for the success of Essex in his Irish expedition (3-4). And in 1593 and 1594 he had dedicated first *Venus and Adonis* and then *The Rape of Lucrece* to Southampton in the language of a devotee. I offer no opinion on the possibility that Southampton was "the onelie begetter" (whatever that phrase in the dedication means) of the *Sonnets*. They were not published till 1609; and in 1601 comparatively few people would know that they were being written.

The behaviour of James VI at this critical time was characteristically complicated. His policy was mainly directed to making secure his accession to the English crown on Elizabeth's death. Such a hope was not a certainty by any means, since the enactment of Henry VIII against a Scottish successor descended from his sister Margaret had never been revoked. James tried to conciliate opinions and win friends in as many quarters as possible. He courted Sir Robert Cecil with some success. His cautious moves towards a Scottish Episcopacy were likely to find favour in England. At the same time, he did his best to disarm Catholic hostility at home by conferring offices and honours on noblemen of that persuasion. In his foreign exchanges with the Earl of Tyrone in Ireland, Henry IV of France, and the Pope, he used language which implied the possibility of his conversion. And he seems to have allowed his Queen to send an envoy to Rome to make some sort of profession of her adherence to Catholicism.

But James's most daring manœuvres were in relation to Essex and his conspiracy. About 1595 Essex had established an office to gather foreign intelligence and no doubt to pass on home news in exchange. As a result a contact was made with James in Scotland. Indeed James may have been assured that, in certain as-yet-imprecise circumstances, he was to play the Bolingbroke to Elizabeth's Richard II. At any rate early in 1601 James sent his close friend, John Erskine, Earl of Mar, who had attended him throughout the Gowrie Conspiracy, as Ambassador to Elizabeth, but with the covert purpose as well of co-operating with Essex. Associated with Mar as envoy was Edward Bruce, lay Abbot or Commendator of Kinloss (later Lord Bruce of Kinloss), who knew the London ropes well, having been twice before on missions to Elizabeth. Mar and Bruce went about their double-dealing with caution. On the question which interested James most, Sir Robert Cecil, Mar, and Bruce reached a friendly understanding. Through the two Scottish envoys, Cecil assured James of the succession, provided that James himself did nothing about the matter and left it in Cecil's experienced hands.

Two years later, the latter was as good as his promise. Shortly before Elizabeth's death, he prepared a proclamation of James as the lawful inheritor of the English Crown; and shortly after it, he secured the approval of the Privy Council.

But James received the momentous news he had been so long waiting for some days before the official intelligence arrived. The Lord Chamberlain's brother, Sir Robert Carey (later Earl of Monmouth) had privately pre-arranged for relays of horses to carry him north. He set out from London on the very day of Elizabeth's death, which was Thursday, 24th March 1603, and arrived to greet his new King at Holyroodhouse on Saturday, 26th March.

Let me conclude by adopting as a cryptic epilogue some words of Old Siward:

> The time approaches
> That will with due decision make us know
> What we shall say we have and what we owe.
> Thoughts speculative their unsure hopes relate,
> But certain issue strokes must arbitrate:
> Towards which advance the war. (V, iv, 16-21).

Notes

A. It may be worth noting that, whereas Holinshed has "*Makdowald*" (I, 335), Shakespeare has "Macdonwald" (I, ii, 9). Also Holinshed says "out of the westerne iles" came a great multitude "and out of *Ireland* no small number of *Kernes* and *Galloglasses*" (I, 335); but Shakespeare drops any reference to Ireland and derives "from the western isles" his "kernes and gallowglasses" (I, ii, 12-13).

B. *Cf.* J. W. Draper, '*Macbeth*' *as a Compliment to James I* in *Englische Studien*, 1937-38, 207 *et seq.*; and 40, note 63 *supra*.

C. *Cf.* Stopes, 102.

D. The "credible person" is said by William Oldys (in a note in his copy of Thomas Fuller's *Worthies of England*) to have had the story from D'Avenant himself and to have been John Sheffield, Duke of Buckingham. Buckingham was a great admirer of Shakespeare, who out of his admiration "altered" *Julius Caesar* into two plays, *The Tragedy of Julius Caesar* and *The Tragedy of Marcus Brutus*.

E. According to John Aubrey's *Brief Lives*, Shakespeare often stopped on his journeys between London and Stratford at the inn in Oxford (subsequently called the Crown Tavern) kept by John Davenant. His son Sir William (who spelled his name D'Avenant to suggest some link with the river Avon) "would sometimes when he was pleasant over a glasse of wine with his most intimate friends . . . say that it seemed to him that he writt with the very spirit that Shakespeare did, and seemed contented enough to be thought his Son; he would tell them the story as above, in which way his mother had a very light report". It is only fair to add that Mrs. Davenant had the reputation during her lifetime of being a woman of excellent character.

D'Avenant transmitted several theatrical traditions about his god-father.

F. Halliday, 480.

G. *Ibid.*, 349. Elizabeth must have been referring to performances of *Richard II* some years earlier.

A copy in the Folger Library of Lambarde's Ἀρχαιονομία, *Sive de priscis anglorum legibus libri*, 1568, has a signature "W. Shakspere" which some handwriting experts believe to be genuine.